MznLnx

Missing Links Exam Preps

Exam Prep for

Investments

Bodie, Kane & Marcus, 7th Edition

The MznLnx Exam Prep is your link from the texbook and lecture to your exams.
The MznLnx Exam Preps are unauthorized and comprehensive reviews of your textbooks.

All material provided by MznLnx and Rico Publications (c) 2010
Textbook publishers and textbook authors do not particpate in or contribute to these reviews.

MznLnx

Rico Publications

Exam Prep for Investments
7th Edition
Bodie, Kane & Marcus

Publisher: Raymond Houge	*Product Manager:* Dave Mason
Assistant Editor: Michael Rouger	*Editorial Assitant:* Rachel Guzmanji
Text and Cover Designer: Lisa Buckner	*Pedagogy:* Debra Long
Marketing Manager: Sara Swagger	*Cover Image:* Jim Reed/Getty Images
Project Manager, Editorial Production: Jerry Emerson	*Text and Cover Printer:* City Printing, Inc.
Art Director: Vernon Lowerui	*Compositor:* Media Mix, Inc.

(c) 2010 Rico Publications

ALL RIGHTS RESERVED. No part of this work covered by the copyright may be reproduced or used in any form or by an means--graphic, electronic, or mechanical, including photocopying, recording, taping, Web distribution, information storage, and retrieval systems, or in any other manner--without the written permission of the publisher.

Printed in the United States
ISBN:

For more information about our products, contact us at:
Dave.Mason@RicoPublications.com

For permission to use material from this text or product, submit a request online to:
Dave.Mason@RicoPublications.com

Contents

CHAPTER 1
The Investment Environment — 1

CHAPTER 2
Asset Classes and Financial Instruments — 12

CHAPTER 3
How Securities are Traded — 32

CHAPTER 4
Mutual Funds and Other Investment Companies — 48

CHAPTER 5
Learning About Return and Risk from the Historical Record — 55

CHAPTER 6
Risk Aversion and Capital Allocation to Risky Assets — 65

CHAPTER 7
Optimal Risky Portfolios — 72

CHAPTER 8
Index Models — 81

CHAPTER 9
The Capital Asset Pricing Model — 90

CHAPTER 10
Arbitrage Pricing Theory and Multifactor Models of Risk and Return — 101

CHAPTER 11
The Efficient Market Hypothesis — 106

CHAPTER 12
Behavioral Finance and Technical Analysis — 114

CHAPTER 13
Empirical Evidence on Security Returns — 119

CHAPTER 14
Bond Prices and Yields — 130

CHAPTER 15
The Term Structure of Interest Rates — 146

CHAPTER 16
Managing Bond Portfolios — 151

CHAPTER 17
Macroeconomic and Industry Analysis — 160

CHAPTER 18
Equity Valuation Models — 170

CHAPTER 19
Financial Statement Analysis — 179

CHAPTER 20
Options Markets: Introduction — 196

Contents (Cont.)

CHAPTER 21
Option Valuation — 207

CHAPTER 22
Futures Markets — 212

CHAPTER 23
Futures and Swaps: Markets and Applications — 219

CHAPTER 24
Portfolio Performance Evaluation — 228

CHAPTER 25
International Diversification — 236

CHAPTER 26
Investment Policy and the Framework of the CFA Institute — 243

CHAPTER 27
The Theory of Active Portfolio Management — 257

ANSWER KEY — 262

TO THE STUDENT

COMPREHENSIVE

The *MznLnx* Exam Prep series is designed to help you pass your exams. Editors at MznLnx review your textbooks and then prepare these practice exams to help you master the textbook material. Unlike study guides, workbooks, and practice tests provided by the texbook publisher and textbook authors, *MznLnx* gives you **all** of the material in each chapter in exam form, not just samples, so you can be sure to nail your exam.

MECHANICAL

The MznLnx Exam Prep series creates exams that will help you learn the subject matter as well as test you on your understanding. Each question is designed to help you master the concept. Just working through the exams, you gain an understanding of the subject--its a simple mechanical process that produces success.

INTEGRATED STUDY GUIDE AND REVIEW

MznLnx is not just a set of exams designed to test you, its also a comprehensive review of the subject content. Each exam question is also a review of the concept, making sure that you will get the answer correct without having to go to other sources of material. You learn as you go! Its the easiest way to pass an exam.

HUMOR

Studying can be tedious and dry. MznLnx's instructional design includes moderate humor within the exam questions on occassion, to break the tedium and revitalize the brain

Chapter 1. The Investment Environment

1. _____ are made by investors and investment managers.

Investors commonly perform investment analysis by making use of fundamental analysis, technical analysis and gut feel.

_____ are often supported by decision tools.

   a. Investment decisions
   b. Asset allocation
   c. Investing online
   d. Investment performance

2. In business and accounting, _____s are everything of value that is owned by a person or company. The balance sheet of a firm records the monetary value of the _____s owned by the firm. The two major _____ classes are tangible _____s and intangible _____s.
   a. EBITDA
   b. Income
   c. Accounts payable
   d. Asset

3. The term _____ or replacement value refers to the amount that an entity would have to pay, at the present time, to replace any one of its assets.

In the insurance industry, '_____' is a method of computing the value of an item insured. _____ is not market value, but is instead the cost to replace an item or structure at its pre-loss condition.

   a. January effect
   b. False billing
   c. Bonus share
   d. Replacement cost

4. The _____ is the relationship between the amount of return gained on an investment and the amount of risk undertaken in that investment. The more return sought, the more risk that must be undertaken.

There are various classes of possible investments, each with their own positions on the overall _____.

   a. Fiscal sponsorship
   b. Post earnings announcement drift
   c. Blank endorsement
   d. Risk-return spectrum

5. In financial accounting, a _____ or statement of financial position is a summary of a person's or organization's balances. Assets, liabilities and ownership equity are listed as of a specific date, such as the end of its financial year. A _____ is often described as a snapshot of a company's financial condition.

   a. Statement of retained earnings
   b. Statement on Auditing Standards No. 70: Service Organizations
   c. Balance sheet
   d. Financial statements

6. In economics, business, and accounting, a _____ is the value of money that has been used up to produce something, and hence is not available for use anymore. In business, the _____ may be one of acquisition, in which case the amount of money expended to acquire it is counted as _____. In this case, money is the input that is gone in order to acquire the thing.
   a. Cost
   b. Sliding scale fees
   c. Fixed costs
   d. Marginal cost

Chapter 1. The Investment Environment

7. A _____ is a situation that involves losing one quality or aspect of something in return for gaining another quality or aspect. It implies a decision to be made with full comprehension of both the upside and downside of a particular choice.

In economics the term is expressed as opportunity cost, referring the most preferred alternative given up.

 a. Total revenue
 b. Capital outflow
 c. Trade-off
 d. Break-even point

8. In business, _____ is the total assets minus total outside liabilities of an individual or a company. For a company, this is called shareholders' equity and may be referred to as book value. _____ is stated as at a particular point in time.
 a. Moneylender
 b. Net worth
 c. Restructuring
 d. Certified International Investment Analyst

9. In finance, a _____ is a debt security, in which the authorized issuer owes the holders a debt and, depending on the terms of the _____, is obliged to pay interest (the coupon) and/or to repay the principal at a later date, termed maturity.

Thus a _____ is a loan: the issuer is the borrower, the _____ holder is the lender, and the coupon is the interest. _____s provide the borrower with external funds to finance long-term investments, or, in the case of government _____s, to finance current expenditure.

 a. Convertible bond
 b. Catastrophe bonds
 c. Bond
 d. Puttable bond

10. A _____ is a financial contract between two parties, the buyer and the seller of this type of option. Often it is simply labeled a 'call'. The buyer of the option has the right, but not the obligation to buy an agreed quantity of a particular commodity or financial instrument (the underlying instrument) from the seller of the option at a certain time (the expiration date) for a certain price (the strike price.)
 a. Bull spread
 b. Bear spread
 c. Bear call spread
 d. Call option

11. The _____ is the market for securities, where companies and governments can raise longterm funds. The _____ includes the stock market and the bond market. Financial regulators, such as the U.S. Securities and Exchange Commission, oversee the _____s in their designated countries to ensure that investors are protected against fraud.
 a. Spot rate
 b. Delta neutral
 c. Forward market
 d. Capital market

12. A _____s a time deposit, a financial product commonly offered to consumers by banks, thrift institutions, and credit unions.

They are similar to savings accounts in that they are insured and thus virtually risk-free; they are 'money in the bank'. They are different from savings accounts in that they have a specific, fixed term (often three months, six months, or one to five years), and, usually, a fixed interest rate.

a. Variable rate mortgage	b. Time deposit
c. Certificate of deposit	d. Reserve requirement

13. _____ is a form of corporation equity ownership represented in the securities. It is dangerous in comparison to preferred shares and some other investment options, in that in the event of bankruptcy, _____ investors receive their funds after preferred stockholders, bondholders, creditors, etc. On the other hand, common shares on average perform better than preferred shares or bonds over time.

a. Stop-limit order	b. Stock split
c. Common stock	d. Stock market bubble

14. A _____ is a bond issued by a corporation. The term is usually applied to longer-term debt instruments, generally with a maturity date falling at least a year after their issue date. (The term 'commercial paper' is sometimes used for instruments with a shorter maturity.)

a. Brady bonds	b. Corporate bond
c. Government bond	d. Serial bond

15. A _____ is a financial contract whose value is derived from the value of something else (known as the underlying.) The underlying on which a _____ is based can be an asset, weather conditions bonds or other forms of credit.

a. 7-Eleven	b. Derivative
c. 4-4-5 Calendar	d. 529 plan

16. _____ refers to any type of investment that yields a regular (or fixed) return.

For example, if you lend money to a borrower and the borrower has to pay interest once a month, you have been issued a fixed-income security. When a company does this, it is often called a bond or corporate bank debt (although preferred stock is also sometimes considered to be _____).

a. 529 plan	b. Bond market
c. Fixed income	d. 4-4-5 Calendar

17. In finance, a _____ (non-investment grade bond, speculative grade bond or junk bond) is a bond that is rated below investment grade at the time of purchase. These bonds have a higher risk of default or other adverse credit events, but typically pay higher yields than better quality bonds in order to make them attractive to investors.

a. Sharpe ratio	b. Private equity
c. High yield bond	d. Volatility

18. In finance, the _____ is the global financial market for short-term borrowing and lending. It provides short-term liquidity funding for the global financial system. The _____ is where short-term obligations such as Treasury bills, commercial paper and bankers' acceptances are bought and sold.

a. Money market	b. Consumer debt
c. Cramdown	d. Debt-for-equity swap

19. _____ mature in one year or less. Like zero-coupon bonds, they do not pay interest prior to maturity; instead they are sold at a discount of the par value to create a positive yield to maturity. Many regard _____ as the least risky investment available to U.S. investors.

a. Treasury securities
b. 4-4-5 Calendar
c. Treasury Inflation Protected Securities
d. Treasury bills

20. The _____ is a financial market where participants buy and sell debt securities, usually in the form of bonds. As of 2006, the size of the international _____ is an estimated $45 trillion, of which the size of the outstanding U.S. _____ debt was $25.2 trillion.

Nearly all of the $923 billion average daily trading volume in the U.S. _____ takes place between broker-dealers and large institutions in a decentralized, over-the-counter market.

a. Fixed income
b. 529 plan
c. 4-4-5 Calendar
d. Bond market

21. An _____ is a contract written by a seller that conveys to the buyer the right -- but not the obligation -- to buy (in the case of a call _____) or to sell (in the case of a put _____) a particular asset, such as a piece of property such as, among others, a futures contract. In return for granting the _____, the seller collects a payment (the premium) from the buyer.

For example, buying a call _____ provides the right to buy a specified quantity of a security at a set strike price at some time on or before expiration, while buying a put _____ provides the right to sell.

a. Annuity
b. AT'T Mobility LLC
c. Amortization
d. Option

22. A _____ is a fungible, negotiable instrument representing financial value. They are broadly categorized into debt securities (such as banknotes, bonds and debentures), and equity securities; e.g., common stocks. The company or other entity issuing the _____ is called the issuer.

a. Book entry
b. Securities lending
c. Security
d. Tracking stock

23. In economics, a _____ is a mechanism that allows people to easily buy and sell (trade) financial securities (such as stocks and bonds), commodities (such as precious metals or agricultural goods), and other fungible items of value at low transaction costs and at prices that reflect the efficient-market hypothesis.

_____s have evolved significantly over several hundred years and are undergoing constant innovation to improve liquidity.

Both general markets (where many commodities are traded) and specialized markets (where only one commodity is traded) exist.

a. Financial market
b. Cost of carry
c. Delta hedging
d. Secondary market

24. In political science and economics, the _____ or agency dilemma treats the difficulties that arise under conditions of incomplete and asymmetric information when a principal hires an agent. Various mechanisms may be used to try to align the interests of the agent with those of the principal, such as piece rates/commissions, profit sharing, efficiency wages, performance measurement (including financial statements), the agent posting a bond, or fear of firing. The _____ is found in most employer/employee relationships, for example, when stockholders hire top executives of corporations.
   a. 529 plan
   b. 7-Eleven
   c. 4-4-5 Calendar
   d. Principal-agent problem

25. The _____ (NYSE: FNM), commonly known as Fannie Mae, is a stockholder-owned corporation chartered by Congress in 1968 as a government sponsored enterprise (GSE), but founded in 1938 during the Great Depression. The corporation's purpose is to purchase and securitize mortgages in order to ensure that funds are consistently available to the institutions that lend money to home buyers.

On September 7, 2008, James Lockhart, director of the Federal Housing Finance Agency (FHFA), announced that Fannie Mae and Freddie Mac were being placed into conservatorship of the FHFA.

   a. The Depository Trust ' Clearing Corporation
   b. General partnership
   c. SPDR
   d. Federal National Mortgage Association

26. In business, a _____ is the purchase of one company (the target) by another (the acquirer or bidder). In the UK the term refers to the acquisition of a public company whose shares are listed on a stock exchange, in contrast to the acquisition of a private company.

Before a bidder makes an offer for another company, it usually first informs that company's board of directors.

   a. 4-4-5 Calendar
   b. Stock swap
   c. 529 plan
   d. Takeover

27. _____ LLP, based in Chicago, was once one of the 'Big Five' accounting firms among PricewaterhouseCoopers, Deloitte Touche Tohmatsu, Ernst ' Young and KPMG, providing auditing, tax, and consulting services to large corporations. In 2002, the firm voluntarily surrendered its licenses to practice as Certified Public Accountants in the United States after being found guilty of criminal charges relating to the firm's handling of the auditing of Enron, the energy corporation, resulting in the loss of 85,000 jobs. Although the verdict was subsequently overturned by the Supreme Court of the United States, it has not returned as a viable business.
   a. Accion USA
   b. Arthur Andersen
   c. Institute of Financial Accountants
   d. Information Systems Audit and Control Association

28. _____ is the set of processes, customs, policies, laws and institutions affecting the way a corporation is directed, administered or controlled. _____ also includes the relationships among the many stakeholders involved and the goals for which the corporation is governed. The principal stakeholders are the shareholders, management and the board of directors.
   a. Patent
   b. Due diligence
   c. Foreign Corrupt Practices Act
   d. Corporate governance

29. An _____ is an investment vehicle traded on stock exchanges, much like stocks. An ETF holds assets such as stocks or bonds and trades at approximately the same price as the net asset value of its underlying assets over the course of the trading day. Most ETFs track an index, such as the Dow Jones Industrial Average or the S'P 500.

   a. ABN Amro   b. Exchange-traded fund
   c. A Random Walk Down Wall Street   d. AAB

30. _____ is a term used to refer to how an investor distributes his or her investments among various classes of investment vehicles (e.g., stocks and bonds.)

A large part of financial planning is finding an _____ that is appropriate for a given person in terms of their appetite for and ability to shoulder risk. This can depend on various factors; see investor profile.

   a. Asset allocation   b. Investing online
   c. Alternative investment   d. Investment performance

31. The _____ of 2002 (Pub.L. 107-204, 116 Stat. 745, enacted July 30, 2002), also known as the Public Company Accounting Reform and Investor Protection Act of 2002 and commonly called Sarbanes-Oxley, Sarbox or SOX, is a United States federal law enacted on July 30, 2002 in response to a number of major corporate and accounting scandals including those affecting Enron, Tyco International, Adelphia, Peregrine Systems and WorldCom.

   a. Foreign Corrupt Practices Act   b. Blue sky law
   c. Duty of loyalty   d. Sarbanes-Oxley Act

32. The _____ is the weighted-average most likely outcome in gambling, probability theory, economics or finance.

In gambling and probability theory, there is usually a discrete set of possible outcomes. In this case, _____ is a measure of the relative balance of win or loss weighted by their chances of occurring.

   a. A Random Walk Down Wall Street   b. ABN Amro
   c. Expected return   d. AAB

33. _____, authored by professors Benjamin Graham and David Dodd of Columbia Business School, laid the intellectual foundation for what would later be called value investing. The work was first published in 1934, following unprecedented losses on Wall Street. In summing up lessons learned, Graham and Dodd chided Wall Street for its myopic focus on a company's reported earnings per share, and were particularly harsh on the favored 'earnings trends.' They encouraged investors to take an entirely different approach by gauging the rough value of the operating business that lay behind the security.

   a. Stock valuation   b. Security analysis
   c. Growth stocks   d. 4-4-5 Calendar

34. _____ refers to a portfolio management strategy where the manager makes specific investments with the goal of outperforming an investment benchmark index. Investors or mutual funds that do not aspire to create a return in excess of a benchmark index will often invest in an index fund that replicates as closely as possible the investment weighting and returns of that index; this is called passive management. _____ is the opposite of passive management, because in passive management the manager does not seek to outperform the benchmark index.

a. ABN Amro
b. A Random Walk Down Wall Street
c. AAB
d. Active management

35. _____ in finance is a risk management technique, related to hedging, that mixes a wide variety of investments within a portfolio. Because the fluctuations of a single security have less impact on a diverse portfolio, _____ minimizes the risk from any one investment.

A simple example of _____ is the following: On a particular island the entire economy consists of two companies: one that sells umbrellas and another that sells sunscreen.

a. Diversification
b. 4-4-5 Calendar
c. 529 plan
d. 7-Eleven

36. _____ proposes how rational investors will use diversification to optimize their portfolios, and how a risky asset should be priced. The basic concepts of the theory are Markowitz diversification, the efficient frontier, capital asset pricing model, the alpha and beta coefficients, the Capital Market Line and the Securities Market Line.

_____ models an asset's return as a random variable, and models a portfolio as a weighted combination of assets so that the return of a portfolio is the weighted combination of the assets' returns.

a. Market value
b. Payback period
c. Modern portfolio theory
d. Consumer basket

37. A _____ is an institution, firm or individual who mediates between two or more parties in a financial context. Typically the first party is a provider of a product or service and the second party is a consumer or customer.

In the U.S., a _____ is typically an institution that facilitates the channelling of funds between lenders and borrowers indirectly.

a. Mutual fund
b. Savings and loan association
c. Net asset value
d. Financial intermediary

38. In finance, a _____ is the party in a loan agreement which receives money or other instrument from a lender and promises to repay the lender in a specified time.
a. Debt management plan
b. Cash credit
c. Line of credit
d. Borrower

39.

A _____ is a type of financial intermediary and a type of bank. Commercial banking is also known as business banking. It is a bank that provides checking accounts, savings accounts, and money market accounts and that accepts time deposits.

a. 4-4-5 Calendar
b. 529 plan
c. Commercial bank
d. 7-Eleven

40. _____ is the provision of resources (such as granting a loan) by one party to another party where that second party does not reimburse the first party immediately, thereby generating a debt, and instead arranges either to repay or return those resources (or material(s) of equal value) at a later date. The first party is called a creditor, also known as a lender, while the second party is called a debtor, also known as a borrower.

Movements of financial capital are normally dependent on either _____ or equity transfers.

a. Clearing house
b. Warrant
c. Credit
d. Comparable

41. A _____ is a cooperative financial institution that is owned and controlled by its members, and operated for the purpose of promoting thrift, providing credit at reasonable rates, and providing other financial services to its members. Many _____s exist to further community development or sustainable international development on a local level. Worldwide, _____ systems vary significantly in terms of total system assets and average institution asset size since _____s exist in a wide range of sizes, ranging from volunteer operations with a handful of members to institutions with several billion dollars in assets and hundreds of thousands of members.

a. Credit Union Service Organization
b. Credit union
c. Corporate credit union
d. Fi-linx

42. An _____ is a company whose main business is holding securities of other companies purely for investment purposes. The _____ invests money on behalf of its shareholders who in turn share in the profits and losses.

a. AAB
b. A Random Walk Down Wall Street
c. Unit investment trust
d. Investment company

43. A _____ or bank is a financial institution whose primary activity is to act as a payment agent for customers and to borrow and lend money.

The first modern bank was founded in Italy in Genoa in 1406, its name was Banco di San Giorgio (Bank of St. George.)

Many other financial activities were added over time.

a. Bought deal
b. 4-4-5 Calendar
c. Black Sea Trade and Development Bank
d. Banker

44. _____, in microeconomics, are the cost advantages that a business obtains due to expansion. _____ may be utilized by any size firm expanding its scale of operation.

a. Articles of incorporation
b. Uniform Commercial Code
c. Employee Retirement Income Security Act
d. Economies of scale

45. The _____ is that part of the capital markets that deals with the issuance of new securities. Companies, governments or public sector institutions can obtain funding through the sale of a new stock or bond issue. This is typically done through a syndicate of securities dealers.

Chapter 1. The Investment Environment

a. Volatility clustering
b. Sector rotation
c. Peer group analysis
d. Primary market

46. The _____ is the financial market where previously issued securities and financial instruments such as stock, bonds, options, and futures are bought and sold. The term '_____' is also used refer to the market for any used goods or assets, or an alternative use for an existing product or asset where the customer base is the second market

With primary issuances of securities or financial instruments, or the primary market, investors purchase these securities directly from issuers such as corporations issuing shares in an IPO or private placement, or directly from the federal government in the case of treasuries.

a. Financial market
b. Secondary market
c. Delta neutral
d. Performance attribution

47. An _____ represents the ownership in the shares of a foreign company trading on US financial markets. The stock of many non-US companies trades on US exchanges through the use of _____s. _____s enable US investors to buy shares in foreign companies without undertaking cross-border transactions.

a. AAB
b. American Depository Receipt
c. A Random Walk Down Wall Street
d. ABN Amro

48. A _____ is a professionally managed type of collective investment scheme that pools money from many investors and invests it in stocks, bonds, short-term money market instruments, and/or other securities. The _____ will have a fund manager that trades the pooled money on a regular basis. Currently, the worldwide value of all _____s totals more than $26 trillion.

Since 1940, there have been three basic types of investment companies in the United States: open-end funds, also known in the US as _____s; unit investment trusts (UITs); and closed-end funds.

a. Net asset value
b. Financial intermediary
c. Trust company
d. Mutual fund

49. In business and finance, a _____ (also referred to as equity _____) of stock means a _____ of ownership in a corporation (company.) In the plural, stocks is often used as a synonym for _____s especially in the United States, but it is less commonly used that way outside of North America.

In the United Kingdom, South Africa, and Australia, stock can also refer to completely different financial instruments such as government bonds or, less commonly, to all kinds of marketable securities.

a. Procter ' Gamble
b. Bucket shop
c. Margin
d. Share

50. A _____, securities exchange or (in Europe) bourse is a corporation or mutual organization which provides 'trading' facilities for stock brokers and traders, to trade stocks and other securities. _____s also provide facilities for the issue and redemption of securities as well as other financial instruments and capital events including the payment of income and dividends. The securities traded on a _____ include: shares issued by companies, unit trusts and other pooled investment products and bonds.

a. 529 plan
b. 4-4-5 Calendar
c. 7-Eleven
d. Stock Exchange

51. The institution most often referenced by the word '_____' is a public or publicly traded _____, the shares of which are traded on a public stock exchange (e.g., the New York Stock Exchange or Nasdaq in the United States) where shares of stock of _____s are bought and sold by and to the general public. Most of the largest businesses in the world are publicly traded _____s. However, the majority of _____s are said to be closely held, privately held or close _____s, meaning that no ready market exists for the trading of shares.
   a. Protect
   b. Depository Trust Company
   c. Federal Home Loan Mortgage Corporation
   d. Corporation

52. The _____ (NYSE: FRE) is an insolvent government sponsored enterprise (GSE) of the United States federal government.

The _____ was created in 1970 to expand the secondary market for mortgages in the US. Along with other GSEs, Freddie Mac buys mortgages on the secondary market, pools them, and sells them as mortgage-backed securities to investors on the open market.

   a. Federal Home Loan Mortgage Corporation
   b. Public company
   c. Governmental Accounting Standards Board
   d. The Depository Trust ' Clearing Corporation

53. The _____ is a U.S. government-owned corporation within the Department of Housing and Urban Development

Ginnie Mae provides guarantees on mortgage-backed securities backed by federally insured or guaranteed loans, mainly loans issued by the Federal Housing Administration, Department of Veterans Affairs, Rural Housing Service, and Office of Public and Indian Housing. Ginnie Mae securities are the only MBS that are guaranteed by the United States government.

   a. GNMA
   b. Certified Emission Reductions
   c. Case-Shiller Home Price Indices
   d. Cash budget

54. The _____ is a U.S. government-owned corporation within the Department of Housing and Urban Development

Ginnie Mae provides guarantees on mortgage-backed securities backed by federally insured or guaranteed loans, mainly loans issued by the Federal Housing Administration, Department of Veterans Affairs, Rural Housing Service, and Office of Public and Indian Housing. Ginnie Mae securities are the only MBS that are guaranteed by the United States government.

   a. Jumbo mortgage
   b. Government National Mortgage Association
   c. 4-4-5 Calendar
   d. Graduated payment mortgage

55. A _____ is an asset-backed security whose cash flows are backed by the principal and interest payments of a set of mortgage loans. Payments are typically made monthly over the lifetime of the underlying loans.
   a. Shared appreciation mortgage
   b. Conforming loan
   c. Mortgage-backed security
   d. Home equity line of credit

Chapter 1. The Investment Environment

56. _____ is a structured finance process that involves pooling and repackaging of cash-flow-producing financial assets into securities, which are then sold to investors. The term '_____' is derived from the fact that the form of financial instruments used to obtain funds from the investors are securities. As a portfolio risk backed by amortizing cash flows - and unlike general corporate debt - the credit quality of securitized debt is non-stationary due to changes in volatility that are time- and structure-dependent.

a. Special journals
b. Reputational risk
c. The Glass-Steagall Act of 1933
d. Securitization

57. _____ are dollar-denominated bonds, issued mostly by Latin American countries in the 1980s, named after U.S. Treasury Secretary Nicholas Brady.

_____ were created in March 1989 in order to convert bonds issued by mostly Latin American countries into a variety or 'menu' of new bonds after many of those countries defaulted on their debt in the 1980's. At that time, the market for sovereign debt was small and illiquid, and the standardization of emerging-market debt facilitated risk-spreading and trading.

a. Municipal bond
b. Nominal yield
c. Coupon rate
d. Brady bonds

58. _____ has become the norm for individual investors and traders over the past decade with many, if not all brokers now offering online services with unique trading platforms.

In the past, investors had to call up their brokers and place an order on the phone. The broker would then enter the order in their system which was linked to trading floors and exchanges.

a. Investing online
b. Alternative investment
c. Asset allocation
d. Investment decisions

59. _____ is typically a higher ranking stock than voting shares, and its terms are negotiated between the corporation and the investor.

_____ usually carry no voting rights, but may carry superior priority over common stock in the payment of dividends and upon liquidation. _____ may carry a dividend that is paid out prior to any dividends to common stock holders.

a. Preferred stock
b. Second lien loan
c. Trade-off theory
d. Follow-on offering

60. An _____ is the term used in financial circles for a type of computer system that facilitates trading of financial products outside of stock exchanges. The primary products that are traded on an _____ are stocks and currencies. They came into existence in 1998 when the SEC authorized their creation.

a. Open outcry
b. Electronic communication network
c. Insider trading
d. Intellidex

Chapter 2. Asset Classes and Financial Instruments

1. In business and accounting, _____s are everything of value that is owned by a person or company. The balance sheet of a firm records the monetary value of the _____s owned by the firm. The two major _____ classes are tangible _____s and intangible _____s.

   a. Income
   b. Asset
   c. Accounts payable
   d. EBITDA

2. _____ is a term used to refer to how an investor distributes his or her investments among various classes of investment vehicles (e.g., stocks and bonds.)

   A large part of financial planning is finding an _____ that is appropriate for a given person in terms of their appetite for and ability to shoulder risk. This can depend on various factors; see investor profile.

   a. Asset allocation
   b. Investment performance
   c. Investing online
   d. Alternative investment

3. In finance, the _____ is used to determine a theoretically appropriate required rate of return of an asset, if that asset is to be added to an already well-diversified portfolio, given that asset's non-diversifiable risk. The model takes into account the asset's sensitivity to non-diversifiable risk (also known as systemic risk or market risk), often represented by the quantity beta (β) in the financial industry, as well as the expected return of the market and the expected return of a theoretical risk-free asset.

   The model was introduced by Jack Treynor (1961, 1962), William Sharpe (1964), John Lintner (1965a,b) and Jan Mossin (1966) independently, building on the earlier work of Harry Markowitz on diversification and modern portfolio theory.

   a. Hull-White model
   b. Random walk hypothesis
   c. Cox-Ingersoll-Ross model
   d. Capital asset pricing model

4. The term _____ has three unrelated technical definitions, and is also used in a variety of non-technical ways.

   - In financial economics, it refers to any asset used to make money, as opposed to assets used for personal enjoyment or consumption. This is an important distinction because two people can disagree sharply about the value of personal assets, one person might think a sports car is more valuable than a pickup truck, another person might have the opposite taste. But if an asset is held for the purpose of making money, taste has nothing to do with it, only differences of opinion about how much money the asset will produce. With the further assumption that people agree on the probability distribution of future cash flows, it is possible to have an objective _____ pricing model. Even without the assumption of agreement, it is possible to set rational limits on _____ value.
   - In governmental accounting, it is defined as any asset used in operations with an initial useful life extending beyond one reporting period. Generally, government managers have a 'stewardship' duty to maintain _____s under their control. See International Public Sector Accounting Standards for details.
   - In US tax accounting, it is defined as any property other than a list of exceptions. The main exceptions are anything held for sale, and any real estate or depreciable property used in business. Almost everything you own and use for personal purposes, pleasure or investment is a _____. If something is a _____ for tax purposes, gains or losses on sale or disposition are capital gains or capital losses. For individuals, however, capital losses on property held for personal use are generally not deductible. See the IRS publication Tax Facts about Capital Gains and Losses for details.

Chapter 2. Asset Classes and Financial Instruments

A well-known financial accounting textbook advises that the term be avoided except in tax accounting because it is used in so many different senses, not all of them well-defined. For example it is often used as a synonym for fixed assets or for investments in securities.

A common non-technical usage occurs when people ask that employees or the environment or something else be treated as a _____.

a. Political risk
c. Settlement date
b. Solvency
d. Capital asset

5. The _____ is the market for securities, where companies and governments can raise longterm funds. The _____ includes the stock market and the bond market. Financial regulators, such as the U.S. Securities and Exchange Commission, oversee the _____s in their designated countries to ensure that investors are protected against fraud.

a. Spot rate
c. Forward market
b. Delta neutral
d. Capital market

6. Cash and _____ are the most liquid assets found within the asset portion of a company's balance sheet. _____ are assets that are readily convertible into cash, such as money market holdings, short-term government bonds or Treasury bills, marketable securities and commercial paper. _____ are distinguished from other investments through their short-term existence; they mature within 3 months whereas short-term investments are 12 months or less, and long-term investments are any investments that mature in excess of 12 months.

a. Par value
c. Tick size
b. Secured debt
d. Cash equivalents

7. In finance, the _____ is the global financial market for short-term borrowing and lending. It provides short-term liquidity funding for the global financial system. The _____ is where short-term obligations such as Treasury bills, commercial paper and bankers' acceptances are bought and sold.

a. Consumer debt
c. Debt-for-equity swap
b. Cramdown
d. Money market

8. A _____ is a fungible, negotiable instrument representing financial value. They are broadly categorized into debt securities (such as banknotes, bonds and debentures), and equity securities; e.g., common stocks. The company or other entity issuing the _____ is called the issuer.

a. Security
c. Securities lending
b. Book entry
d. Tracking stock

9. In finance, _____ is the process of estimating the potential market value of a financial asset or liability. they can be done on assets (for example, investments in marketable securities such as stocks, options, business enterprises, or intangible assets such as patents and trademarks) or on liabilities (e.g., Bonds issued by a company.) _____s are required in many contexts including investment analysis, capital budgeting, merger and acquisition transactions, financial reporting, taxable events to determine the proper tax liability, and in litigation.

a. Procter ' Gamble
c. Share
b. Margin
d. Valuation

Chapter 2. Asset Classes and Financial Instruments

10. _____ mature in one year or less. Like zero-coupon bonds, they do not pay interest prior to maturity; instead they are sold at a discount of the par value to create a positive yield to maturity. Many regard _____ as the least risky investment available to U.S. investors.

  a. Treasury bills
  b. Treasury Inflation Protected Securities
  c. 4-4-5 Calendar
  d. Treasury securities

11. In finance, a _____ is a debt security, in which the authorized issuer owes the holders a debt and, depending on the terms of the _____, is obliged to pay interest (the coupon) and/or to repay the principal at a later date, termed maturity.

Thus a _____ is a loan: the issuer is the borrower, the _____ holder is the lender, and the coupon is the interest. _____s provide the borrower with external funds to finance long-term investments, or, in the case of government _____s, to finance current expenditure.

  a. Catastrophe bonds
  b. Convertible bond
  c. Puttable bond
  d. Bond

12. The _____ is a financial market where participants buy and sell debt securities, usually in the form of bonds. As of 2006, the size of the international _____ is an estimated $45 trillion, of which the size of the outstanding U.S. _____ debt was $25.2 trillion.

Nearly all of the $923 billion average daily trading volume in the U.S. _____ takes place between broker-dealers and large institutions in a decentralized, over-the-counter market.

  a. 529 plan
  b. 4-4-5 Calendar
  c. Fixed income
  d. Bond market

13. _____ offer, asking price is a price a seller of a good is willing to accept for that particular good.

In bid and ask, the term _____ is used in contrast to the term bid price. The difference between the _____ and the bid price is called the spread.

  a. AAB
  b. A Random Walk Down Wall Street
  c. Interest rate parity
  d. Ask price

14. A _____ is the highest price that a buyer (i.e., bidder) is willing to pay for a good. It is usually referred to simply as the 'bid.'

In bid and ask, the _____ stands in contrast to the ask price or 'offer', and the difference between the two is called the bid/ask spread.

An unsolicited bid or offer is when a person or company receives a bid even though they are not looking to sell.

a. Mid price
c. Political risk
b. Settlement date
d. Bid price

15. A _____ or market-based mechanism is any of a wide variety of ways to match up buyers and sellers.

An example of a _____ uses announced bid and ask prices. Generally speaking, when two parties wish to engage in a trade, the purchaser will announce a price he is willing to pay (the bid price) and seller will announce a price he is willing to accept (the ask price).

a. 4-4-5 Calendar
c. 7-Eleven
b. 529 plan
d. Price mechanism

16. The _____ for securities is the difference between the price quoted by a market maker for an immediate sale and an immediate purchase The size of the bid-offer spread in a given commodity is a measure of the liquidity of the market.

The trader initiating the transaction is said to demand liquidity, and the other party to the transaction supplies liquidity.

a. Trade-off
c. Defined contribution plan
b. Capital outflow
d. Bid/offer spread

17. The _____ for an investment is a calculated annual yield for an investment, which may not pay out yearly. This allows investments which payout with different frequencies to be compared.
a. Bond equivalent yield
c. 4-4-5 Calendar
b. 7-Eleven
d. 529 plan

18. A _____ s a time deposit, a financial product commonly offered to consumers by banks, thrift institutions, and credit unions.

They are similar to savings accounts in that they are insured and thus virtually risk-free; they are 'money in the bank'. They are different from savings accounts in that they have a specific, fixed term (often three months, six months, or one to five years), and, usually, a fixed interest rate.

a. Variable rate mortgage
c. Reserve requirement
b. Time deposit
d. Certificate of deposit

19. In the global money market, _____ is an unsecured promissory note with a fixed maturity of one to 270 days. _____ is a money-market security issued (sold) by large banks and corporations to get money to meet short term debt obligations (for example, payroll), and is only backed by an issuing bank or corporation's promise to pay the face amount on the maturity date specified on the note. Since it is not backed by collateral, only firms with excellent credit ratings from a recognized rating agency will be able to sell their _____ at a reasonable price.
a. Trade-off theory
c. Commercial paper
b. Book building
d. Financial distress

Chapter 2. Asset Classes and Financial Instruments

20. The institution most often referenced by the word '_____' is a public or publicly traded _____, the shares of which are traded on a public stock exchange (e.g., the New York Stock Exchange or Nasdaq in the United States) where shares of stock of _____s are bought and sold by and to the general public. Most of the largest businesses in the world are publicly traded _____s. However, the majority of _____s are said to be closely held, privately held or close _____s, meaning that no ready market exists for the trading of shares.
    a. Protect
    b. Federal Home Loan Mortgage Corporation
    c. Depository Trust Company
    d. Corporation

21. Explicit _____ is a measure implemented in many countries to protect bank depositors, in full or in part, from losses caused by a bank's inability to pay its debts when due. _____ systems are one component of a financial system safety net that promotes financial stability.
    a. Banking panic
    b. Reserve requirement
    c. Time deposit
    d. Deposit Insurance

22. _____s are deposits denominated in United States dollars at banks outside the United States, and thus are not under the jurisdiction of the Federal Reserve. Consequently, such deposits are subject to much less regulation than similar deposits within the United States, allowing for higher margins. There is nothing 'European' about _____ deposits; a US dollar-denominated deposit in Tokyo or Caracas would likewise be deemed _____ deposits.
    a. A Random Walk Down Wall Street
    b. AAB
    c. Eurodollar
    d. ABN Amro

23. The _____ is a United States government corporation created by the Glass-Steagall Act of 1933. It provides deposit insurance, which guarantees the safety of checking and savings deposits in member banks, currently up to $250,000 per depositor per bank. Insured deposits are backed by the full faith and credit of the United States.
    a. Federal Deposit Insurance Corporation
    b. FASB
    c. Ford Foundation
    d. NYSE Group

24. The U.S. _____ is an independent agency of the United States government which holds primary responsibility for enforcing the federal securities laws and regulating the securities industry, the nation's stock and options exchanges, and other electronic securities markets. The SEC was created by section 4 of the SEC of 1934 (now codified as 15 U.S.C. Â§ 78d and commonly referred to as the 1934 Act.)
    a. 7-Eleven
    b. 529 plan
    c. Securities and Exchange Commission
    d. 4-4-5 Calendar

25. In finance, the term _____ describes the amount in cash that returns to the owners of a security. Normally it does not include the price variations, at the difference of the total return. _____ applies to various stated rates of return on stocks (common and preferred, and convertible), fixed income instruments (bonds, notes, bills, strips, zero coupon), and some other investment type insurance products (e.g. annuities).
    a. Yield to maturity
    b. Macaulay duration
    c. 4-4-5 Calendar
    d. Yield

26. In the United States, _____ are overnight borrowings by banks to maintain their bank reserves at the Federal Reserve. Banks keep reserves at Federal Reserve Banks to meet their reserve requirements and to clear financial transactions. Transactions in the _____ market enable depository institutions with reserve balances in excess of reserve requirements to lend reserves to institutions with reserve deficiencies.

Chapter 2. Asset Classes and Financial Instruments

a. Federal funds rate
b. 4-4-5 Calendar
c. Federal funds
d. Regulation T

27. A _____ allows a borrower to use a financial security as collateral for a cash loan at a fixed rate of interest. In a repo, the borrower agrees to immediately sell a security to a lender and also agrees to buy the same security from the lender at a fixed price at some later date. A repo is equivalent to a cash transaction combined with a forward contract.

a. Volatility arbitrage
b. Total return swap
c. Contango
d. Repurchase agreement

28. The _____ (or Euribor) is a daily reference rate based on the averaged interest rates at which banks offer to lend unsecured funds to other banks in the euro wholesale money market (or interbank market.)

Euribor rates are used as a reference rate for euro-denominated forward rate agreements, short term interest rate futures contracts and interest rate swaps, in very much the same way as LIBOR rates are commonly used for Sterling and US dollar-denominated instruments. They thus provide the basis for some of the world's most liquid and active interest rate markets.

a. Exchange Rate Mechanism
b. A Random Walk Down Wall Street
c. European Monetary System
d. Euro Interbank Offered Rate

29. _____ are cash, evidence of an ownership interest in an entity or deliver, cash or another financial instrument.

_____ can be categorized by form depending on whether they are cash instruments or derivative instruments:

- Cash instruments are _____ whose value is determined directly by markets. They can be divided into securities, which are readily transferable, and other cash instruments such as loans and deposits, where both borrower and lender have to agree on a transfer.
- Derivative instruments are _____ which derive their value from the value and characteristics of one or more underlying assets. They can be divided into exchange-traded derivatives and over-the-counter (OTC) derivatives.

Alternatively, _____ can be categorized by 'asset class' depending on whether they are equity based (reflecting ownership of the issuing entity) or debt based (reflecting a loan the investor has made to the issuing entity.) If it is debt, it can be further categorised into short term (less than one year) or long term.

Foreign Exchange instruments and transactions are neither debt nor equity based and belong in their own category.

a. Financial services
b. Cost of carry
c. Secondary market
d. Financial instruments

30. The _____ is a daily reference rate based on the interest rates at which banks borrow unsecured funds from banks in the London wholesale money market (or interbank market.) It is roughly comparable to the U.S. Federal funds rate.

Chapter 2. Asset Classes and Financial Instruments

During 1984 it became apparent that an increasing number of banks were trading actively in a variety of relatively new market instruments, notably interest rate swaps, foreign currency options and forward rate agreements.

a. Shanghai Interbank Offered Rate
b. Risk-free interest rate
c. Fixed interest
d. London Interbank Offered Rate

31. A _____ is a private or public market for the trading of company stock and derivatives of company stock at an agreed price; these are securities listed on a stock exchange as well as those only traded privately.

The size of the world _____ is estimated at about $36.6 trillion US at the beginning of October 2008 . The world derivatives market has been estimated at about $480 trillion face or nominal value, 12 times the size of the entire world economy.

a. Anton Gelonkin
b. Adolph Coors
c. Andrew Tobias
d. Stock market

32. A _____ is a sudden dramatic decline of stock prices across a significant cross-section of a stock market. Crashes are driven by panic as much as by underlying economic factors. They often follow speculative stock market bubbles.

a. 4-4-5 Calendar
b. 7-Eleven
c. Stock market crash
d. 529 plan

33. The coupon or _____ of a bond is the amount of interest paid per year expressed as a percentage of the face value of the bond.

For example if you hold $10,000 nominal of a bond described as a 4.5% loan stock, you will receive $450 in interest each year (probably in two installments of $225 each.)

Not all bonds have coupons.

a. Puttable bond
b. Zero-coupon bond
c. Revenue bonds
d. Coupon rate

34. _____ refers to any type of investment that yields a regular (or fixed) return.

For example, if you lend money to a borrower and the borrower has to pay interest once a month, you have been issued a fixed-income security. When a company does this, it is often called a bond or corporate bank debt (although preferred stock is also sometimes considered to be _____).

a. 4-4-5 Calendar
b. Fixed income
c. 529 plan
d. Bond market

Chapter 2. Asset Classes and Financial Instruments

35. _____ are government bonds issued by the United States Department of the Treasury through the Bureau of the Public Debt. They are the debt financing instruments of the U.S. Federal government, and they are often referred to simply as Treasuries or Treasurys. There are four types of marketable _____: Treasury bills, Treasury notes, Treasury bonds, and Treasury Inflation Protected Securities (TIPS.)

   a. 4-4-5 Calendar
   b. Treasury Inflation Protected Securities
   c. Treasury Inflation-Protected Securities
   d. Treasury securities

36. _____ is the strategy of making buy or sell decisions of financial assets (often stocks) by attempting to predict future market price movements. The prediction may be based on an outlook of market or economic conditions resulting from technical or fundamental analysis. This is an investment strategy based on the outlook for an aggregate market, rather than for a particular financial asset.

   a. Divestment
   b. Portable alpha
   c. Late trading
   d. Market timing

37. _____ are the inflation-indexed bonds issued by the U.S. Treasury. The principal is adjusted to the Consumer Price Index, the commonly used measure of inflation. The coupon rate is constant, but generates a different amount of interest when multiplied by the inflation-adjusted principal, thus protecting the holder against inflation. _____ are currently offered in 5-year, 10-year and 20-year maturities.

   a. 4-4-5 Calendar
   b. Treasury securities
   c. Treasury Inflation Protected Securities
   d. Treasury Inflation-Protected Securities

38. The _____ or redemption yield is the yield promised to the bondholder on the assumption that the bond or other fixed-interest security such as gilts will be held to maturity, that all coupon and principal payments will be made and coupon payments are reinvested at the bond's promised yield at the same rate as invested. It is a measure of the return of the bond. This technique in theory allows investors to calculate the fair value of different financial instruments.

   a. Macaulay duration
   b. Yield
   c. 4-4-5 Calendar
   d. Yield to maturity

39. _____ is that which is owed; usually referencing assets owed, but the term can cover other obligations. In the case of assets, _____ is a means of using future purchasing power in the present before a summation has been earned. Some companies and corporations use _____ as a part of their overall corporate finance strategy.

   a. Cross-collateralization
   b. Credit cycle
   c. Debt
   d. Partial Payment

40. _____ is a life of security. It may also refer to the final payment date of a loan or other financial instrument, at which point all remaining interest and principal is due to be paid.

1, 3, 6 months _____ band can be calculated by using 30-day per month periods.

   a. Maturity
   b. Replacement cost
   c. Primary market
   d. False billing

41. The _____ (NYSE: FNM), commonly known as Fannie Mae, is a stockholder-owned corporation chartered by Congress in 1968 as a government sponsored enterprise (GSE), but founded in 1938 during the Great Depression. The corporation's purpose is to purchase and securitize mortgages in order to ensure that funds are consistently available to the institutions that lend money to home buyers.

Chapter 2. Asset Classes and Financial Instruments

On September 7, 2008, James Lockhart, director of the Federal Housing Finance Agency (FHFA), announced that Fannie Mae and Freddie Mac were being placed into conservatorship of the FHFA.

a. SPDR
b. General partnership
c. The Depository Trust ' Clearing Corporation
d. Federal National Mortgage Association

42. The _____ provide stable, on-demand, low-cost funding to American financial institutions for home mortgage loans, small business, rural, agricultural, and economic development lending. With their members, the _____ank System represents the largest collective source of home mortgage and community credit in the United States. The banks do not provide loans directly to individuals, only to other banks.

a. 529 plan
b. 4-4-5 Calendar
c. Federal Home Loan Banks
d. 7-Eleven

43. The _____ (NYSE: FRE) is an insolvent government sponsored enterprise (GSE) of the United States federal government.

The _____ was created in 1970 to expand the secondary market for mortgages in the US. Along with other GSEs, Freddie Mac buys mortgages on the secondary market, pools them, and sells them as mortgage-backed securities to investors on the open market.

a. Governmental Accounting Standards Board
b. Public company
c. The Depository Trust ' Clearing Corporation
d. Federal Home Loan Mortgage Corporation

44. The _____ is a U.S. government-owned corporation within the Department of Housing and Urban Development

Ginnie Mae provides guarantees on mortgage-backed securities backed by federally insured or guaranteed loans, mainly loans issued by the Federal Housing Administration, Department of Veterans Affairs, Rural Housing Service, and Office of Public and Indian Housing. Ginnie Mae securities are the only MBS that are guaranteed by the United States government.

a. Case-Shiller Home Price Indices
b. GNMA
c. Cash budget
d. Certified Emission Reductions

45. The _____ is a U.S. government-owned corporation within the Department of Housing and Urban Development

Ginnie Mae provides guarantees on mortgage-backed securities backed by federally insured or guaranteed loans, mainly loans issued by the Federal Housing Administration, Department of Veterans Affairs, Rural Housing Service, and Office of Public and Indian Housing. Ginnie Mae securities are the only MBS that are guaranteed by the United States government.

a. Graduated payment mortgage
b. Jumbo mortgage
c. 4-4-5 Calendar
d. Government National Mortgage Association

Chapter 2. Asset Classes and Financial Instruments

46. A _____ is an international bond that is denominated in a currency not native to the country where it is issued. It can be categorised according to the currency in which it is issued. London is one of the centers of the _____ market, but _____s may be traded throughout the world - for example in Singapore or Tokyo.

   a. Interest rate option
   b. Eurobond
   c. Education production function
   d. Economic entity

47. A _____ is a legal pledge in United States municipal finance, in which an entity pledges its full faith and credit to repay its debt, typically a _____ bond.

   a. Covenant
   b. Financial Institutions Reform Recovery and Enforcement Act
   c. Letter of credit
   d. General obligation

48. In the United States, a _____ is a bond issued by a city or other local government, or their agencies. Potential issuers of these bonds include cities, counties, redevelopment agencies, school districts, publicly owned airports and seaports, and any other governmental entity (or group of governments) below the state level. They may be general obligations of the issuer or secured by specified revenues.

   a. Puttable bond
   b. Premium bond
   c. Senior debt
   d. Municipal bond

49. In business, _____ is income that a company receives from its normal business activities, usually from the sale of goods and services to customers. Some companies also receive _____ from interest, dividends or royalties paid to them by other companies. _____ may refer to business income in general, or it may refer to the amount, in a monetary unit, received during a period of time, as in 'Last year, Company X had _____ of $32 million.'

   In many countries, including the UK, _____ is referred to as turnover.

   a. Revenue
   b. Furniture, Fixtures and Equipment
   c. Bottom line
   d. Matching principle

50. _____ are bonds issued by governments, authorities, or public benefit corporations that are guaranteed by the revenue flow of the issuing agency.

   The Supreme Court decision of Pollock versus Farmer's Loan and Trust Company of 1895 initiated a wave or series of innovations for the financial services community in both tax-treatment and regulation from government. This specific case, according to a leading investment bank's research, resulted in the 'intergovernmental tax immunity doctrine,' ultimately leading to 'tax-free status.' Municipal bonds are generally exempt from federal tax on their interest payments (not capital gains.)

   a. Gilts
   b. Private activity bond
   c. Callable bond
   d. Revenue bonds

51. A _____ is an exemption from all or certain taxes of a state or nation in which part of the taxes that would normally be collected from an individual or an organization are instead foregone.

Normally a _____ is provided to an individual or organization which falls within a class which the government wishes to promote economically, such as charitable organizations. _____s are usually meant to either reduce the tax burden on a particular segment of society in the interests of fairness or to promote some type of economic activity through reducing the tax burden on those organizations or individuals who are involved in that activity.

  a. Tax incidence
  b. Federal Open Market Committee
  c. Tax compliance solution
  d. Tax exemption

52. _____ are the divisions at which tax rates change in a progressive tax system (or an explicitly regressive tax system, although this is much rarer.) Essentially, they are the cutoff values for taxable income -- income past a certain point will be taxed at a higher rate.

Imagine that there are three _____: 10%, 20%, and 30%.

  a. Capital gains tax
  b. Tax holiday
  c. Payroll tax
  d. Tax brackets

53. An _____ is a mortgage loan where the interest rate on the note is periodically adjusted based on a variety of indices. Among the most common indices are the rates on 1-year constant-maturity Treasury (CMT) securities, the Cost of Funds Index (COFI), and the London Interbank Offered Rate (LIBOR.) A few lenders use their own cost of funds as an index, rather than using other indices.

  a. A Random Walk Down Wall Street
  b. ABN Amro
  c. AAB
  d. Adjustable rate mortgage

54. _____ is a type of bond that allows the issuer of the bond to retain the privilege of redeeming the bond at some point before the bond reaches the date of maturity. In other words, on the call dates, the issuer has the right, but not the obligation, to buy back the bonds from the bond holders at the call price. Technically speaking, the bonds are not really bought and held by the issuer but cancelled immediately.

  a. Gilts
  b. Callable bond
  c. Coupon rate
  d. Bond fund

55. In finance, a _____ is a type of bond that can be converted into shares of stock in the issuing company, usually at some pre-announced ratio. It is a hybrid security with debt- and equity-like features. Although it typically has a low coupon rate, the holder is compensated with the ability to convert the bond to common stock, usually at a substantial discount to the stock's market value.

  a. Gilts
  b. Bond fund
  c. Convertible bond
  d. Corporate bond

56. A _____ is a bond issued by a corporation. The term is usually applied to longer-term debt instruments, generally with a maturity date falling at least a year after their issue date. (The term 'commercial paper' is sometimes used for instruments with a shorter maturity.)

  a. Corporate bond
  b. Government bond
  c. Serial bond
  d. Brady bonds

Chapter 2. Asset Classes and Financial Instruments

57. A _____ is defined as a certificate of agreement of loans which is given under the company's stamp and carries an undertaking that the _____ holder will get a fixed return (fixed on the basis of interest rates) and the principal amount whenever the _____ matures.

In finance, a _____ is a long-term debt instrument used by governments and large companies to obtain funds. It is defined as 'a debt secured only by the debtor's earning power, not by a lien on any specific asset.' It is similar to a bond except the securitization conditions are different.

a. Collateral Management
c. Partial Payment
b. Debenture
d. Collection agency

58. In finance, _____ occurs when a debtor has not met its legal obligations according to the debt contract, e.g. it has not made a scheduled payment, or has violated a loan covenant (condition) of the debt contract. _____ may occur if the debtor is either unwilling or unable to pay their debt. This can occur with all debt obligations including bonds, mortgages, loans, and promissory notes.

a. Debt validation
c. Credit crunch
b. Vendor finance
d. Default

59. _____ is the risk of loss due to a debtor's non-payment of a loan or other line of credit (either the principal or interest (coupon) or both)

Most lenders employ their own models (credit scorecards) to rank potential and existing customers according to risk, and then apply appropriate strategies. With products such as unsecured personal loans or mortgages, lenders charge a higher price for higher risk customers and vice versa. With revolving products such as credit cards and overdrafts, risk is controlled through careful setting of credit limits.

a. Transaction risk
c. Market risk
b. Liquidity risk
d. Credit risk

60. A _____ is an asset-backed security whose cash flows are backed by the principal and interest payments of a set of mortgage loans. Payments are typically made monthly over the lifetime of the underlying loans.

a. Home equity line of credit
c. Conforming loan
b. Shared appreciation mortgage
d. Mortgage-backed security

61. In financial accounting, _____s are precautions for which the amount or probability of occurrence are not known. Typical examples are _____s for warranty costs and _____ for taxes the term reserve is used instead of term _____; such a use, however, is inconsistent with the terminology suggested by International Accounting Standards Board.

a. Money measurement concept
c. Petty cash
b. Momentum Accounting and Triple-Entry Bookkeeping
d. Provision

62. _____ is a form of corporation equity ownership represented in the securities. It is dangerous in comparison to preferred shares and some other investment options, in that in the event of bankruptcy, _____ investors receive their funds after preferred stockholders, bondholders, creditors, etc. On the other hand, common shares on average perform better than preferred shares or bonds over time.

a. Stop-limit order
c. Stock market bubble
b. Stock split
d. Common stock

63. In business and finance, a _____ (also referred to as equity _____) of stock means a _____ of ownership in a corporation (company.) In the plural, stocks is often used as a synonym for _____s especially in the United States, but it is less commonly used that way outside of North America.

In the United Kingdom, South Africa, and Australia, stock can also refer to completely different financial instruments such as government bonds or, less commonly, to all kinds of marketable securities.

   a. Margin
   c. Procter ' Gamble
   b. Share
   d. Bucket shop

64. In political science and economics, the _____ or agency dilemma treats the difficulties that arise under conditions of incomplete and asymmetric information when a principal hires an agent. Various mechanisms may be used to try to align the interests of the agent with those of the principal, such as piece rates/commissions, profit sharing, efficiency wages, performance measurement (including financial statements), the agent posting a bond, or fear of firing. The _____ is found in most employer/employee relationships, for example, when stockholders hire top executives of corporations.
   a. Principal-agent problem
   c. 529 plan
   b. 4-4-5 Calendar
   d. 7-Eleven

65. A _____ is a profit that results from investments into a capital asset, such as stocks, bonds or real estate, which exceeds the purchase price. It is the difference between a higher selling price and a lower purchase price, resulting in a financial gain for the seller. Conversely, a capital loss arises if the proceeds from the sale of a capital asset are less than the purchase price.
   a. Capital gain
   c. Tax brackets
   b. Payroll tax
   d. Capital gains tax

66. _____ is a concept whereby a person's financial liability is limited to a fixed sum, most commonly the value of a person's investment in a company or partnership with _____. A shareholder in a limited company is not personally liable for any of the debts of the company, other than for the value of his investment in that company. The same is true for the members of a _____ partnership and the limited partners in a limited partnership.
   a. Sarbanes-Oxley Act
   c. Personal property
   b. Beneficial owner
   d. Limited liability

67. The _____ is a stock exchange based in New York City, New York. It is the largest stock exchange in the world by dollar value of its listed companies securities. As of October 2008, the combined capitalization of all domestic _____ listed companies was $10.1 trillion.
   a. New York Stock Exchange
   c. 4-4-5 Calendar
   b. 529 plan
   d. 7-Eleven

Chapter 2. Asset Classes and Financial Instruments 25

68. A _____, securities exchange or (in Europe) bourse is a corporation or mutual organization which provides 'trading' facilities for stock brokers and traders, to trade stocks and other securities. _____s also provide facilities for the issue and redemption of securities as well as other financial instruments and capital events including the payment of income and dividends. The securities traded on a _____ include: shares issued by companies, unit trusts and other pooled investment products and bonds.

   a. 7-Eleven
   b. 529 plan
   c. 4-4-5 Calendar
   d. Stock Exchange

69. In the most general sense, a _____ is anything that is a hindrance, or puts individuals at a disadvantage.

Before we discuss the financial terms, we should note that a _____ can also have a much more important slang meaning.

This is best described in an example.

   a. Covenant
   b. McFadden Act
   c. Limited liability
   d. Liability

70. The _____ of a stock is a measure of the price paid for a share relative to the annual income or profit earned by the firm per share. It is a financial ratio used for valuation: a higher _____ means that investors are paying more for each unit of income, so the stock is more expensive compared to one with lower _____.

The _____ has units of years, which can be interpreted as 'number of years of earnings to pay back purchase price'.

   a. Quick ratio
   b. Sustainable growth rate
   c. Return of capital
   d. P/E ratio

71. _____ is typically a higher ranking stock than voting shares, and its terms are negotiated between the corporation and the investor.

_____ usually carry no voting rights, but may carry superior priority over common stock in the payment of dividends and upon liquidation. _____ may carry a dividend that is paid out prior to any dividends to common stock holders.

   a. Preferred stock
   b. Follow-on offering
   c. Trade-off theory
   d. Second lien loan

72. A _____ is a payment made by a corporation to its shareholder members. When a corporation earns a profit or surplus, that money can be put to two uses: it can either be re-invested in the business (called retained earnings), or it can be paid to the shareholders as a _____. Many corporations retain a portion of their earnings and pay the remainder as a _____.

   a. Dividend puzzle
   b. Dividend
   c. Dividend yield
   d. Special dividend

73. An _____ represents the ownership in the shares of a foreign company trading on US financial markets. The stock of many non-US companies trades on US exchanges through the use of _____s. _____s enable US investors to buy shares in foreign companies without undertaking cross-border transactions.
   a. A Random Walk Down Wall Street
   b. AAB
   c. ABN Amro
   d. American Depository Receipt

74. The _____ is one of several stock market indices, created by nineteenth-century Wall Street Journal editor and Dow Jones ' Company co-founder Charles Dow. Dow compiled the index to gauge the performance of the industrial sector of the American stock market. It is the second-oldest U.S. market index, after the Dow Jones Transportation Average, which Dow also created.
   a. 4-4-5 Calendar
   b. Dow Jones Industrial Average
   c. 7-Eleven
   d. 529 plan

75. _____ is a stock market index for the Tokyo Stock Exchange (TSE.) It has been calculated daily by the Nihon Keizai Shimbun (Nikkei) newspaper since 1950. It is a price-weighted average (the unit is Yen), and the components are reviewed once a year.
   a. 4-4-5 Calendar
   b. 7-Eleven
   c. 529 plan
   d. Nikkei 225

76. A _____ index is a stock market index where each constituent makes up a fraction of the index that is proportional to its price. For a stock market index this implies that stocks are included in proportions based on their quoted prices. A stock trading at $100 will thus be making up 10 times more of the total index compared to a stock trading at $10.
   a. Product life cycle
   b. Golden parachute
   c. Price-weighted
   d. Trade finance

77. A _____ is a method of measuring a section of the stock market. Many indices are cited by news or financial services firms and are used to benchmark the performance of portfolios such as mutual funds.
   a. Program trading
   b. Stop order
   c. Trading curb
   d. Stock market index

78. A _____ is a listing of bonds or fixed income instruments and a statistic reflecting the composite value of its components. It is used as a tool to represent the characteristics of its component fixed income instruments. They differ from stock market indices in their complexity.
   a. 7-Eleven
   b. 529 plan
   c. Bond market index
   d. 4-4-5 Calendar

79. The _____ of a public company is an estimate of the proportion of shares that are not held by large owners and that are not stock with sales restrictions (restricted stock that cannot be sold until they become unrestricted stock.)

The _____ or a public float is usually defined as being all shares held by investors other than:

- shares held by owners owning more than 5% of all shares (those could be institutional investors, 'strategic shareholders,' founders, executives, and other insiders' holdings)
- restricted stocks (granted to executives that can be, but don't have to be, registered insiders)
- insider holdings (it is assumed that insiders hold stock for the very long term)

The _____ is an important criterion in quoting a share on the stock market.

To float a company means to list its shares on a public stock exchange through an initial public offering (or 'flotation'.)

- Open market
- Outstanding shares
- Market capitalization
- Public float
- Reverse takeover

a. Free float
b. Proxy fight
c. Product life cycle
d. Counting house

80. An _____ or index tracker is a collective investment scheme (usually a mutual fund or exchange-traded fund) that aims to replicate the movements of an index of a specific financial market regardless of market conditions.

Tracking can be achieved by trying to hold all of the securities in the index, in the same proportions as the index. Other methods include statistically sampling the market and holding 'representative' securities.

a. Index fund
b. AAB
c. Investment company
d. A Random Walk Down Wall Street

81. The free _____ of a public company is an estimate of the proportion of shares that are not held by large owners and that are not stock with sales restrictions (restricted stock that cannot be sold until they become unrestricted stock.)

The free _____ or a public _____ is usually defined as being all shares held by investors other than:

- shares held by owners owning more than 5% of all shares (those could be institutional investors, 'strategic shareholders,' founders, executives, and other insiders' holdings)
- restricted stocks (granted to executives that can be, but don't have to be, registered insiders)
- insider holdings (it is assumed that insiders hold stock for the very long term)

The free _____ is an important criterion in quoting a share on the stock market.

Chapter 2. Asset Classes and Financial Instruments

To _____ a company means to list its shares on a public stock exchange through an initial public offering (or 'flotation'.)

- Open market
- Outstanding shares
- Market capitalization
- Public _____ loat
- Reverse takeover

a. Synthetic CDO
b. Float
c. Trade finance
d. Golden parachute

82. An _____ is an investment vehicle traded on stock exchanges, much like stocks. An ETF holds assets such as stocks or bonds and trades at approximately the same price as the net asset value of its underlying assets over the course of the trading day. Most ETFs track an index, such as the Dow Jones Industrial Average or the S'P 500.

a. ABN Amro
b. A Random Walk Down Wall Street
c. Exchange-traded fund
d. AAB

83. A _____ is a professionally managed type of collective investment scheme that pools money from many investors and invests it in stocks, bonds, short-term money market instruments, and/or other securities. The _____ will have a fund manager that trades the pooled money on a regular basis. Currently, the worldwide value of all _____s totals more than $26 trillion.

Since 1940, there have been three basic types of investment companies in the United States: open-end funds, also known in the US as _____s; unit investment trusts (UITs); and closed-end funds.

a. Trust company
b. Mutual fund
c. Financial intermediary
d. Net asset value

84. In the United States, the Financial Industry Regulatory Authority (FINRA) is a self-regulatory organization (SRO) under the Securities Exchange Act of 1934, successor to the _____, Inc.

FINRA is responsible for regulatory oversight of all securities firms that do business with the public; professional training, testing and licensing of registered persons; arbitration and mediation; market regulation by contract for The NASDAQ Stock Market, Inc., the American Stock Exchange LLC, and the International Securities Exchange, LLC; and industry utilities, such as Trade Reporting Facilities and other over-the-counter operations.

a. 7-Eleven
b. 4-4-5 Calendar
c. 529 plan
d. National Association of Securities Dealers

Chapter 2. Asset Classes and Financial Instruments

85. A _____ is a financial contract between two parties, the buyer and the seller of this type of option. Often it is simply labeled a 'call'. The buyer of the option has the right, but not the obligation to buy an agreed quantity of a particular commodity or financial instrument (the underlying instrument) from the seller of the option at a certain time (the expiration date) for a certain price (the strike price.)

   a. Call option
   c. Bear call spread
   b. Bull spread
   d. Bear spread

86. A _____ is a financial contract whose value is derived from the value of something else (known as the underlying.) The underlying on which a _____ is based can be an asset, weather conditions bonds or other forms of credit.

   a. 529 plan
   c. Derivative
   b. 4-4-5 Calendar
   d. 7-Eleven

87. In options, the _____ is a key variable in a derivatives contract between two parties. Where the contract requires delivery of the underlying instrument, the trade will be at the _____, regardless of the spot price (market price) of the underlying instrument at that time.

Definition - The fixed price at which the owner of an option can purchase, in the case of a call in the case of a put, the underlying security or commodity.

   a. Swaption
   c. Moneyness
   b. Naked put
   d. Strike price

88. A bond is considered _____ if its credit rating is BBB- or higher by Standard and Poor's or Baa3 or higher by Moody's or BBB(low) or higher by DBRS. Generally they are bonds that are judged by the rating agency as likely enough to meet payment obligations that banks are allowed to invest in them.

Ratings play a critical role in determining how much companies and other entities that issue debt, including sovereign governments, have to pay to access credit markets, i.e., the amount of interest they pay on their issued debt.

   a. Investment Grade
   c. AAB
   b. A Random Walk Down Wall Street
   d. ABN Amro

89. The _____ is a broad base index, maintained by Lehman Brothers, often used to represent investment grade bonds being traded in United States. Index funds and exchange-traded funds are available that track this bond index.

The _____ is a market capitalization-weighted index, meaning the securities in the index are weighted according to the market size of each bond type.

   a. 529 plan
   c. 4-4-5 Calendar
   b. 7-Eleven
   d. Lehman Aggregate Bond Index

Chapter 2. Asset Classes and Financial Instruments

90. An _____ is a contract written by a seller that conveys to the buyer the right -- but not the obligation -- to buy (in the case of a call _____) or to sell (in the case of a put _____) a particular asset, such as a piece of property such as, among others, a futures contract. In return for granting the _____, the seller collects a payment (the premium) from the buyer.

For example, buying a call _____ provides the right to buy a specified quantity of a security at a set strike price at some time on or before expiration, while buying a put _____ provides the right to sell.

   a. Option
   c. Amortization
   b. Annuity
   d. AT'T Mobility LLC

91. A _____ is a financial contract between two parties, the seller (writer) and the buyer of the option. The put allows its buyer the right but not the obligation to sell a commodity or financial instrument (the underlying instrument) to the writer (seller) of the option at a certain time for a certain price (the strike price.) The writer (seller) has the obligation to purchase the underlying asset at that strike price, if the buyer exercises the option.
   a. Put option
   c. Debit spread
   b. Bear spread
   d. Bear call spread

92. The _____ is an American financial and commodity derivative exchange based in Chicago. The _____ was founded in 1898 as the Chicago Butter and Egg Board. Originally, the exchange was a non-profit organization.
   a. Financial Crimes Enforcement Network
   c. Public Company Accounting Oversight Board
   b. Gamelan Council
   d. Chicago Mercantile Exchange

93. In finance, a _____ is a standardized contract, to buy or sell a specified commodity of standardized quality at a certain date in the future, at a market determined price (the futures price.)

The price is determined by the instantaneous equilibrium between the forces of supply and demand among competing buy and sell orders on the exchange at the time of the purchase or sale of the contract.

In many cases, the items may be such non-traditional 'commodities' as foreign currencies, commercial or government paper [e.g., bonds], or 'baskets' of corporate equity ['stock indices'] or other financial instruments.

   a. Financial future
   c. Futures contract
   b. Repurchase agreement
   d. Heston model

94. Days to Cover (DTC) is a numerical term that describes the relationship between the amount of shares in a given equity that have been short sold and the number of days of typical trading that it would require to 'cover' all _____ outstanding. For example, if there are ten million shares of XYZ Inc. that are currently short sold and the average daily volume of XYZ shares traded each day is one million, it would require ten days of trading for all _____ to be covered (10 million / 1 million.)
   a. Stock or scrip dividends
   c. Guaranteed investment contracts
   b. Cash budget
   d. Short positions

95. A _____ is an exchange of promises between two or more parties to do an act which is enforceable in a court of law. It is where an unqualified offer meets a qualified acceptance and the parties reach Consensus ad Idem. The parties must have the necessary capacity to _____ and the _____ must not be either trifling, indeterminate, impossible or illegal.
    a. Contract
    b. 4-4-5 Calendar
    c. 7-Eleven
    d. 529 plan

Chapter 3. How Securities are Traded

1. The free _____ of a public company is an estimate of the proportion of shares that are not held by large owners and that are not stock with sales restrictions (restricted stock that cannot be sold until they become unrestricted stock.)

The free _____ or a public _____ is usually defined as being all shares held by investors other than:

- shares held by owners owning more than 5% of all shares (those could be institutional investors, 'strategic shareholders,' founders, executives, and other insiders' holdings)
- restricted stocks (granted to executives that can be, but don't have to be, registered insiders)
- insider holdings (it is assumed that insiders hold stock for the very long term)

The free _____ is an important criterion in quoting a share on the stock market.

To _____ a company means to list its shares on a public stock exchange through an initial public offering (or 'flotation'.)

- Open market
- Outstanding shares
- Market capitalization
- Public _____ loat
- Reverse takeover

    a. Synthetic CDO   b. Golden parachute
    c. Trade finance   d. Float

2. The _____ is that part of the capital markets that deals with the issuance of new securities. Companies, governments or public sector institutions can obtain funding through the sale of a new stock or bond issue. This is typically done through a syndicate of securities dealers.

    a. Peer group analysis   b. Primary market
    c. Sector rotation   d. Volatility clustering

3. The _____ is the financial market where previously issued securities and financial instruments such as stock, bonds, options, and futures are bought and sold. The term '_____' is also used refer to the market for any used goods or assets, or an alternative use for an existing product or asset where the customer base is the second market

With primary issuances of securities or financial instruments, or the primary market, investors purchase these securities directly from issuers such as corporations issuing shares in an IPO or private placement, or directly from the federal government in the case of treasuries.

    a. Delta neutral   b. Performance attribution
    c. Financial market   d. Secondary market

4. A _____ is a fungible, negotiable instrument representing financial value. They are broadly categorized into debt securities (such as banknotes, bonds and debentures), and equity securities; e.g., common stocks. The company or other entity issuing the _____ is called the issuer.

a. Security	b. Book entry
c. Securities lending	d. Tracking stock

5. In the _____ contract the underwriter guarantees the sale of the issued stock at the agreed-upon price. For the issuer, it is the safest but the most expensive type of the contracts, since the underwriter takes the risk of sale.

In the best efforts contract the underwriter agrees to sell as many shares as possible at the agreed-upon price.

a. Special purpose entity	b. Rights issue
c. Participating preferred stock	d. Firm commitment

6. _____, is when a company issues common stock or shares to the public for the first time. They are often issued by smaller, younger companies seeking capital to expand, but can also be done by large privately-owned companies looking to become publicly traded.

In an _____ the issuer may obtain the assistance of an underwriting firm, which helps it determine what type of security to issue (common or preferred), best offering price and time to bring it to market.

a. Asian Financial Crisis	b. Insolvency
c. Interest	d. Initial public offering

7. In the United States, a _____ is an offering of securities that are not registered with the Securities and Exchange Commission (SEC.) Such offerings exploit an exemption offered by the Securities Act of 1933 that comes with several restrictions, including a prohibition against general solicitation. This exemption allows companies to avoid quarterly reporting requirements and many of the legal liabilities associated with the Sarbanes-Oxley Act.

a. 7-Eleven	b. 529 plan
c. 4-4-5 Calendar	d. Private placement

8. The U.S. _____ is an independent agency of the United States government which holds primary responsibility for enforcing the federal securities laws and regulating the securities industry, the nation's stock and options exchanges, and other electronic securities markets. The SEC was created by section 4 of the SEC of 1934 (now codified as 15 U.S.C. § 78d and commonly referred to as the 1934 Act.)

a. 7-Eleven	b. Securities and Exchange Commission
c. 4-4-5 Calendar	d. 529 plan

9. Unemployment occurs when a person is available to work and currently seeking work, but the person is without work. The prevalence of unemployment is usually measured using the _____, which is defined as the percentage of those in the labor force who are unemployed. The _____ is also used in economic studies and economic indexes such as the United States' Conference Board's Index of Leading Indicators as a measure of the state of the macroeconomics.

a. AAB	b. A Random Walk Down Wall Street
c. ABN Amro	d. Unemployment rate

10. _____, adopted pursuant to the U.S. Securities Act of 1933, as amended (the 'Securities Act') provides a safe harbor from the registration requirements of the Securities Act of 1933 for certain private resales of restricted securities to QIBs (qualified institutional buyers), which generally are large institutional investors with over $100 million in investable assets. When a broker or dealer is selling securities in reliance on _____, it is subject to the condition that it may not make offers to persons other than those it reasonably believes to be QIBs.

Since its adoption, _____ has greatly increased the liquidity of the securities affected.

   a. Securities Investor Protection Corporation   b. SIPC
   c. Prudent man rule   d. Rule 144A

11. _____ is an arrangement with the U.S. Securities and Exchange Commission that allows a single registration document to be filed that permits the issuance of multiple securities.

_____ is a registration of a new issue which can be prepared up to two years in advance, so that the issue can be offered quickly as soon as funds are needed or market conditions are favorable.

For example, current market conditions in the housing market are not favorable for a specific firm to issue a public offering.

   a. Black Sea Trade and Development Bank   b. 4-4-5 Calendar
   c. Bought deal   d. Shelf registration

12. In finance, a _____ is a debt security, in which the authorized issuer owes the holders a debt and, depending on the terms of the _____, is obliged to pay interest (the coupon) and/or to repay the principal at a later date, termed maturity.

Thus a _____ is a loan: the issuer is the borrower, the _____ holder is the lender, and the coupon is the interest. _____s provide the borrower with external funds to finance long-term investments, or, in the case of government _____s, to finance current expenditure.

   a. Convertible bond   b. Catastrophe bonds
   c. Puttable bond   d. Bond

13. _____ is basically the process of generating a book of investor demand for the shares during an IPO for efficient price discovery. Usually, the issuer appoints a major investment bank to act as a book runner.

_____ is a common practice in developed countries and has recently been making inroads into emerging markets as well, including India.

   a. Book building   b. Gross profit margin
   c. Preferred stock   d. Gross profit

14. In finance, the term _____ describes the amount in cash that returns to the owners of a security. Normally it does not include the price variations, at the difference of the total return. _____ applies to various stated rates of return on stocks (common and preferred, and convertible), fixed income instruments (bonds, notes, bills, strips, zero coupon), and some other investment type insurance products (e.g. annuities.)
   a. Yield to maturity
   b. 4-4-5 Calendar
   c. Macaulay duration
   d. Yield

15. The _____ or redemption yield is the yield promised to the bondholder on the assumption that the bond or other fixed-interest security such as gilts will be held to maturity, that all coupon and principal payments will be made and coupon payments are reinvested at the bond's promised yield at the same rate as invested. It is a measure of the return of the bond. This technique in theory allows investors to calculate the fair value of different financial instruments.
   a. 4-4-5 Calendar
   b. Macaulay duration
   c. Yield
   d. Yield to maturity

16. A _____, in its most general sense, is a solemn promise to engage in or refrain from a specified action.

More specifically, a _____, in contrast to a contract, is a one-way agreement whereby the _____er is the only party bound by the promise. A _____ may have conditions and prerequisites that qualify the undertaking, including the actions of second or third parties, but there is no inherent agreement by such other parties to fulfill those requirements.

   a. Partnership
   b. Covenant
   c. Clayton Antitrust Act
   d. Federal Trade Commission Act

17. _____ is a life of security. It may also refer to the final payment date of a loan or other financial instrument, at which point all remaining interest and principal is due to be paid.

1, 3, 6 months _____ band can be calculated by using 30-day per month periods.

   a. Maturity
   b. False billing
   c. Primary market
   d. Replacement cost

18. A _____ is a bond bought at a price lower than its face value, with the face value repaid at the time of maturity. It does not make periodic interest payments, or have so-called 'coupons,' hence the term _____. Investors earn return from the compounded interest all paid at maturity plus the difference between the discounted price of the bond and its par value.
   a. Corporate bond
   b. Clean price
   c. Zero-coupon bond
   d. Bond fund

19. A _____ is a type of auction where the auctioneer begins with a high asking price which is lowered until some participant is willing to accept the auctioneer's price, or a predetermined reserve price (the seller's minimum acceptable price) is reached. The winning participant pays the last announced price. This is also known as a 'clock auction' or an open-outcry descending-price auction.
   a. 7-Eleven
   b. 529 plan
   c. 4-4-5 Calendar
   d. Dutch auction

20. _____ most frequently refers to the standard deviation of the continuously compounded returns of a financial instrument with a specific time horizon. It is often used to quantify the risk of the instrument over that time period. _____ is typically expressed in annualized terms, and it may either be an absolute number ($5) or a fraction of the mean (5%).
   a. Volatility
   b. Seasoned equity offering
   c. Currency swap
   d. Portfolio insurance

21. _____ in financial markets is the likelihood of fluctuations in the exchange rate of currencies. Therefore, it is a probability measure of the threat that an exchange rate movement poses to an investor's portfolio in a foreign currency. The volatility of the exchange rate is measured as standard deviation over a dataset of exchange rate movements.
   a. Volatility risk
   b. 7-Eleven
   c. 4-4-5 Calendar
   d. 529 plan

22. In economics, a _____ is a mechanism that allows people to easily buy and sell (trade) financial securities (such as stocks and bonds), commodities (such as precious metals or agricultural goods), and other fungible items of value at low transaction costs and at prices that reflect the efficient-market hypothesis.

_____s have evolved significantly over several hundred years and are undergoing constant innovation to improve liquidity.

Both general markets (where many commodities are traded) and specialized markets (where only one commodity is traded) exist.

   a. Financial market
   b. Cost of carry
   c. Delta hedging
   d. Secondary market

23. The _____ is a stock exchange based in New York City, New York. It is the largest stock exchange in the world by dollar value of its listed companies securities. As of October 2008, the combined capitalization of all domestic _____ listed companies was $10.1 trillion.
   a. 7-Eleven
   b. 529 plan
   c. 4-4-5 Calendar
   d. New York Stock Exchange

24. A _____, securities exchange or (in Europe) bourse is a corporation or mutual organization which provides 'trading' facilities for stock brokers and traders, to trade stocks and other securities. _____s also provide facilities for the issue and redemption of securities as well as other financial instruments and capital events including the payment of income and dividends. The securities traded on a _____ include: shares issued by companies, unit trusts and other pooled investment products and bonds.
   a. 4-4-5 Calendar
   b. Stock Exchange
   c. 7-Eleven
   d. 529 plan

25. _____ offer, asking price is a price a seller of a good is willing to accept for that particular good.

In bid and ask, the term _____ is used in contrast to the term bid price. The difference between the _____ and the bid price is called the spread.

Chapter 3. How Securities are Traded 37

a. A Random Walk Down Wall Street
b. AAB
c. Interest rate parity
d. Ask price

26. A _____ is the highest price that a buyer (i.e., bidder) is willing to pay for a good. It is usually referred to simply as the 'bid.'

In bid and ask, the _____ stands in contrast to the ask price or 'offer', and the difference between the two is called the bid/ask spread.

An unsolicited bid or offer is when a person or company receives a bid even though they are not looking to sell.

a. Mid price
b. Bid price
c. Settlement date
d. Political risk

27. A _____ or market-based mechanism is any of a wide variety of ways to match up buyers and sellers.

An example of a _____ uses announced bid and ask prices. Generally speaking, when two parties wish to engage in a trade, the purchaser will announce a price he is willing to pay (the bid price) and seller will announce a price he is willing to accept (the ask price).

a. 529 plan
b. 7-Eleven
c. 4-4-5 Calendar
d. Price mechanism

28. The _____ for securities is the difference between the price quoted by a market maker for an immediate sale and an immediate purchase The size of the bid-offer spread in a given commodity is a measure of the liquidity of the market.

The trader initiating the transaction is said to demand liquidity, and the other party to the transaction supplies liquidity.

a. Capital outflow
b. Defined contribution plan
c. Trade-off
d. Bid/offer spread

29. A _____ is an order to buy a security at no more (or sell at no less) than a specific price. This gives the customer some control over the price at which the trade is executed, but may prevent the order from being executed ('filled'.)

A buy _____ can only be executed by the broker at the limit price or lower.

a. Limit order
b. Common stock
c. Block premium
d. Commercial mortgage-backed securities

30. A _____ is a buy or sell order to be executed by the broker immediately at current market prices. As long as there are willing sellers and buyers, _____ s are filled.

A _____ is the simplest of the order types.

Chapter 3. How Securities are Traded

a. Block premium
c. Market order
b. Trading curb
d. Stockholder

31. _____ is a measure of the ability of a debtor to pay their debts as and when they fall due. It is usually expressed as a ratio or a percentage of current liabilities.

For a corporation with a published balance sheet there are various ratios used to calculate a measure of liquidity.

a. Operating profit margin
c. Invested capital
b. Operating leverage
d. Accounting liquidity

32. In the United States, the Financial Industry Regulatory Authority (FINRA) is a self-regulatory organization (SRO) under the Securities Exchange Act of 1934, successor to the _____, Inc.

FINRA is responsible for regulatory oversight of all securities firms that do business with the public; professional training, testing and licensing of registered persons; arbitration and mediation; market regulation by contract for The NASDAQ Stock Market, Inc., the American Stock Exchange LLC, and the International Securities Exchange, LLC; and industry utilities, such as Trade Reporting Facilities and other over-the-counter operations.

a. 529 plan
c. National Association of Securities Dealers
b. 7-Eleven
d. 4-4-5 Calendar

33. In finance, _____ or 'shorting' is the practice of selling a financial instrument that the seller does not own at the time of the sale. _____ is done with intent of later purchasing the financial instrument at a lower price. Short-sellers attempt to profit from an expected decline in the price of a financial instrument.

a. 529 plan
c. Short ratio
b. Short selling
d. 4-4-5 Calendar

34. A _____ is an order to buy (or sell) a security once the price of the security has climbed above (or dropped below) a specified stop price. When the specified stop price is reached, the _____ is entered as a market order (no limit.)

With a _____, the customer does not have to actively monitor how a stock is performing.

a. Share price
c. Stock split
b. Wash sale
d. Stop order

35. An _____ is the term used in financial circles for a type of computer system that facilitates trading of financial products outside of stock exchanges. The primary products that are traded on an _____ are stocks and currencies. They came into existence in 1998 when the SEC authorized their creation.

a. Open outcry
c. Insider trading
b. Intellidex
d. Electronic communication network

36. NYSE Euronext, Inc. is a Euro-American for-profit corporation that operates multiple securities exchanges, most notably Euronext, New York Stock Exchange (NYSE), and NYSE Arca (formerly known as ArcaEx.) _____ also operates NYSE Regulation, which is a non-profit Self-Regulatory Organization that oversees securities firms and companies listed on the New York Stock Exchange and NYSE Arca.

NYSE completed its acquisition of Archipelago Holdings via reverse takeover on March 7, 2006 in a 10 billion USD deal to create the _____.

  a. NYSE Group   b. Gold exchange-traded fund
  c. PlaNet Finance   d. Federal National Mortgage Association

37. The _____ is an American stock exchange. It is the largest electronic screen-based equity securities trading market in the United States. With approximately 3,200 companies, it has more trading volume per day than any other stock exchange in the world.

  a. 529 plan   b. 7-Eleven
  c. 4-4-5 Calendar   d. Nasdaq

38. A _____ is a private or public market for the trading of company stock and derivatives of company stock at an agreed price; these are securities listed on a stock exchange as well as those only traded privately.

The size of the world _____ is estimated at about $36.6 trillion US at the beginning of October 2008 . The world derivatives market has been estimated at about $480 trillion face or nominal value, 12 times the size of the entire world economy.

  a. Adolph Coors   b. Andrew Tobias
  c. Stock market   d. Anton Gelonkin

39. The _____ is an American financial and commodity derivative exchange based in Chicago. The _____ was founded in 1898 as the Chicago Butter and Egg Board. Originally, the exchange was a non-profit organization.

  a. Financial Crimes Enforcement Network   b. Gamelan Council
  c. Public Company Accounting Oversight Board   d. Chicago Mercantile Exchange

40. An _____ is a contract written by a seller that conveys to the buyer the right -- but not the obligation -- to buy (in the case of a call _____) or to sell (in the case of a put _____) a particular asset, such as a piece of property such as, among others, a futures contract. In return for granting the _____, the seller collects a payment (the premium) from the buyer.

For example, buying a call _____ provides the right to buy a specified quantity of a security at a set strike price at some time on or before expiration, while buying a put _____ provides the right to sell.

  a. Annuity   b. AT'T Mobility LLC
  c. Amortization   d. Option

41. A _____ is a financial services company that provides clearing and settlement services for financial transactions, usually on a futures exchange, and often acts as central counterparty (the payor actually pays the _____, which then pays the payee). A _____ may also offer novation, the substitution of a new contract or debt for an old, or other credit enhancement services to its members.

The term is also used for banks like Suffolk Bank that acted as a restraint on the over-issuance of private bank notes.

a. Bucket shop
c. Clearing house
b. Warrant
d. Valuation

42. In finance, _____ is that risk which is common to an entire market and not to any individual entity or component thereof. It should be distinguished from systemic risk which is the risk that the entire financial system will collapse as a result of some catastrophic event.

Risks can be reduced in four main ways: Avoidance, Reduction, Retention and Transfer.

a. Conglomerate merger
c. Systematic risk
b. Capital surplus
d. Primary market

43. The _____ is overseen by the _____ Association.

Tape C contains over-the-counter stocks listed on the NASDAQ National Market or NASDAQ Small Cap Market, and is overseen by the OTC/UTP Operating Committee.

a. Liquidating dividend
c. Consolidated Tape
b. January effect
d. Peer group analysis

44. _____ N.V. is a pan-European stock exchange based in Paris and with subsidiaries in Belgium, France, Netherlands, Luxembourg, Portugal and the United Kingdom. In addition to equities and derivatives markets, the _____ group provides clearing and information services. As of 31 January 2006, markets run by _____ had a market capitalization of US$2.9 trillion, making it the 5th largest exchange on the planet.

a. A Random Walk Down Wall Street
c. AAB
b. ABN Amro
d. Euronext

45. A _____ is a futures contract on a short term interest rate (STIR.) Contracts vary, but are often defined on an interest rate index such as 3-month sterling or US dollar LIBOR.

They are traded across a wide range of currencies, including the G12 country currencies and many others.

a. Notional amount
c. Dual currency deposit
b. Financial Future
d. Real estate derivatives

46. In finance, a _____ is a standardized contract, to buy or sell a specified commodity of standardized quality at a certain date in the future, at a market determined price (the futures price.)

The price is determined by the instantaneous equilibrium between the forces of supply and demand among competing buy and sell orders on the exchange at the time of the purchase or sale of the contract.

In many cases, the items may be such non-traditional 'commodities' as foreign currencies, commercial or government paper [e.g., bonds], or 'baskets' of corporate equity ['stock indices'] or other financial instruments.

Chapter 3. How Securities are Traded

a. Heston model
b. Repurchase agreement
c. Financial future
d. Futures contract

47. The _____ Options Exchange is a futures exchange based in London. _____ is now part of NYSE Euronext following its takeover by Euronext in January 2002 and Euronext's merger with New York Stock Exchange in April 2007.

The _____ started life on September 30, 1982, to take advantage of the removal of currency controls in the UK in 1979.

a. LIFFE
b. 529 plan
c. 7-Eleven
d. 4-4-5 Calendar

48. _____ or amalgamation is the act of merging many things into one. In business, it often refers to the mergers or acquisitions of many smaller companies into much larger ones. The financial accounting term of _____ refers to the aggregated financial statements of a group company as consolidated account.

a. Retained earnings
b. Consolidation
c. Cost of goods sold
d. Write-off

49. A '_____' is a 'Charge' that is paid to obtain the right to delay a payment. Essentially, the payer purchases the right to make a given payment in the future instead of in the Present. The '_____', or 'Charge' that must be paid to delay the payment, is simply the difference between what the payment amount would be if it were paid in the present and what the payment amount would be paid if it were paid in the future.

a. Value at risk
b. Risk aversion
c. Discount
d. Risk modeling

50. _____, in bookkeeping, refers to assets, liabilities, income, and expenses recorded on individual pages of the so called book of final entry or ledger. Changes in _____ value are made by chronologically posting debit (DR) and credit (CR) entries to its page. Examples of _____s are cash, _____s receivable, mortgages, loans, land and buildings, common stock, sales, services provided, wages, and payroll overhead.

a. Account
b. Accretion
c. Option
d. Alpha

51. In economics, business, and accounting, a _____ is the value of money that has been used up to produce something, and hence is not available for use anymore. In business, the _____ may be one of acquisition, in which case the amount of money expended to acquire it is counted as _____. In this case, money is the input that is gone in order to acquire the thing.

a. Sliding scale fees
b. Marginal cost
c. Fixed costs
d. Cost

52. _____ is buying securities with cash borrowed from a broker, using other securities as collateral. This has the effect of magnifying any profit or loss made on the securities. The securities serve as collateral for the loan.

a. SPI 200 futures contract
b. Margin buying
c. Triple witching hour
d. Risk-neutral measure

Chapter 3. How Securities are Traded

53. In finance, a _____ is collateral that the holder of a position in securities, options, or futures contracts has to deposit to cover the credit risk of his counterparty (most often his broker.) This risk can arise if the holder has done any of the following:

- borrowed cash from the counterparty to buy securities or options,
- sold securities or options short, or
- entered into a futures contract.

The collateral can be in the form of cash or securities, and it is deposited in a _____ account. On U.S. futures exchanges, '_____' was formally called performance bond.

_____ buying is buying securities with cash borrowed from a broker, using other securities as collateral.

    a. Share   b. Credit
    c. Procter ' Gamble   d. Margin

54. In financial accounting, the term _____ is most commonly used to describe any part of shareholders' equity, except for basic share capital. Sometimes, the term is used instead of the term provision; such a use, however, is inconsistent with the terminology suggested by International Accounting Standards Board. For more information about provisions, see provision (accounting.)

    a. Reserve   b. Treasury stock
    c. FIFO and LIFO accounting   d. Closing entries

55. The variation margin or _____ is not collateral, but a daily offsetting of profits and losses. Futures are marked-to-market every day, so the current price is compared to the previous day's price. The profit or loss on the day of a position is then paid to or debited from the holder by the futures exchange.

    a. Delivery month   b. Total return swap
    c. SPI 200 futures contract   d. Maintenance margin

56. The _____ is the amount required to be collateralized in order to open a position. Thereafter, the amount required to be kept in collateral until the position is closed is the maintenance requirement. The maintenance requirement is the minimum amount to be collateralized in order to keep an open position.

    a. AAB   b. ABN Amro
    c. A Random Walk Down Wall Street   d. Initial margin requirement

57. _____ is the balance of the amounts of cash being received and paid by a business during a defined period of time, sometimes tied to a specific project. Measurement of _____ can be used

- to evaluate the state or performance of a business or project.
- to determine problems with liquidity. Being profitable does not necessarily mean being liquid. A company can fail because of a shortage of cash, even while profitable.
- to generate project rate of returns. The time of _____s into and out of projects are used as inputs to financial models such as internal rate of return, and net present value.
- to examine income or growth of a business when it is believed that accrual accounting concepts do not represent economic realities. Alternately, _____ can be used to 'validate' the net income generated by accrual accounting.

Chapter 3. How Securities are Traded

_____ as a generic term may be used differently depending on context, and certain _____ definitions may be adapted by analysts and users for their own uses. Common terms include operating _____ and free _____.

_____s can be classified into:

1. Operational _____s: Cash received or expended as a result of the company's core business activities.
2. Investment _____s: Cash received or expended through capital expenditure, investments or acquisitions.
3. Financing _____s: Cash received or expended as a result of financial activities, such as interests and dividends.

All three together - the net _____ - are necessary to reconcile the beginning cash balance to the ending cash balance. Loan draw downs or equity injections, that is just shifting of capital but no expenditure as such, are not considered in the net _____.

   a. Shareholder value
   b. Corporate finance
   c. Real option
   d. Cash flow

58. _____ refers to a business or organization attempting to acquire goods or services to accomplish the goals of the enterprise. Though there are several organizations that attempt to set standards in the _____ process, processes can vary greatly between organizations. Typically the word '_____' is not used interchangeably with the word 'procurement', since procurement typically includes Expediting, Supplier Quality, and Traffic and Logistics (T'L) in addition to _____.
   a. 529 plan
   b. 7-Eleven
   c. 4-4-5 Calendar
   d. Purchasing

59. Days to Cover (DTC) is a numerical term that describes the relationship between the amount of shares in a given equity that have been short sold and the number of days of typical trading that it would require to 'cover' all _____ outstanding. For example, if there are ten million shares of XYZ Inc. that are currently short sold and the average daily volume of XYZ shares traded each day is one million, it would require ten days of trading for all _____ to be covered (10 million / 1 million.)
   a. Stock or scrip dividends
   b. Guaranteed investment contracts
   c. Short positions
   d. Cash budget

60. The _____ of 1934 is a law governing the secondary trading of securities (stocks, bonds, and debentures) in the United States of America. The Act, 48 Stat. 881 (enacted June 6, 1934), codified at 15 U.S.C. § 78a et seq., was a sweeping piece of legislation. The Act and related statutes form the basis of regulation of the financial markets and their participants in the United States.
   a. 529 plan
   b. 4-4-5 Calendar
   c. Securities Exchange Act
   d. 7-Eleven

Chapter 3. How Securities are Traded

61. A _____ is a state law in the United States that regulates the offering and sale of securities to protect the public from fraud. Though the specific provisions of these laws vary among states, they all require the registration of all securities offerings and sales, as well as of stock brokers and brokerage firms. Each state's _____ is administered by its appropriate regulatory agency, and most also provide private causes of action for private investors who have been injured by securities fraud.

   a. Bundesrechnungshof
   b. Blue sky law
   c. Patent
   d. Court of Audit of Belgium

62. _____ is an international professional designation offered by the _____ Institute (formerly known as AIMR) to financial analysts who complete a series of three examinations. In order to become a '_____ Charterholder' candidates must pass all three six-hour exams, possess a bachelor's degree (or equivalent, as assessed by the _____ institute) and have 48 months of work experience in an investment decision-making position. _____ charterholders are also obligated to adhere to a strict Code of Ethics and Standards governing their professional conduct.

   a. 4-4-5 Calendar
   b. 7-Eleven
   c. 529 plan
   d. Chartered Financial Analyst

63. In the original and simplified sense, _____ were things of value, of uniform quality, that were produced in large quantities by many different producers; the items from each different producer are considered equivalent. It is the contract and this underlying standard that define the commodity, not any quality inherent in the product.

_____ exchanges include:

- Chicago Board of Trade
- Kansas City Board of Trade
- Euronext.liffe
- Kuala Lumpur Futures Exchange
- Bhatinda Om ' Oil Exchange
- London Metal Exchange
- New York Mercantile Exchange
- Multi Commodity Exchange
- Dalian Commodity Exchange

Markets for trading _____ can be very efficient, particularly if the division into pools matches demand segments. These markets will quickly respond to changes in supply and demand to find an equilibrium price and quantity.

   a. 529 plan
   b. 7-Eleven
   c. Commodities
   d. 4-4-5 Calendar

64. The institution most often referenced by the word '_____' is a public or publicly traded _____, the shares of which are traded on a public stock exchange (e.g., the New York Stock Exchange or Nasdaq in the United States) where shares of stock of _____s are bought and sold by and to the general public. Most of the largest businesses in the world are publicly traded _____s. However, the majority of _____s are said to be closely held, privately held or close _____s, meaning that no ready market exists for the trading of shares.

Chapter 3. How Securities are Traded

a. Federal Home Loan Mortgage Corporation
b. Depository Trust Company
c. Protect
d. Corporation

65. Explicit _____ is a measure implemented in many countries to protect bank depositors, in full or in part, from losses caused by a bank's inability to pay its debts when due. _____ systems are one component of a financial system safety net that promotes financial stability.

a. Deposit Insurance
b. Time deposit
c. Reserve requirement
d. Banking panic

66. The _____ is a United States government corporation created by the Glass-Steagall Act of 1933. It provides deposit insurance, which guarantees the safety of checking and savings deposits in member banks, currently up to $250,000 per depositor per bank. Insured deposits are backed by the full faith and credit of the United States.

a. Ford Foundation
b. FASB
c. NYSE Group
d. Federal Deposit Insurance Corporation

67. A _____, securities analyst, research analyst, equity analyst, or investment analyst is a person who performs financial analysis for external or internal clients as a core part of the job.

An analyst studies companies and other entities to arrive at the estimate of their financial value. It is normally done by analyzing financial reports, aided by follow-up interviews with company representatives and industry experts.

a. Portfolio manager
b. Stockbroker
c. Purchasing manager
d. Financial Analyst

68. The _____ of 1970 codified at 15 U.S.C. Â§ 78aaa through 15 U.S.C. Â§ 78lll, established the Securities Investor Protection Corporation (SIPC). Most brokers and dealers registered under the Securities Exchange Act of 1934 are required to be members of the SIPC.

The SIPC maintains a fund that is intended to protect investors against the misappropriation of their funds and of most types of securities in the event of the failure of their broker.

a. Securities Investor Protection Act
b. McFadden Act
c. Fiduciary
d. Quiet period

69. The _____ is a federally mandated non-profit corporation in the United States that protects securities investors from harm if a broker-dealer company fails. Investors are not insured for any potential loss while invested in the market.

Congress created _____ in 1970 through the Securities Investor Protection Act (15 U.S.C.

a. Prudent man rule
b. Rule 144A
c. SIPC
d. Securities Investor Protection Corporation

70. The _____ is a model statute designed to guide each state in drafting its state securities law. It was created by the National Conference of Commissioners on Uniform State Laws (NCCUSL.)

The purpose of the _____ is to provide model legislation that can be adopted by a state to deal with securities fraud at the state level, supplementing enforcement and regulation efforts of the U.S. Securities and Exchange Commission (SEC.)

   a. Economies of scale
   c. External risks
   b. Employee Retirement Income Security Act
   d. Uniform Securities Act

71. A _____ is a point at which a stock market will stop trading for a period of time in response to substantial drops in value.

On the New York Stock Exchange, one type of _____ is referred to as a 'circuit breaker.' These limits were put in place after Black Monday in order to reduce market volatility and massive panic sell-offs, giving traders time to reconsider their transactions.

At the start of each quarter, the NYSE sets three circuit breaker levels at levels of 10%, 20%, and 30% of the average closing price of the Dow Jones Industrial Average for the month preceding the start of the quarter, rounded to the nearest 50-point interval.

   a. Common stock
   c. Trading curb
   b. Stock repurchase
   d. Stock market index

72. An _____ is an investment vehicle traded on stock exchanges, much like stocks. An ETF holds assets such as stocks or bonds and trades at approximately the same price as the net asset value of its underlying assets over the course of the trading day. Most ETFs track an index, such as the Dow Jones Industrial Average or the S'P 500.
   a. ABN Amro
   c. A Random Walk Down Wall Street
   b. AAB
   d. Exchange-traded fund

73. The _____ of 2002 (Pub.L. 107-204, 116 Stat. 745, enacted July 30, 2002), also known as the Public Company Accounting Reform and Investor Protection Act of 2002 and commonly called Sarbanes-Oxley, Sarbox or SOX, is a United States federal law enacted on July 30, 2002 in response to a number of major corporate and accounting scandals including those affecting Enron, Tyco International, Adelphia, Peregrine Systems and WorldCom.
   a. Foreign Corrupt Practices Act
   c. Duty of loyalty
   b. Sarbanes-Oxley Act
   d. Blue sky law

74. A _____ or chief executive is one of the highest-ranking corporate officer (executive) or administrator in charge of total management. An individual selected as President and _____ of a corporation, company, organization, or agency, reports to the board of directors. In internal communication and press releases, many companies capitalize the term and those of other high positions, even when they are not proper nouns.
   a. Chief executive officer
   c. Portfolio manager
   b. Stockbroker
   d. Purchasing manager

75. _____ is the set of processes, customs, policies, laws and institutions affecting the way a corporation is directed, administered or controlled. _____ also includes the relationships among the many stakeholders involved and the goals for which the corporation is governed. The principal stakeholders are the shareholders, management and the board of directors.

a. Patent
b. Foreign Corrupt Practices Act
c. Corporate governance
d. Due diligence

76. The _____ is one of several stock market indices, created by nineteenth-century Wall Street Journal editor and Dow Jones ' Company co-founder Charles Dow. Dow compiled the index to gauge the performance of the industrial sector of the American stock market. It is the second-oldest U.S. market index, after the Dow Jones Transportation Average, which Dow also created.
   a. 4-4-5 Calendar
   b. 7-Eleven
   c. 529 plan
   d. Dow Jones Industrial Average

77. The U.S. Securities and Exchange Commission's (SEC's) Regulation Fair Disclosure, also commonly referred to as _____ was an SEC ruling implemented in October 2000 (.) It mandated that all publicly traded companies must disclose material information to all investors at the same time.

The regulation sought to stamp out selective disclosure, in which some investors (often large institutional investors) received market moving information before others (often smaller, individual investors.)

   a. Revenue recognition
   b. Regulation Fair Disclosure
   c. Commodity Pool Operator
   d. Regulation FD

78. A _____ is a sudden dramatic decline of stock prices across a significant cross-section of a stock market. Crashes are driven by panic as much as by underlying economic factors. They often follow speculative stock market bubbles.
   a. 7-Eleven
   b. Stock market crash
   c. 4-4-5 Calendar
   d. 529 plan

79. _____ is the trading of a corporation's stock or other securities (e.g. bonds or stock options) by individuals with potential access to non-public information about the company. In most countries, trading by corporate insiders such as officers, key employees, directors, and large shareholders may be legal, if this trading is done in a way that does not take advantage of non-public information. However, the term is frequently used to refer to a practice in which an insider or a related party trades based on material non-public information obtained during the performance of the insider's duties at the corporation, or otherwise in breach of a fiduciary duty or other relationship of trust and confidence or where the non-public information was misappropriated from the company.
   a. Equity investment
   b. Open outcry
   c. Intellidex
   d. Insider trading

48   Chapter 4. Mutual Funds and Other Investment Companies

1. An _____ is a company whose main business is holding securities of other companies purely for investment purposes. The _____ invests money on behalf of its shareholders who in turn share in the profits and losses.
   a. A Random Walk Down Wall Street
   b. Unit investment trust
   c. AAB
   d. Investment company

2. A _____ is a professionally managed type of collective investment scheme that pools money from many investors and invests it in stocks, bonds, short-term money market instruments, and/or other securities. The _____ will have a fund manager that trades the pooled money on a regular basis. Currently, the worldwide value of all _____s totals more than $26 trillion.

   Since 1940, there have been three basic types of investment companies in the United States: open-end funds, also known in the US as _____s; unit investment trusts (UITs); and closed-end funds.

   a. Net asset value
   b. Financial intermediary
   c. Trust company
   d. Mutual Fund

3. _____ is a term used to describe the value of an entity's assets less the value of its liabilities. The term is commonly used in relation to collective investment schemes. It may also be used as a synonym for the book value of a firm.
   a. Financial intermediary
   b. Passive management
   c. Retail broker
   d. Net asset value

4. In business and accounting, _____s are everything of value that is owned by a person or company. The balance sheet of a firm records the monetary value of the _____s owned by the firm. The two major _____ classes are tangible _____s and intangible _____s.
   a. Income
   b. Accounts payable
   c. EBITDA
   d. Asset

5. _____ in finance is a risk management technique, related to hedging, that mixes a wide variety of investments within a portfolio. Because the fluctuations of a single security have less impact on a diverse portfolio, _____ minimizes the risk from any one investment.

   A simple example of _____ is the following: On a particular island the entire economy consists of two companies: one that sells umbrellas and another that sells sunscreen.

   a. 4-4-5 Calendar
   b. Diversification
   c. 7-Eleven
   d. 529 plan

6. _____ refers to a portfolio management strategy where the manager makes specific investments with the goal of outperforming an investment benchmark index. Investors or mutual funds that do not aspire to create a return in excess of a benchmark index will often invest in an index fund that replicates as closely as possible the investment weighting and returns of that index; this is called passive management. _____ is the opposite of passive management, because in passive management the manager does not seek to outperform the benchmark index.
   a. AAB
   b. A Random Walk Down Wall Street
   c. ABN Amro
   d. Active management

7. A _____, is a collective investment scheme with a limited number of shares.

Chapter 4. Mutual Funds and Other Investment Companies 49

New shares are rarely issued after the fund is launched; shares are not normally redeemable for cash or securities until the fund liquidates. Typically an investor can acquire shares in a _____ by buying shares on a secondary market from a broker, market maker, or other investor as opposed to an open-end fund where all transactions eventually involve the fund company creating new shares on the fly (in exchange for either cash or securities) or redeeming shares (for cash or securities.)

- a. Stock fund
- b. Money market funds
- c. Mutual fund fees and expenses
- d. Closed-end fund

8. The institution most often referenced by the word '_____' is a public or publicly traded _____, the shares of which are traded on a public stock exchange (e.g., the New York Stock Exchange or Nasdaq in the United States) where shares of stock of _____s are bought and sold by and to the general public. Most of the largest businesses in the world are publicly traded _____s. However, the majority of _____s are said to be closely held, privately held or close _____s, meaning that no ready market exists for the trading of shares.
- a. Protect
- b. Depository Trust Company
- c. Federal Home Loan Mortgage Corporation
- d. Corporation

9. A _____ is a US investment company offering a fixed (unmanaged) portfolio of securities having a definite life. _____s are assembled by a sponsor and sold through brokers to investors.

A _____ portfolio may contain one of several different types of securities.

- a. A Random Walk Down Wall Street
- b. AAB
- c. Investment company
- d. Unit investment trust

10. In finance, a _____ is a position established in one market in an attempt to offset exposure to the price risk of an equal but opposite obligation or position in another market -- usually, but not always, in the context of one's commercial activity. Hedging is a strategy designed to minimize exposure to such business risks as a sharp contraction in demand for one's inventory, while still allowing the business to profit from producing and maintaining that inventory. A typical hedger might be a farmer with 2000 acres of unharvested wheat in the ground, who would rather tend his crop without the distraction of uncertain prices.
- a. Hedge
- b. 529 plan
- c. 7-Eleven
- d. 4-4-5 Calendar

11. A _____ is a private investment fund open to a limited range of investors that is permitted by regulators to undertake a wider range of activities than other investment funds and also pays a performance fee to its investment manager. Each fund will have its own strategy which determines the type of investments and the methods of investment it undertakes. _____s as a class invest in a broad range of investments extending over shares, debt, commodities and beyond.
- a. 7-Eleven
- b. Hedge fund
- c. 4-4-5 Calendar
- d. 529 plan

Chapter 4. Mutual Funds and Other Investment Companies

12. A _____ or _____ is a tax designation for a corporation investing in real estate that reduces or eliminates corporate income taxes. In return, _____s are required to distribute 95% of their income, which may be taxable in the hands of the investors. The _____ structure was designed to provide a similar structure for investment in real estate as mutual funds provide for investment in stocks.
    a. Real estate investing
    b. Tenancy
    c. Liquidation value
    d. Real estate investment trust

13. A '_____' (FoF) is an investment fund that uses an investment strategy of holding a portfolio of other investment funds rather than investing directly in shares, bonds or other securities. This type of investing is often referred to as multi-manager investment.

    There are different types of '_____', each investing in a different type of collective investment scheme (typically one type per FoF), eg.

    a. Fund of funds
    b. Limited liability company
    c. Leverage
    d. Pension fund

14. In finance, a _____ is a debt security, in which the authorized issuer owes the holders a debt and, depending on the terms of the _____, is obliged to pay interest (the coupon) and/or to repay the principal at a later date, termed maturity.

    Thus a _____ is a loan: the issuer is the borrower, the _____ holder is the lender, and the coupon is the interest. _____s provide the borrower with external funds to finance long-term investments, or, in the case of government _____s, to finance current expenditure.

    a. Catastrophe bonds
    b. Convertible bond
    c. Puttable bond
    d. Bond

15. A _____ is a collective investment scheme that invests in bonds and other debt securities. _____s yield monthly dividends that include interest payments on the fund's underlying securities plus any capital appreciation in the prices of the portfolio's bonds. _____s tend to pay higher dividends than CDs and money market accounts, and they generally pay out dividends more frequently and regularly than individual bonds.
    a. Gilts
    b. Bond fund
    c. Private activity bond
    d. Premium bond

16. A _____ or equity fund is a fund that invests in Equities more commonly known as stocks. Such funds are typically held either in stock or cash, as opposed to Bonds, notes, or other securities. This may be a mutual fund or exchange-traded fund.
    a. Mutual fund fees and expenses
    b. Stock fund
    c. Closed-end fund
    d. Money market funds

17. _____, refers to consumption opportunity gained by an entity within a specified time frame, which is generally expressed in monetary terms. However, for households and individuals, '_____ is the sum of all the wages, salaries, profits, interests payments, rents and other forms of earnings received... in a given period of time.' For firms, _____ generally refers to net-profit: what remains of revenue after expenses have been subtracted.

a. Accrual
b. OIBDA
c. Income
d. Annual report

18. In finance, a _____ (non-investment grade bond, speculative grade bond or junk bond) is a bond that is rated below investment grade at the time of purchase. These bonds have a higher risk of default or other adverse credit events, but typically pay higher yields than better quality bonds in order to make them attractive to investors.
   a. Volatility
   b. Private equity
   c. High yield bond
   d. Sharpe ratio

19. In finance, the _____ is the global financial market for short-term borrowing and lending. It provides short-term liquidity funding for the global financial system. The _____ is where short-term obligations such as Treasury bills, commercial paper and bankers' acceptances are bought and sold.
   a. Money market
   b. Cramdown
   c. Consumer debt
   d. Debt-for-equity swap

20. Money funds (or _____, money market mutual funds) are mutual funds that invest in short-term debt instruments.

   _____, also known as principal stability funds, seek to limit exposure to losses due to credit, market and liquidity risks.
   _____, in the United States, are regulated by the Securities and Exchange Commission's (SEC) Investment Company Act of 1940.

   a. Mutual fund fees and expenses
   b. Money market funds
   c. Stock fund
   d. Closed-end fund

21. An _____ or index tracker is a collective investment scheme (usually a mutual fund or exchange-traded fund) that aims to replicate the movements of an index of a specific financial market regardless of market conditions.

Tracking can be achieved by trying to hold all of the securities in the index, in the same proportions as the index. Other methods include statistically sampling the market and holding 'representative' securities.

   a. A Random Walk Down Wall Street
   b. Index fund
   c. Investment company
   d. AAB

22. _____ is the strategy of making buy or sell decisions of financial assets (often stocks) by attempting to predict future market price movements. The prediction may be based on an outlook of market or economic conditions resulting from technical or fundamental analysis. This is an investment strategy based on the outlook for an aggregate market, rather than for a particular financial asset.
   a. Portable alpha
   b. Market timing
   c. Divestment
   d. Late trading

23. _____ is a term used to refer to how an investor distributes his or her investments among various classes of investment vehicles (e.g., stocks and bonds.)

A large part of financial planning is finding an _____ that is appropriate for a given person in terms of their appetite for and ability to shoulder risk. This can depend on various factors; see investor profile.

a. Asset allocation
b. Alternative investment
c. Investment performance
d. Investing online

24. In business, _____ is income that a company receives from its normal business activities, usually from the sale of goods and services to customers. Some companies also receive _____ from interest, dividends or royalties paid to them by other companies. _____ may refer to business income in general, or it may refer to the amount, in a monetary unit, received during a period of time, as in 'Last year, Company X had _____ of $32 million.'

In many countries, including the UK, _____ is referred to as turnover.

a. Bottom line
b. Matching principle
c. Revenue
d. Furniture, Fixtures and Equipment

25. In business, _____ refers to the sharing of profits and losses among different groups. One form shares between the general partner(s) and limited partners in a limited partnership. Another form shares with a company's employees, and another between companies in a business alliance.

a. 4-4-5 Calendar
b. Revenue sharing
c. 7-Eleven
d. 529 plan

26. _____ also known as Deferred Sales Charge, is a fee paid when shares are sold. This fee typically goes to the brokers that sell the fund's shares. The amount of this type of load will depend on how long the investor holds his or her shares and typically decreases to zero if the investor holds his or her shares long enough.

a. Closed-end fund
b. Money market funds
c. Back-end load
d. Mutual fund fees and expenses

27. An _____, operating expenditure, operational expense, operational expenditure or OPEX is an on-going cost for running a product, business, or system. Its counterpart, a capital expenditure (CAPEX), is the cost of developing or providing non-consumable parts for the product or system. For example, the purchase of a photocopier is the CAPEX, and the annual paper and toner cost is the OPEX.

a. A Random Walk Down Wall Street
b. AAB
c. ABN Amro
d. Operating expense

28. In economics, business, and accounting, a _____ is the value of money that has been used up to produce something, and hence is not available for use anymore. In business, the _____ may be one of acquisition, in which case the amount of money expended to acquire it is counted as _____. In this case, money is the input that is gone in order to acquire the thing.

a. Fixed costs
b. Marginal cost
c. Sliding scale fees
d. Cost

29. _____, in accrual accounting, is any account where the asset or liability is not realized until a future date, e.g. annuities, charges, taxes, income, etc. The _____ item may be carried, dependent on type of deferral, as either an asset or liability. See also: accrual

_____ is also used in the university admissions process. It is the action by which a school rejects a student for early admission but still opts to review that student in the general admissions pool.

a. Revenue
b. Net profit
c. Current asset
d. Deferred

30. The _____ is the national association of U.S. investment companies. _____ encourages adherence to high ethical standards, promotes public understanding of funds and investing, and advances the interests of investment funds and their shareholders, directors, and advisers.

As of July 1, 2008, _____ membership included 9,067 mutual funds, 675 closed-end funds, 625 exchange-traded funds (ETFs), and three sponsors of unit investment trust (UITs.)

a. A Random Walk Down Wall Street
b. ABN Amro
c. AAB
d. Investment Company Institute

31. _____ is trading executed after the standard local national exchanges have closed. This is distinct from after-hours trading, as they have in context specific meanings, the former may be illegal while the latter is legal.

In the mutual fund context, _____ involves placing orders for mutual fund shares after the close of the stock market, 4:00 p.m for the New York Stock Exchange, but still getting that day's closing price, rather than the next day's opening price.

a. Divestment
b. Certificate in Investment Performance Measurement
c. Tactical asset allocation
d. Late trading

32. An _____ is a tax levied on the financial income of people, corporations, or other legal entities. Various _____ systems exist, with varying degrees of tax incidence. Income taxation can be progressive, proportional, or regressive.

a. Income Tax
b. AAB
c. A Random Walk Down Wall Street
d. ABN Amro

33. A _____ is a fungible, negotiable instrument representing financial value. They are broadly categorized into debt securities (such as banknotes, bonds and debentures), and equity securities; e.g., common stocks. The company or other entity issuing the _____ is called the issuer.

a. Security
b. Tracking stock
c. Book entry
d. Securities lending

34. An _____ is an investment vehicle traded on stock exchanges, much like stocks. An ETF holds assets such as stocks or bonds and trades at approximately the same price as the net asset value of its underlying assets over the course of the trading day. Most ETFs track an index, such as the Dow Jones Industrial Average or the S'P 500.

a. AAB
b. ABN Amro
c. A Random Walk Down Wall Street
d. Exchange-traded fund

35. _____ Â® funds are shares of a family of exchange-traded funds (ETFs) traded in the United States and managed by State Street Global Advisors (SSgA.) Informally, they are also known as Spyders or Spiders. _____ Â® is a trademark of the McGraw-Hill Companies, Inc.

a. SPDR
b. Federal Agricultural Mortgage Corporation
c. Federal Deposit Insurance Corporation
d. Microfinance

36. _____ is the return on an investment portfolio. The investment portfolio can contain a single asset or multiple assets. The _____ is measured over a specific period of time and in a specific currency.
    a. Investment performance
    b. Asset allocation
    c. Investment decisions
    d. Alternative investment

37. The U.S. _____ is an independent agency of the United States government which holds primary responsibility for enforcing the federal securities laws and regulating the securities industry, the nation's stock and options exchanges, and other electronic securities markets. The SEC was created by section 4 of the SEC of 1934 (now codified as 15 U.S.C. Â§ 78d and commonly referred to as the 1934 Act.)
    a. 7-Eleven
    b. 4-4-5 Calendar
    c. 529 plan
    d. Securities and Exchange Commission

38. In finance, _____ are stocks that appreciate in value and yield a high return on equity (ROE.) Analysts compute ROE by taking the company's net income and dividing it by the company's equity. To be classified as a growth stock, analysts expect to see at least 15 percent return on equity.
    a. 4-4-5 Calendar
    b. Stock valuation
    c. Security Analysis
    d. Growth stocks

39. In business and finance, a _____ (also referred to as equity _____) of stock means a _____ of ownership in a corporation (company.) In the plural, stocks is often used as a synonym for _____s especially in the United States, but it is less commonly used that way outside of North America.

In the United Kingdom, South Africa, and Australia, stock can also refer to completely different financial instruments such as government bonds or, less commonly, to all kinds of marketable securities.

    a. Margin
    b. Bucket shop
    c. Share
    d. Procter ' Gamble

Chapter 5. Learning About Return and Risk from the Historical Record

1. In economics, _____ is a rise in the general level of prices of goods and services in an economy over a period of time. The term '_____' once referred to increases in the money supply (monetary _____); however, economic debates about the relationship between money supply and price levels have led to its primary use today in describing price _____. _____ can also be described as a decline in the real value of money--a loss of purchasing power in the medium of exchange which is also the monetary unit of account.
    a. AAB
    b. A Random Walk Down Wall Street
    c. Inflation
    d. ABN Amro

2. _____ is a fee paid on borrowed assets. It is the price paid for the use of borrowed money, or, money earned by deposited funds. Assets that are sometimes lent with _____ include money, shares, consumer goods through hire purchase, major assets such as aircraft, and even entire factories in finance lease arrangements.
    a. Insolvency
    b. A Random Walk Down Wall Street
    c. AAB
    d. Interest

3. _____ relates to the cost of borrowing money. It is the price that a lender charges a borrower for the use of the lender's money. _____ is different from OPEX and CAPEX, for it relates to the capital structure of a company.
    a. AAB
    b. A Random Walk Down Wall Street
    c. Interest expense
    d. ABN Amro

4. _____ are made by investors and investment managers.

    Investors commonly perform investment analysis by making use of fundamental analysis, technical analysis and gut feel.

    _____ are often supported by decision tools.

    a. Investing online
    b. Investment decisions
    c. Investment performance
    d. Asset allocation

5. In finance and economics _____ refers to the rate of interest before adjustment for inflation (in contrast with the real interest rate); or, for interest balls stated' without adjustment for the full effect of compounding (also referred to as the nominal annual rate.) An interest rate is called nominal if the frequency of compounding (e.g. a month) is not identical to the basic time unit (normally a year.)

    The real interest rate includes compensation for the lender's lost value due to inflation, whereas the _____ excludes inflation.

    a. SIBOR
    b. Shanghai Interbank Offered Rate
    c. Cash accumulation equation
    d. Nominal interest rate

6. The '_____' is approximately the nominal interest rate minus the inflation rate Since the inflation rate over the course of a loan is not known initially, volatility in inflation represents a risk to both the lender and the borrower.

    In economics and finance, an individual who lends money for repayment at a later point in time expects to be compensated for the time value of money, or not having the use of that money while it is lent.

56   *Chapter 5. Learning About Return and Risk from the Historical Record*

a. 7-Eleven
c. 4-4-5 Calendar
b. 529 plan
d. Real interest rate

7. In finance, the yield curve is the relation between the interest rate (or cost of borrowing) and the time to maturity of the debt for a given borrower in a given currency. For example, the current U.S. dollar interest rates paid on U.S. Treasury securities for various maturities are closely watched by many traders, and are commonly plotted on a graph such as the one on the right which is informally called 'the yield curve.' More formal mathematical descriptions of this relation are often called the _____.

The yield of a debt instrument is the annualized percentage increase in the value of the investment.

a. Term structure of interest rates
c. 7-Eleven
b. 529 plan
d. 4-4-5 Calendar

8. An _____ is the price a borrower pays for the use of money they do not own, and the return a lender receives for deferring the use of funds, by lending it to the borrower. _____s are normally expressed as a percentage rate over the period of one year.

_____s targets are also a vital tool of monetary policy and are used to control variables like investment, inflation, and unemployment.

a. A Random Walk Down Wall Street
c. Interest rate
b. AAB
d. ABN Amro

9. _____ is a mathematical science pertaining to the collection, analysis, interpretation or explanation, and presentation of data. It also provides tools for prediction and forecasting based on data. It is applicable to a wide variety of academic disciplines, from the natural and social sciences to the humanities, government and business.

a. Covariance
c. Sample size
b. Mean
d. Statistics

10. The _____ in financial mathematics and economics estimates the relationship between nominal and real interest rates under inflation. It is named after Irving Fisher who was famous for his works on the theory of interest. In finance, the _____ is primarily used in YTM calculations of bonds or IRR calculations of investments.

Letting *r* denote the real interest rate, *i* denote the nominal interest rate, and let >π denote the inflation rate, the _____ is:

[×]>

a. Binomial options pricing model
c. Fisher equation
b. Treynor-Black model
d. Discount rate

11. In financial accounting, the term _____ is most commonly used to describe any part of shareholders' equity, except for basic share capital. Sometimes, the term is used instead of the term provision; such a use, however, is inconsistent with the terminology suggested by International Accounting Standards Board. For more information about provisions, see provision (accounting.)

Chapter 5. Learning About Return and Risk from the Historical Record

a. Treasury stock
c. FIFO and LIFO accounting
b. Closing entries
d. Reserve

12. In economic models, the _____ time frame assumes no fixed factors of production. Firms can enter or leave the marketplace, and the cost (and availability) of land, labor, raw materials, and capital goods can be assumed to vary. In contrast, in the short-run time frame, certain factors are assumed to be fixed, because there is not sufficient time for them to change.
a. 4-4-5 Calendar
c. 529 plan
b. Long-run
d. Short-run

13. _____ describes the process by which inflation pushes wages and salaries into higher tax brackets.

Many progressive tax systems are not adjusted for inflation. As wages and salaries rise in nominal terms under the influence of inflation they become more highly taxed, even though in real terms the value of the wages and salaries has not increased at all.

a. Payroll tax
c. Capital gain
b. Tax brackets
d. Bracket creep

14. A _____, reserve bank, or monetary authority is the entity responsible for the monetary policy of a country or of a group of member states. It is a bank that can lend money to other banks in times of need. Its primary responsibility is to maintain the stability of the national currency and money supply, but more active duties include controlling subsidized-loan interest rates, and acting as a lender of last resort to the banking sector during times of financial crisis (private banks often being integral to the national financial system.)
a. 7-Eleven
c. 529 plan
b. Central bank
d. 4-4-5 Calendar

15. In finance, a _____ is a debt security, in which the authorized issuer owes the holders a debt and, depending on the terms of the _____, is obliged to pay interest (the coupon) and/or to repay the principal at a later date, termed maturity.

Thus a _____ is a loan: the issuer is the borrower, the _____ holder is the lender, and the coupon is the interest. _____ s provide the borrower with external funds to finance long-term investments, or, in the case of government _____ s, to finance current expenditure.

a. Catastrophe bonds
c. Puttable bond
b. Convertible bond
d. Bond

16. _____ are the divisions at which tax rates change in a progressive tax system (or an explicitly regressive tax system, although this is much rarer.) Essentially, they are the cutoff values for taxable income -- income past a certain point will be taxed at a higher rate.

Imagine that there are three _____: 10%, 20%, and 30%.

a. Capital gains tax
b. Payroll tax
c. Tax holiday
d. Tax brackets

17. The _____, effective annual interest rate, Annual Equivalent Rate (AER) or simply effective rate is the interest rate on a loan or financial product restated from the nominal interest rate as an interest rate with annual compound interest. It is used to compare the annual interest between loans with different compounding terms (daily, monthly, annually, or other.)

The _____ differs in two important respects from the annual percentage rate (APR):

1. the _____ generally does not incorporate one-time charges such as front-end fees;
2. the _____ is (generally) not defined by legal or regulatory authorities (as APR is in many jurisdictions.)

By contrast, the 'effective APR' is used as a legal term, where front-fees and other costs can be included, as defined by local law.

Annual Percentage Yield or effective annual yield is the analogous concept used for savings or investment products, such as a certificate of deposit.

a. ABN Amro
b. A Random Walk Down Wall Street
c. AAB
d. Effective interest rate

18. A _____ is a bond bought at a price lower than its face value, with the face value repaid at the time of maturity. It does not make periodic interest payments, or have so-called 'coupons,' hence the term _____. Investors earn return from the compounded interest all paid at maturity plus the difference between the discounted price of the bond and its par value.
   a. Clean price
   b. Corporate bond
   c. Zero-coupon bond
   d. Bond fund

19. In finance, _____, also known as return on investment is the ratio of money gained or lost on an investment relative to the amount of money invested. The amount of money gained or lost may be referred to as interest, profit/loss, gain/loss, or net income/loss. The money invested may be referred to as the asset, capital, principal, or the cost basis of the investment.
   a. Rate of return
   b. Doctrine of the Proper Law
   c. Composiition of Creditors
   d. Stock or scrip dividends

20. The terms _____ , nominal _____, and effective _____ describe the interest rate for a whole year (annualized), rather than just a monthly fee/rate, as applied on a loan, mortgage, credit card, etc. Those terms have formal, legal definitions in some countries or legal jurisdictions, but in general:

   - The nominal _____ is the simple-interest rate (for a year.)
   - The effective _____ is the fee+compound interest rate (calculated across a year.)

Chapter 5. Learning About Return and Risk from the Historical Record 59

The nominal _____ is calculated as: the rate, for a payment period, multiplied by the number of payment periods in a year. However, the exact legal definition of 'effective _____' can vary greatly in each jurisdiction, depending on the type of fees included, such as participation fees, loan origination fees, monthly service charges, or late fees. The effective _____ has been called the 'mathematically-true' interest rate for each year. The computation for the effective _____, as the fee+compound interest rate, can also vary depending on whether the up-front fees, such as origination or participation fees, are added to the entire amount, or treated as a short-term loan due in the first payment.

a. AAB
b. ABN Amro
c. Annual percentage rate
d. A Random Walk Down Wall Street

21. _____ is the concept of adding accumulated interest back to the principal, so that interest is earned on interest from that moment on. The act of declaring interest to be principal is called compounding (i.e., interest is compounded.) A loan, for example, may have its interest compounded every month: in this case, a loan with $100 principal and 1% interest per month would have a balance of $101 at the end of the first month.

a. 4-4-5 Calendar
b. Risk management
c. Penny stock
d. Compound interest

22. _____ mature in one year or less. Like zero-coupon bonds, they do not pay interest prior to maturity; instead they are sold at a discount of the par value to create a positive yield to maturity. Many regard _____ as the least risky investment available to U.S. investors.

a. Treasury bills
b. Treasury Inflation Protected Securities
c. Treasury securities
d. 4-4-5 Calendar

23.

In finance, the _____ can be the expected rate of return above the risk-free interest rate. When measuring risk, a common sense approach is to compare the risk-free return on T-bills and the very risky return on other investments. The difference between these two returns can be interpreted as a measure of the excess return on the average risky asset. This excess return is known as the _____.

a. Risk adjusted return on capital
b. Risk modeling
c. Risk aversion
d. Risk premium

24. A _____ is a payment made by a corporation to its shareholder members. When a corporation earns a profit or surplus, that money can be put to two uses: it can either be re-invested in the business (called retained earnings), or it can be paid to the shareholders as a _____. Many corporations retain a portion of their earnings and pay the remainder as a _____.

a. Special dividend
b. Dividend puzzle
c. Dividend yield
d. Dividend

25. The _____ on a company stock is the company's annual dividend payments divided by its market cap, or the dividend per share divided by the price per share. It is often expressed as a percentage.

Dividend payments on preferred shares are stipulated by the prospectus.

a. Dividend imputation
b. Dividend yield
c. Dividend reinvestment plan
d. Special dividend

26. The _____ is the weighted-average most likely outcome in gambling, probability theory, economics or finance.

In gambling and probability theory, there is usually a discrete set of possible outcomes. In this case, _____ is a measure of the relative balance of win or loss weighted by their chances of occurring.

a. ABN Amro
b. Expected return
c. AAB
d. A Random Walk Down Wall Street

27. In probability and statistics, the _____ of a collection of numbers is a measure of the dispersion of the numbers from their expected (mean) value. It can apply to a probability distribution, a random variable, a population or a data set. The _____ is usually denoted with the letter σ (lowercase sigma.)

a. Mean
b. Sample size
c. Standard deviation
d. Kurtosis

28. In finance, the term _____ describes the amount in cash that returns to the owners of a security. Normally it does not include the price variations, at the difference of the total return. _____ applies to various stated rates of return on stocks (common and preferred, and convertible), fixed income instruments (bonds, notes, bills, strips, zero coupon), and some other investment type insurance products (e.g. annuities.)

a. Yield to maturity
b. 4-4-5 Calendar
c. Macaulay duration
d. Yield

29. _____ is a risk-adjusted measure of the so-called active return on an investment. It is the return in excess of the compensation for the risk borne, and thus commonly used to assess active managers' performances. Often, the return of a benchmark is subtracted in order to consider relative performance, which yields Jensen's _____.

a. Annuity
b. Alpha
c. Option
d. Amortization

30. _____ is a concept in economics, finance, and psychology related to the behaviour of consumers and investors under uncertainty. _____ is the reluctance of a person to accept a bargain with an uncertain payoff rather than another bargain with a more certain, but possibly lower, expected payoff.

The inverse of a person's _____ is sometimes called their risk tolerance

a. Risk adjusted return on capital
b. Discount factor
c. Risk aversion
d. Risk premium

31. _____ is a process of analyzing possible future events by considering alternative possible outcomes (scenarios.) The analysis is designed to allow improved decision-making by allowing consideration of outcomes and their implications.

For example, in economics and finance, a financial institution might attempt to forecast several possible scenarios for the economy (e.g. rapid growth, moderate growth, slow growth) and it might also attempt to forecast financial market returns (for bonds, stocks and cash) in each of those scenarios.

Chapter 5. Learning About Return and Risk from the Historical Record 61

    a. Scenario analysis
    b. Detection Risk
    c. 529 plan
    d. 4-4-5 Calendar

32. In probability theory and statistics, the _____ of a random variable, probability distribution averaging the squared distance of its possible values from the expected value (mean.) Whereas the mean is a way to describe the location of a distribution, the _____ is a way to capture its scale or degree of being spread out. The unit of _____ is the square of the unit of the original variable.

    a. Monte Carlo methods
    b. Harmonic mean
    c. Semivariance
    d. Variance

33. _____ is a graph created by investors to measure the risk of risky and risk-free assets. The graph displays to the investors on the return they can make by taking on a certain level of risk. It is also known as a 'reward-to-variability ratio'.

    a. Portfolio investment
    b. Divestment
    c. Dollar cost averaging
    d. Capital allocation line

34. The _____ is a measure of the excess return (or Risk Premium) per unit of risk in an investment asset or a trading strategy it is defined as:

$$S = \frac{R - R_f}{\sigma} = \frac{E[R - R_f]}{\sqrt{\mathrm{var}[R - R_f]}},$$

where R is the asset return, R_f is the return on a benchmark asset, such as the risk free rate of return, $E[R - R_f]$ is the expected value of the excess of the asset return over the benchmark return, and σ is the standard deviation of the asset excess return.

Note, if R_f is a constant risk free return throughout the period,

$$\sqrt{\mathrm{var}[R - R_f]} = \sqrt{\mathrm{var}[R]}.$$

The _____ is used to characterize how well the return of an asset compensates the investor for the risk taken. When comparing two assets each with the expected return E[R] against the same benchmark with return R_f, the asset with the higher _____ gives more return for the same risk.

    a. Sharpe ratio
    b. P/E ratio
    c. Current ratio
    d. Receivables turnover ratio

35. _____ is a failure analysis in which an undesired state of a system is analyzed using boolean logic to combine a series of lower-level events. This analysis method is mainly used in the field of safety engineering to quantitatively determine the probability of a safety hazard.

_____ attempts to model and analyze failure processes of engineering and biological systems.

a. 529 plan
c. 7-Eleven
b. 4-4-5 Calendar
d. Fault tree analysis

36. The _____ is an important family of continuous probability distributions, applicable in many fields. Each member of the family may be defined by two parameters, location and scale: the mean and variance respectively. The standard _____ is the _____ with a mean of zero and a variance of one
   a. Normal distribution
   c. Random variables
   b. Probability distribution
   d. Correlation

37. In probability theory and statistics, _____ is a measure of the 'peakedness' of the probability distribution of a real-valued random variable. Higher _____ means more of the variance is due to infrequent extreme deviations, as opposed to frequent modestly-sized deviations. The far red light has no effect on the average speed of the gravitropic reaction in wheat coleoptiles, but it changes _____ from platykurtic to leptokurtic (-0.194 → 0.055)

The fourth standardized moment is defined as

$$\frac{\mu_4}{\sigma^4},$$

where μ_4 is the fourth moment about the mean and σ is the standard deviation.

   a. Kurtosis
   c. Correlation
   b. Mean
   d. Random variables

38. A _____ is a fungible, negotiable instrument representing financial value. They are broadly categorized into debt securities (such as banknotes, bonds and debentures), and equity securities; e.g., common stocks. The company or other entity issuing the _____ is called the issuer.
   a. Security
   c. Securities lending
   b. Book entry
   d. Tracking stock

39. _____ are government bonds issued by the United States Department of the Treasury through the Bureau of the Public Debt. They are the debt financing instruments of the U.S. Federal government, and they are often referred to simply as Treasuries or Treasurys. There are four types of marketable _____: Treasury bills, Treasury notes, Treasury bonds, and Treasury Inflation Protected Securities (TIPS.)
   a. Treasury Inflation Protected Securities
   c. Treasury securities
   b. 4-4-5 Calendar
   d. Treasury Inflation-Protected Securities

40. A _____ is a government debt issued by the United States Department of the Treasury through the Bureau of the Public Debt. They are the debt financing instruments of the United States Federal government, and they are often referred to simply as Treasuries. There are four types of marketable treasury securities: Treasury bills, Treasury notes, Treasury bonds, and Treasury Inflation Protected Securities (TIPS.)
   a. International trade
   c. OTC Bulletin Board
   b. Insolvency
   d. United States Treasury security

Chapter 5. Learning About Return and Risk from the Historical Record 63

41. In business and finance, a _____ (also referred to as equity _____) of stock means a _____ of ownership in a corporation (company.) In the plural, stocks is often used as a synonym for _____s especially in the United States, but it is less commonly used that way outside of North America.

In the United Kingdom, South Africa, and Australia, stock can also refer to completely different financial instruments such as government bonds or, less commonly, to all kinds of marketable securities.

- a. Margin
- b. Procter ' Gamble
- c. Bucket shop
- d. Share

42. In probability theory and statistics, _____ indicates the strength and direction of a linear relationship between two random variables. That is in contrast with the usage of the term in colloquial speech, which denotes any relationship, not necessarily linear. In general statistical usage, _____ or co-relation refers to the departure of two random variables from independence.

- a. Geometric mean
- b. Probability distribution
- c. Correlation
- d. Variance

43. The term _____ or economic cycle refers to the fluctuations of economic activity (business fluctuations) around a long-term growth trend. The cycle involves shifts over time between periods of relatively rapid growth of output (recovery and prosperity), and periods of relative stagnation or decline (contraction or recession.) These fluctuations are often measured using the real gross domestic product.

- a. Business cycle
- b. Deflation
- c. Behavioral finance
- d. Fixed exchange rate

44. In probability and statistics, the _____ is the single-tailed probability distribution of any random variable whose logarithm is normally distributed. If X is a random variable with a normal distribution, then Y = exp(X) has a _____; likewise, if Y is log-normally distributed, then log(Y) is normally distributed. (The base of the logarithmic function does not matter: if $\log_a$(Y) is normally distributed, then so is $\log_b$(Y), for any two positive numbers a, b ≠ 1.)

- a. 529 plan
- b. 7-Eleven
- c. 4-4-5 Calendar
- d. Log-normal distribution

45. Depending on the nature of the investment, the type of _____ will vary.

A common concern with any investment is that you may lose the money you invest - your capital. This risk is therefore often referred to as 'capital risk.'

If the assets you invest in are held in another currency there is a risk that currency movements alone may affect the value.

- a. AAB
- b. ABN Amro
- c. A Random Walk Down Wall Street
- d. Investment risk

46. _____ is a method of hedging a portfolio of stocks against the market risk by short selling stock index futures.

This hedging technique is frequently used by institutional investors when the market direction is uncertain or volatile. Short selling index futures can offset any downturns, but it also hinders any gains.

a. Freight derivative
b. PAUG
c. Delivery month
d. Portfolio insurance

47. _____ is a method for constructing a (zero-coupon) fixed-income yield curve from the prices of a set of coupon-bearing products by forward substitution.

Using these zero-coupon products it becomes possible to derive par swap rates (forward and spot) for all maturities by making a few assumptions (including linear interpolation.) The term structure of spot returns is recovered from the bond yields by solving for them recursively, this iterative process is called the BootStrap Method.

a. Probability of default
b. Bootstrapping
c. Reserve requirement
d. Bullet loan

48. In finance, _____ is the process of estimating the potential market value of a financial asset or liability. they can be done on assets (for example, investments in marketable securities such as stocks, options, business enterprises, or intangible assets such as patents and trademarks) or on liabilities (e.g., Bonds issued by a company.) _____s are required in many contexts including investment analysis, capital budgeting, merger and acquisition transactions, financial reporting, taxable events to determine the proper tax liability, and in litigation.

a. Margin
b. Share
c. Procter ' Gamble
d. Valuation

49. In financial mathematics and financial risk management, _____ is a widely used measure of the risk of loss on a specific portfolio of financial assets. For a given portfolio, probability and time horizon, VaR is defined as a threshold value such that the probability that the mark-to-market loss on the portfolio over the given time horizon exceeds this value (assuming normal markets and no trading) is the given probability level.

For example, if a portfolio of stocks has a one-day 5% VaR of $1 million, there is a 5% probability that the portfolio will fall in value by more than $1 million over a one day period, assuming markets are normal and there is no trading.

a. Value at risk
b. Risk aversion
c. Discount factor
d. Risk modeling

Chapter 6. Risk Aversion and Capital Allocation to Risky Assets

1. In business and accounting, _____s are everything of value that is owned by a person or company. The balance sheet of a firm records the monetary value of the _____s owned by the firm. The two major _____ classes are tangible _____s and intangible _____s.
   - a. Accounts payable
   - b. Asset
   - c. Income
   - d. EBITDA

2. _____ is a term used to refer to how an investor distributes his or her investments among various classes of investment vehicles (e.g., stocks and bonds.)

   A large part of financial planning is finding an _____ that is appropriate for a given person in terms of their appetite for and ability to shoulder risk. This can depend on various factors; see investor profile.

   - a. Investing online
   - b. Alternative investment
   - c. Investment performance
   - d. Asset allocation

3. Behavioral economics and _____ are closely related fields that have evolved to be a separate branch of economic and financial analysis which applies scientific research on human and social, cognitive and emotional factors to better understand economic decisions by, say, consumers, borrowers, investors, and how they affect market prices, returns and the allocation of resources.

   The field is primarily concerned with the bounds of rationality (selfishness, self-control) of economic agents. Behavioral models typically integrate insights from psychology with neo-classical economic theory.

   - a. Medium of exchange
   - b. Recession
   - c. Market structure
   - d. Behavioral finance

4. In economics, _____ is a measure of the relative satisfaction from or desirability of consumption of various goods and services. Given this measure, one may speak meaningfully of increasing or decreasing _____, and thereby explain economic behavior in terms of attempts to increase one's _____. For illustrative purposes, changes in _____ are sometimes expressed in units called utils.
   - a. A Random Walk Down Wall Street
   - b. Utility function
   - c. AAB
   - d. Utility

5. While preferences are the conventional foundation of microeconomics, it is often convenient to represent preferences with a _____ and reason indirectly about preferences with _____s. Let X be the consumption set, the set of all mutually-exclusive packages the consumer could conceivably consume (such as an indifference curve map without the indifference curves.) The consumer's _____ $u : X \to \mathbf{R}$ ranks each package in the consumption set.
   - a. Utility
   - b. Utility function
   - c. AAB
   - d. A Random Walk Down Wall Street

6. _____ is a graph created by investors to measure the risk of risky and risk-free assets. The graph displays to the investors on the return they can make by taking on a certain level of risk. It is also known as a 'reward-to-variability ratio'.
   - a. Capital allocation line
   - b. Divestment
   - c. Dollar cost averaging
   - d. Portfolio investment

Chapter 6. Risk Aversion and Capital Allocation to Risky Assets

7. _____ proposes how rational investors will use diversification to optimize their portfolios, and how a risky asset should be priced. The basic concepts of the theory are Markowitz diversification, the efficient frontier, capital asset pricing model, the alpha and beta coefficients, the Capital Market Line and the Securities Market Line.

_____ models an asset's return as a random variable, and models a portfolio as a weighted combination of assets so that the return of a portfolio is the weighted combination of the assets' returns.

a. Market value
b. Consumer basket
c. Payback period
d. Modern portfolio theory

8. _____ is a concept in economics, finance, and psychology related to the behaviour of consumers and investors under uncertainty. _____ is the reluctance of a person to accept a bargain with an uncertain payoff rather than another bargain with a more certain, but possibly lower, expected payoff.

The inverse of a person's _____ is sometimes called their risk tolerance

a. Risk adjusted return on capital
b. Risk aversion
c. Discount factor
d. Risk premium

9.

In finance, the _____ can be the expected rate of return above the risk-free interest rate. When measuring risk, a common sense approach is to compare the risk-free return on T-bills and the very risky return on other investments. The difference between these two returns can be interpreted as a measure of the excess return on the average risky asset. This excess return is known as the _____.

a. Risk aversion
b. Risk premium
c. Risk adjusted return on capital
d. Risk modeling

10. _____ (in a financial context) is the assumption of the risk of loss, in return for the uncertain possibility of a reward. Only if one may safely say that a particular position involves no risk may one say, strictly speaking, that such a position represents an 'investment.' Financial _____ involves the buying, holding, selling, and short-selling of stocks, bonds, commodities, currencies, collectibles, real estate, derivatives, or any valuable financial instrument to profit from fluctuations in its price as opposed to buying it for use or for income via methods such as dividends or interest. _____ represents one of four market roles in Western financial markets, distinct from hedging, long- or short-term investing, and arbitrage.

a. Market anomaly
b. Speculation
c. Central Securities Depository
d. Forward market

11. _____ is an international professional designation offered by the _____ Institute (formerly known as AIMR) to financial analysts who complete a series of three examinations. In order to become a '_____ Charterholder' candidates must pass all three six-hour exams, possess a bachelor's degree (or equivalent, as assessed by the _____ institute) and have 48 months of work experience in an investment decision-making position. _____ charterholders are also obligated to adhere to a strict Code of Ethics and Standards governing their professional conduct.

a. Chartered Financial Analyst
b. 4-4-5 Calendar
c. 7-Eleven
d. 529 plan

12. A _____, securities analyst, research analyst, equity analyst, or investment analyst is a person who performs financial analysis for external or internal clients as a core part of the job.

An analyst studies companies and other entities to arrive at the estimate of their financial value. It is normally done by analyzing financial reports, aided by follow-up interviews with company representatives and industry experts.

a. Portfolio manager
b. Financial Analyst
c. Purchasing manager
d. Stockbroker

13. The _____ is the guaranteed payoff at which a person is 'indifferent' between accepting the guaranteed payoff and a higher but uncertain payoff. (It is the amount of the higher payout minus the risk premium).

a. 4-4-5 Calendar
b. Certainty equivalent
c. 7-Eleven
d. 529 plan

14. In microeconomic theory, an _____ is a graph showing different bundles of goods, each measured as to quantity, between which a consumer is indifferent. That is, at each point on the curve, the consumer has no preference for one bundle over another. In other words, they are all equally preferred. One can equivalently refer to each point on the _____ as rendering the same level of utility (satisfaction) for the consumer.

a. ABN Amro
b. AAB
c. Indifference curve
d. A Random Walk Down Wall Street

15. In Finance the _____ is a mathematical model for portfolio allocation developed in 1990 at Goldman Sachs by Fischer Black and Robert Litterman, and published in 1992. It seeks to overcome problems that institutional investors have encountered in applying modern portfolio theory in practice. The model starts with the equilibrium assumption that the asset allocation of a representative agent should be proportional to the market values of the available assets, and then modifies that to take into account the 'views' (i.e. the specific opinions about asset returns) of the investor in question to arrive at a bespoke asset allocation.

a. Clientele effect
b. Specific risk
c. Capital surplus
d. Black-Litterman model

16. A _____ s a time deposit, a financial product commonly offered to consumers by banks, thrift institutions, and credit unions.

They are similar to savings accounts in that they are insured and thus virtually risk-free; they are 'money in the bank'. They are different from savings accounts in that they have a specific, fixed term (often three months, six months, or one to five years), and, usually, a fixed interest rate.

a. Reserve requirement
b. Certificate of deposit
c. Variable rate mortgage
d. Time deposit

Chapter 6. Risk Aversion and Capital Allocation to Risky Assets

17. In the global money market, _____ is an unsecured promissory note with a fixed maturity of one to 270 days. _____ is a money-market security issued (sold) by large banks and corporations to get money to meet short term debt obligations (for example, payroll), and is only backed by an issuing bank or corporation's promise to pay the face amount on the maturity date specified on the note. Since it is not backed by collateral, only firms with excellent credit ratings from a recognized rating agency will be able to sell their _____ at a reasonable price.
   a. Financial distress
   b. Trade-off theory
   c. Book building
   d. Commercial paper

18. In finance, the _____ is the global financial market for short-term borrowing and lending. It provides short-term liquidity funding for the global financial system. The _____ is where short-term obligations such as Treasury bills, commercial paper and bankers' acceptances are bought and sold.
   a. Consumer debt
   b. Cramdown
   c. Debt-for-equity swap
   d. Money market

19. Money funds (or _____, money market mutual funds) are mutual funds that invest in short-term debt instruments.

   _____, also known as principal stability funds, seek to limit exposure to losses due to credit, market and liquidity risks. _____, in the United States, are regulated by the Securities and Exchange Commission's (SEC) Investment Company Act of 1940.

   a. Mutual fund fees and expenses
   b. Stock fund
   c. Closed-end fund
   d. Money market funds

20. In finance, _____, also known as return on investment is the ratio of money gained or lost on an investment relative to the amount of money invested. The amount of money gained or lost may be referred to as interest, profit/loss, gain/loss, or net income/loss. The money invested may be referred to as the asset, capital, principal, or the cost basis of the investment.
   a. Doctrine of the Proper Law
   b. Stock or scrip dividends
   c. Composiition of Creditors
   d. Rate of return

21. The _____ is a measure of the excess return (or Risk Premium) per unit of risk in an investment asset or a trading strategy it is defined as:

$$S = \frac{R - R_f}{\sigma} = \frac{E[R - R_f]}{\sqrt{\text{var}[R - R_f]}},$$

where R is the asset return, R_f is the return on a benchmark asset, such as the risk free rate of return, $E[R - R_f]$ is the expected value of the excess of the asset return over the benchmark return, and σ is the standard deviation of the asset excess return.

Note, if R_f is a constant risk free return throughout the period,

$$\sqrt{\mathrm{var}[R - R_f]} = \sqrt{\mathrm{var}[R]}.$$

The _____ is used to characterize how well the return of an asset compensates the investor for the risk taken. When comparing two assets each with the expected return E[R] against the same benchmark with return R_f, the asset with the higher _____ gives more return for the same risk.

a. Receivables turnover ratio
b. Sharpe ratio
c. Current ratio
d. P/E ratio

22. In finance, a _____ is collateral that the holder of a position in securities, options, or futures contracts has to deposit to cover the credit risk of his counterparty (most often his broker.) This risk can arise if the holder has done any of the following:

- borrowed cash from the counterparty to buy securities or options,
- sold securities or options short, or
- entered into a futures contract.

The collateral can be in the form of cash or securities, and it is deposited in a _____ account. On U.S. futures exchanges, '_____' was formally called performance bond.

_____ buying is buying securities with cash borrowed from a broker, using other securities as collateral.

a. Share
b. Credit
c. Procter ' Gamble
d. Margin

23. In finance, _____ is the risk involved in using models to value financial securities. Rebonato considers alternative definitions including:

1) After observing a set of prices for the underlying and hedging instruments, different but identically calibrated models might produce different prices for the same exotic product. 2) Losses will be incurred because of an â€˜incorrectâ€™ hedging strategy suggested by a model.

a. Price-to-book ratio
b. Takeover
c. Duty of loyalty
d. Model risk

24. A _____ is a fungible, negotiable instrument representing financial value. They are broadly categorized into debt securities (such as banknotes, bonds and debentures), and equity securities; e.g., common stocks. The company or other entity issuing the _____ is called the issuer.

a. Securities lending
b. Security
c. Tracking stock
d. Book entry

Chapter 6. Risk Aversion and Capital Allocation to Risky Assets

25. The _____ is the market for securities, where companies and governments can raise longterm funds. The _____ includes the stock market and the bond market. Financial regulators, such as the U.S. Securities and Exchange Commission, oversee the _____s in their designated countries to ensure that investors are protected against fraud.
    a. Capital market
    b. Forward market
    c. Delta neutral
    d. Spot rate

26. An _____ or index tracker is a collective investment scheme (usually a mutual fund or exchange-traded fund) that aims to replicate the movements of an index of a specific financial market regardless of market conditions.

    Tracking can be achieved by trying to hold all of the securities in the index, in the same proportions as the index. Other methods include statistically sampling the market and holding 'representative' securities.

    a. A Random Walk Down Wall Street
    b. Investment company
    c. Index fund
    d. AAB

27. In finance, a _____ is a debt security, in which the authorized issuer owes the holders a debt and, depending on the terms of the _____, is obliged to pay interest (the coupon) and/or to repay the principal at a later date, termed maturity.

    Thus a _____ is a loan: the issuer is the borrower, the _____ holder is the lender, and the coupon is the interest. _____s provide the borrower with external funds to finance long-term investments, or, in the case of government _____s, to finance current expenditure.

    a. Puttable bond
    b. Convertible bond
    c. Catastrophe bonds
    d. Bond

28. In economics, game theory, and decision theory the _____ theorem or _____ hypothesis predicts that the 'betting preferences' of people with regard to uncertain outcomes (gambles) can be described by a mathematical relation which takes into account the size of a payout (whether in money or other goods), the probability of occurrence, risk aversion, and the different utility of the same payout to people with different assets or personal preferences. It is a more sophisticated theory than simply predicting that choices will be made based on expected value (which takes into account only the size of the payout and the probability of occurrence.)

    Daniel Bernoulli described the complete theory in 1738.

    a. A Random Walk Down Wall Street
    b. AAB
    c. Utility
    d. Expected utility

29. In economics, the _____ is a paradox related to probability theory and decision theory. It is based on a particular (theoretical) lottery game (sometimes called St. Petersburg Lottery) that leads to a random variable with infinite expected value, i.e. infinite expected payoff, but would nevertheless be considered to be worth only a very small amount of money. The _____ is a classical situation where a naïve decision criterion (which takes only the expected value into account) would recommend a course of action that no (real) rational person would be willing to take.
    a. 529 plan
    b. 7-Eleven
    c. St. Petersburg Paradox
    d. 4-4-5 Calendar

30. A _____ is an exchange of promises between two or more parties to do an act which is enforceable in a court of law. It is where an unqualified offer meets a qualified acceptance and the parties reach Consensus ad Idem. The parties must have the necessary capacity to _____ and the _____ must not be either trifling, indeterminate, impossible or illegal.
   a. 529 plan
   b. 7-Eleven
   c. 4-4-5 Calendar
   d. Contract

Chapter 7. Optimal Risky Portfolios

1. In business and accounting, _____s are everything of value that is owned by a person or company. The balance sheet of a firm records the monetary value of the _____s owned by the firm. The two major _____ classes are tangible _____s and intangible _____s.

   a. EBITDA
   c. Income
   b. Accounts payable
   d. Asset

2. _____ is a term used to refer to how an investor distributes his or her investments among various classes of investment vehicles (e.g., stocks and bonds.)

   A large part of financial planning is finding an _____ that is appropriate for a given person in terms of their appetite for and ability to shoulder risk. This can depend on various factors; see investor profile.

   a. Investing online
   c. Asset allocation
   b. Investment performance
   d. Alternative investment

3. _____ are made by investors and investment managers.

   Investors commonly perform investment analysis by making use of fundamental analysis, technical analysis and gut feel.

   _____ are often supported by decision tools.

   a. Investment performance
   c. Investing online
   b. Asset allocation
   d. Investment decisions

4. A _____ is a fungible, negotiable instrument representing financial value. They are broadly categorized into debt securities (such as banknotes, bonds and debentures), and equity securities; e.g., common stocks. The company or other entity issuing the _____ is called the issuer.

   a. Securities lending
   c. Book entry
   b. Security
   d. Tracking stock

5. _____ in finance is a risk management technique, related to hedging, that mixes a wide variety of investments within a portfolio. Because the fluctuations of a single security have less impact on a diverse portfolio, _____ minimizes the risk from any one investment.

   A simple example of _____ is the following: On a particular island the entire economy consists of two companies: one that sells umbrellas and another that sells sunscreen.

   a. 4-4-5 Calendar
   c. Diversification
   b. 7-Eleven
   d. 529 plan

6. Behavioral economics and _____ are closely related fields that have evolved to be a separate branch of economic and financial analysis which applies scientific research on human and social, cognitive and emotional factors to better understand economic decisions by, say, consumers, borrowers, investors, and how they affect market prices, returns and the allocation of resources.

Chapter 7. Optimal Risky Portfolios

The field is primarily concerned with the bounds of rationality (selfishness, self-control) of economic agents. Behavioral models typically integrate insights from psychology with neo-classical economic theory.

a. Recession
b. Market structure
c. Medium of exchange
d. Behavioral finance

7. In finance, _____ occurs when a debtor has not met its legal obligations according to the debt contract, e.g. it has not made a scheduled payment, or has violated a loan covenant (condition) of the debt contract. _____ may occur if the debtor is either unwilling or unable to pay their debt. This can occur with all debt obligations including bonds, mortgages, loans, and promissory notes.

a. Debt validation
b. Vendor finance
c. Default
d. Credit crunch

8. _____ is the risk of loss due to a debtor's non-payment of a loan or other line of credit (either the principal or interest (coupon) or both)

Most lenders employ their own models (credit scorecards) to rank potential and existing customers according to risk, and then apply appropriate strategies. With products such as unsecured personal loans or mortgages, lenders charge a higher price for higher risk customers and vice versa. With revolving products such as credit cards and overdrafts, risk is controlled through careful setting of credit limits.

a. Credit risk
b. Market risk
c. Transaction risk
d. Liquidity risk

9. _____ is the risk that the value of an investment will decrease due to moves in market factors. The five standard _____ factors are:

- Equity risk, the risk that stock prices will change.
- Interest rate risk, the risk that interest rates will change.
- Currency risk, the risk that foreign exchange rates will change.
- Commodity risk, the risk that commodity prices (e.g. grains, metals) will change.

As with other forms of risk, _____ may be measured in a number of ways. Traditionally, this is done using a Value at Risk methodology. Value at risk is well established as a risk management technique, but it contains a number of limiting assumptions that constrain its accuracy.

a. Currency risk
b. Tracking error
c. Market risk
d. Transaction risk

10. In finance, _____ is that risk which is common to an entire market and not to any individual entity or component thereof. It should be distinguished from systemic risk which is the risk that the entire financial system will collapse as a result of some catastrophic event.

Risks can be reduced in four main ways: Avoidance, Reduction, Retention and Transfer.

a. Conglomerate merger
c. Primary market
b. Systematic risk
d. Capital surplus

11. The term _____ or economic cycle refers to the fluctuations of economic activity (business fluctuations) around a long-term growth trend. The cycle involves shifts over time between periods of relatively rapid growth of output (recovery and prosperity), and periods of relative stagnation or decline (contraction or recession.) These fluctuations are often measured using the real gross domestic product.

a. Behavioral finance
c. Fixed exchange rate
b. Deflation
d. Business cycle

12. In probability theory and statistics, the _____ of a random variable, probability distribution averaging the squared distance of its possible values from the expected value (mean.) Whereas the mean is a way to describe the location of a distribution, the _____ is a way to capture its scale or degree of being spread out. The unit of _____ is the square of the unit of the original variable.

a. Monte Carlo methods
c. Harmonic mean
b. Semivariance
d. Variance

13. In probability theory and statistics, _____ is a measure of how much two variables change together (variance is a special case of the _____ when the two variables are identical.)

If two variables tend to vary together (that is, when one of them is above its expected value, then the other variable tends to be above its expected value too), then the _____ between the two variables will be positive. On the other hand, when one of them is above its expected value the other variable tends to be below its expected value, then the _____ between the two variables will be negative.

a. Covariance
c. Stratified sampling
b. Probability distribution
d. Frequency distribution

14. In statistics and probability theory, the _____ is a matrix of covariances between elements of a vector. It is the natural generalization to higher dimensions of the concept of the variance of a scalar-valued random variable.

If entries in the column vector

$$X = \begin{bmatrix} X_1 \\ \vdots \\ X_n \end{bmatrix}$$

are random variables, each with finite variance, then the _____ Σ is the matrix whose (i, j) entry is the covariance

$$\Sigma_{ij} = \text{cov}(X_i, X_j) = \text{E}\big[(X_i - \mu_i)(X_j - \mu_j)\big]$$

where

Chapter 7. Optimal Risky Portfolios

$$\mu_i = \mathrm{E}(X_i)$$

is the expected value of the ith entry in the vector X.

a. 7-Eleven
c. Covariance matrix
b. 529 plan
d. 4-4-5 Calendar

15. In finance, a _____ is a position established in one market in an attempt to offset exposure to the price risk of an equal but opposite obligation or position in another market -- usually, but not always, in the context of one's commercial activity. Hedging is a strategy designed to minimize exposure to such business risks as a sharp contraction in demand for one's inventory, while still allowing the business to profit from producing and maintaining that inventory. A typical hedger might be a farmer with 2000 acres of unharvested wheat in the ground, who would rather tend his crop without the distraction of uncertain prices.

a. 529 plan
c. Hedge
b. 7-Eleven
d. 4-4-5 Calendar

16. In probability theory and statistics, _____ indicates the strength and direction of a linear relationship between two random variables. That is in contrast with the usage of the term in colloquial speech, which denotes any relationship, not necessarily linear. In general statistical usage, _____ or co-relation refers to the departure of two random variables from independence.

a. Geometric mean
c. Variance
b. Probability distribution
d. Correlation

17. The _____ is the relationship between the amount of return gained on an investment and the amount of risk undertaken in that investment. The more return sought, the more risk that must be undertaken.

There are various classes of possible investments, each with their own positions on the overall _____.

a. Blank endorsement
c. Post earnings announcement drift
b. Risk-return spectrum
d. Fiscal sponsorship

18. A _____ is a situation that involves losing one quality or aspect of something in return for gaining another quality or aspect. It implies a decision to be made with full comprehension of both the upside and downside of a particular choice.

In economics the term is expressed as opportunity cost, referring the most preferred alternative given up.

a. Break-even point
c. Trade-off
b. Total revenue
d. Capital outflow

19. In Finance the _____ is a mathematical model for portfolio allocation developed in 1990 at Goldman Sachs by Fischer Black and Robert Litterman, and published in 1992. It seeks to overcome problems that institutional investors have encountered in applying modern portfolio theory in practice. The model starts with the equilibrium assumption that the asset allocation of a representative agent should be proportional to the market values of the available assets, and then modifies that to take into account the 'views' (i.e. the specific opinions about asset returns) of the investor in question to arrive at a bespoke asset allocation.

Chapter 7. Optimal Risky Portfolios

a. Black-Litterman model
b. Capital surplus
c. Clientele effect
d. Specific risk

20. _____ refers to any type of investment that yields a regular (or fixed) return.

For example, if you lend money to a borrower and the borrower has to pay interest once a month, you have been issued a fixed-income security. When a company does this, it is often called a bond or corporate bank debt (although preferred stock is also sometimes considered to be _____).

a. 529 plan
b. Bond market
c. 4-4-5 Calendar
d. Fixed income

21. _____ is a concept in economics, finance, and psychology related to the behaviour of consumers and investors under uncertainty. _____ is the reluctance of a person to accept a bargain with an uncertain payoff rather than another bargain with a more certain, but possibly lower, expected payoff.

The inverse of a person's _____ is sometimes called their risk tolerance

a. Risk aversion
b. Risk premium
c. Risk adjusted return on capital
d. Discount factor

22. In business and finance, a _____ (also referred to as equity _____) of stock means a _____ of ownership in a corporation (company.) In the plural, stocks is often used as a synonym for _____ s especially in the United States, but it is less commonly used that way outside of North America.

In the United Kingdom, South Africa, and Australia, stock can also refer to completely different financial instruments such as government bonds or, less commonly, to all kinds of marketable securities.

a. Margin
b. Procter ' Gamble
c. Bucket shop
d. Share

23. In finance, the yield curve is the relation between the interest rate (or cost of borrowing) and the time to maturity of the debt for a given borrower in a given currency. For example, the current U.S. dollar interest rates paid on U.S. Treasury securities for various maturities are closely watched by many traders, and are commonly plotted on a graph such as the one on the right which is informally called 'the yield curve.' More formal mathematical descriptions of this relation are often called the _____.

The yield of a debt instrument is the annualized percentage increase in the value of the investment.

a. 529 plan
b. 7-Eleven
c. 4-4-5 Calendar
d. Term structure of interest rates

24. _____ mature in one year or less. Like zero-coupon bonds, they do not pay interest prior to maturity; instead they are sold at a discount of the par value to create a positive yield to maturity. Many regard _____ as the least risky investment available to U.S. investors.

Chapter 7. Optimal Risky Portfolios

a. Treasury securities
b. Treasury Inflation Protected Securities
c. 4-4-5 Calendar
d. Treasury bills

25. In finance, the term _____ describes the amount in cash that returns to the owners of a security. Normally it does not include the price variations, at the difference of the total return. _____ applies to various stated rates of return on stocks (common and preferred, and convertible), fixed income instruments (bonds, notes, bills, strips, zero coupon), and some other investment type insurance products (e.g. annuities.)

a. Yield to maturity
b. Macaulay duration
c. 4-4-5 Calendar
d. Yield

26. In finance, the _____ is the relation between the interest rate (or cost of borrowing) and the time to maturity of the debt for a given borrower in a given currency. For example, the current U.S. dollar interest rates paid on U.S. Treasury securities for various maturities are closely watched by many traders, and are commonly plotted on a graph such as the one on the right which is informally called 'the _____.' More formal mathematical descriptions of this relation are often called the term structure of interest rates.

The yield of a debt instrument is the annualized percentage increase in the value of the investment.

a. 4-4-5 Calendar
b. 529 plan
c. Yield curve
d. 7-Eleven

27. In finance, _____ is the interest that has accumulated since the principal investment, or since the previous interest payment if there has been one already. For a financial instrument such as a bond, interest is calculated and paid in set intervals.

The primary formula for calculating the interest accrued in a given period is:

$$I_A = T \times P \times R$$

where I_A is the _____, T is the fraction of the year, P is the principal, and R is the annualized interest rate.

a. Accrued interest
b. ABN Amro
c. A Random Walk Down Wall Street
d. AAB

28. In finance, a _____ is a debt security, in which the authorized issuer owes the holders a debt and, depending on the terms of the _____, is obliged to pay interest (the coupon) and/or to repay the principal at a later date, termed maturity.

Thus a _____ is a loan: the issuer is the borrower, the _____ holder is the lender, and the coupon is the interest. _____s provide the borrower with external funds to finance long-term investments, or, in the case of government _____s, to finance current expenditure.

a. Puttable bond
b. Bond
c. Catastrophe bonds
d. Convertible bond

29. The _____ is the market for securities, where companies and governments can raise longterm funds. The _____ includes the stock market and the bond market. Financial regulators, such as the U.S. Securities and Exchange Commission, oversee the _____s in their designated countries to ensure that investors are protected against fraud.
   a. Capital market
   b. Spot rate
   c. Forward market
   d. Delta neutral

30. _____, refers to consumption opportunity gained by an entity within a specified time frame, which is generally expressed in monetary terms. However, for households and individuals, '_____ is the sum of all the wages, salaries, profits, interests payments, rents and other forms of earnings received... in a given period of time.' For firms, _____ generally refers to net-profit: what remains of revenue after expenses have been subtracted.
   a. Annual report
   b. OIBDA
   c. Accrual
   d. Income

31. _____ is a fee paid on borrowed assets. It is the price paid for the use of borrowed money, or, money earned by deposited funds. Assets that are sometimes lent with _____ include money, shares, consumer goods through hire purchase, major assets such as aircraft, and even entire factories in finance lease arrangements.
   a. Insolvency
   b. Interest
   c. AAB
   d. A Random Walk Down Wall Street

32. An _____ is the price a borrower pays for the use of money they do not own, and the return a lender receives for deferring the use of funds, by lending it to the borrower. _____s are normally expressed as a percentage rate over the period of one year.

   _____s targets are also a vital tool of monetary policy and are used to control variables like investment, inflation, and unemployment.

   a. AAB
   b. A Random Walk Down Wall Street
   c. ABN Amro
   d. Interest rate

33. _____ is a graph created by investors to measure the risk of risky and risk-free assets. The graph displays to the investors on the return they can make by taking on a certain level of risk. It is also known as a 'reward-to-variability ratio'.
   a. Portfolio investment
   b. Divestment
   c. Capital allocation line
   d. Dollar cost averaging

34. The _____ is a measure of the excess return (or Risk Premium) per unit of risk in an investment asset or a trading strategy it is defined as:

$$S = \frac{R - R_f}{\sigma} = \frac{E[R - R_f]}{\sqrt{\text{var}[R - R_f]}},$$

where R is the asset return, R_f is the return on a benchmark asset, such as the risk free rate of return, $E[R - R_f]$ is the expected value of the excess of the asset return over the benchmark return, and σ is the standard deviation of the asset excess return.

Chapter 7. Optimal Risky Portfolios

Note, if R_f is a constant risk free return throughout the period,

$$\sqrt{\operatorname{var}[R - R_f]} = \sqrt{\operatorname{var}[R]}.$$

The _____ is used to characterize how well the return of an asset compensates the investor for the risk taken. When comparing two assets each with the expected return E[R] against the same benchmark with return R_f, the asset with the higher _____ gives more return for the same risk.

a. Receivables turnover ratio
b. Sharpe ratio
c. Current ratio
d. P/E ratio

35. Modern portfolio theory (MPT) proposes how rational investors will use diversification to optimize their portfolios, and how a risky asset should be priced. The basic concepts of the theory are Markowitz diversification, the _____, capital asset pricing model, the alpha and beta coefficients, the Capital Market Line and the Securities Market Line.

MPT models an asset's return as a random variable, and models a portfolio as a weighted combination of assets so that the return of a portfolio is the weighted combination of the assets' returns.

a. Efficient frontier
b. A Random Walk Down Wall Street
c. ABN Amro
d. AAB

36. In finance, _____ or 'shorting' is the practice of selling a financial instrument that the seller does not own at the time of the sale. _____ is done with intent of later purchasing the financial instrument at a lower price. Short-sellers attempt to profit from an expected decline in the price of a financial instrument.

a. Short ratio
b. Short selling
c. 529 plan
d. 4-4-5 Calendar

37. In economic models, the _____ time frame assumes no fixed factors of production. Firms can enter or leave the marketplace, and the cost (and availability) of land, labor, raw materials, and capital goods can be assumed to vary. In contrast, in the short-run time frame, certain factors are assumed to be fixed, because there is not sufficient time for them to change.

a. Long-run
b. Short-run
c. 529 plan
d. 4-4-5 Calendar

38. The _____ is the weighted-average most likely outcome in gambling, probability theory, economics or finance.

In gambling and probability theory, there is usually a discrete set of possible outcomes. In this case, _____ is a measure of the relative balance of win or loss weighted by their chances of occurring.

a. AAB
b. A Random Walk Down Wall Street
c. ABN Amro
d. Expected return

39. _____ is a mathematical science pertaining to the collection, analysis, interpretation or explanation, and presentation of data. It also provides tools for prediction and forecasting based on data. It is applicable to a wide variety of academic disciplines, from the natural and social sciences to the humanities, government and business.
   a. Mean
   b. Covariance
   c. Sample size
   d. Statistics

40. In probability and statistics, the _____ of a collection of numbers is a measure of the dispersion of the numbers from their expected (mean) value. It can apply to a probability distribution, a random variable, a population or a data set. The _____ is usually denoted with the letter σ (lowercase sigma.)
   a. Kurtosis
   b. Mean
   c. Sample size
   d. Standard deviation

Chapter 8. Index Models

1. In probability theory and statistics, _____ indicates the strength and direction of a linear relationship between two random variables. That is in contrast with the usage of the term in colloquial speech, which denotes any relationship, not necessarily linear. In general statistical usage, _____ or co-relation refers to the departure of two random variables from independence.
   a. Probability distribution
   b. Variance
   c. Geometric mean
   d. Correlation

2. A _____ is a fungible, negotiable instrument representing financial value. They are broadly categorized into debt securities (such as banknotes, bonds and debentures), and equity securities; e.g., common stocks. The company or other entity issuing the _____ is called the issuer.
   a. Book entry
   b. Tracking stock
   c. Security
   d. Securities lending

3. In probability theory and statistics, a _____, sometimes also called a multivariate Gaussian distribution, is a generalization of the one-dimensional normal distribution to higher dimensions. It is also closely related to matrix normal distribution.

A random vector $X = [X_1, \ldots, X_N]^T$ follows a _____ if it satisfies the following equivalent conditions:

- every linear combination $Y = a_1 X_1 + \cdots + a_N X_N$ is normally distributed

- there is a random vector $Z = [Z_1, \ldots, Z_M]^T$, whose components are independent standard normal random variables, a vector $\mu = [\mu_1, \ldots, \mu_N]^T$ and an $N \times M$ matrix A such that $X = AZ + \mu$.

- there is a vector μ and a symmetric, positive semi-definite matrix Σ such that the characteristic function of X is

$$\phi_X(u; \mu, \Sigma) = \exp\left(i\mu^T u - \frac{1}{2} u^T \Sigma u\right).$$

If Σ is non-singular, then the distribution may be described by the following PDF:

$$f_X(x_1, \ldots, x_N) = \frac{1}{(2\pi)^{N/2} |\Sigma|^{1/2}} \exp\left(-\frac{1}{2}(x-\mu)^T \Sigma^{-1}(x-\mu)\right)$$

where $|\Sigma|$ is the determinant of Σ. Note how the equation above reduces to that of the univariate normal distribution if Σ is a scalar

Chapter 8. Index Models

a. Municipal Okrug #7
c. Certified Emission Reductions
b. FTSE MTIRS Indices
d. Multivariate normal distribution

4. In finance, _____ is that risk which is common to an entire market and not to any individual entity or component thereof. It should be distinguished from systemic risk which is the risk that the entire financial system will collapse as a result of some catastrophic event.

Risks can be reduced in four main ways: Avoidance, Reduction, Retention and Transfer.

a. Primary market
c. Systematic risk
b. Capital surplus
d. Conglomerate merger

5. The _____ is an important family of continuous probability distributions, applicable in many fields. Each member of the family may be defined by two parameters, location and scale: the mean and variance respectively. The standard _____ is the _____ with a mean of zero and a variance of one

a. Random variables
c. Normal distribution
b. Probability distribution
d. Correlation

6. In statistics, regression analysis is a collective name for techniques for the modeling and analysis of numerical data consisting of values of a dependent variable and of one or more independent variables The dependent variable in the _____ is modeled as a function of the independent variables, corresponding parameters, and an error term. The error term is treated as a random variable.

a. 529 plan
c. 4-4-5 Calendar
b. 7-Eleven
d. Regression equation

7. The _____ is an asset pricing model commonly used in the finance industry to measure risk and return of a stock. Mathematically the SIM is expressed as:

where:

$r_{it} - r_f$ is the excess return on the stock
a_i is the company's alpha
B_i is the company's beta
$r_{mt} - r_f$ is the excess return on the market index
E_{it} is the residual return

The accuracy of the model is enhanced by the stock return's influence by market (beta) and firm-specific risk factors (alpha), unexpected returns (residual) and the relation to the performance of a market index (such as the All Ordinaries.) Security analysts often use the SIM for such functions as computing stock betas, evaluating stock selection skills, and conducting event studies.

Chapter 8. Index Models

a. Political risk
b. Capital asset
c. Country risk
d. Single-index model

8. _____ is a risk-adjusted measure of the so-called active return on an investment. It is the return in excess of the compensation for the risk borne, and thus commonly used to assess active managers' performances. Often, the return of a benchmark is subtracted in order to consider relative performance, which yields Jensen's _____.

a. Amortization
b. Annuity
c. Option
d. Alpha

9. In probability theory and statistics, _____ is a measure of how much two variables change together (variance is a special case of the _____ when the two variables are identical.)

If two variables tend to vary together (that is, when one of them is above its expected value, then the other variable tends to be above its expected value too), then the _____ between the two variables will be positive. On the other hand, when one of them is above its expected value the other variable tends to be below its expected value, then the _____ between the two variables will be negative.

a. Frequency distribution
b. Covariance
c. Probability distribution
d. Stratified sampling

10. The _____ is the weighted-average most likely outcome in gambling, probability theory, economics or finance.

In gambling and probability theory, there is usually a discrete set of possible outcomes. In this case, _____ is a measure of the relative balance of win or loss weighted by their chances of occurring.

a. AAB
b. A Random Walk Down Wall Street
c. ABN Amro
d. Expected return

11. In finance, _____ is the risk involved in using models to value financial securities. Rebonato considers alternative definitions including:

1) After observing a set of prices for the underlying and hedging instruments, different but identically calibrated models might produce different prices for the same exotic product. 2) Losses will be incurred because of an 'incorrect' hedging strategy suggested by a model.

a. Takeover
b. Duty of loyalty
c. Price-to-book ratio
d. Model risk

12.

In finance, the _____ can be the expected rate of return above the risk-free interest rate. When measuring risk, a common sense approach is to compare the risk-free return on T-bills and the very risky return on other investments. The difference between these two returns can be interpreted as a measure of the excess return on the average risky asset. This excess return is known as the _____.

a. Risk modeling
b. Risk adjusted return on capital
c. Risk aversion
d. Risk premium

13. In finance, the _____ is used to determine a theoretically appropriate required rate of return of an asset, if that asset is to be added to an already well-diversified portfolio, given that asset's non-diversifiable risk. The model takes into account the asset's sensitivity to non-diversifiable risk (also known as systemic risk or market risk), often represented by the quantity beta (β) in the financial industry, as well as the expected return of the market and the expected return of a theoretical risk-free asset.

The model was introduced by Jack Treynor (1961, 1962), William Sharpe (1964), John Lintner (1965a,b) and Jan Mossin (1966) independently, building on the earlier work of Harry Markowitz on diversification and modern portfolio theory.

a. Cox-Ingersoll-Ross model
b. Hull-White model
c. Capital asset pricing model
d. Random walk hypothesis

14. _____ is a concept in technical analysis that the movement of the price of a security will tend to stop and reverse at certain predetermined price levels.

A support level is a price level where the price tends to find support as it is going down. This means the price is more likely to 'bounce' off this level rather than break through it.

A resistance level is the opposite of a support level. It is where the price tends to find resistance as it is going up. This means the price is more likely to 'bounce' off this level rather than break through it.

a. Dow theory
b. Technical analysis
c. Point and figure
d. Support and resistance

15. _____ in finance is a risk management technique, related to hedging, that mixes a wide variety of investments within a portfolio. Because the fluctuations of a single security have less impact on a diverse portfolio, _____ minimizes the risk from any one investment.

A simple example of _____ is the following: On a particular island the entire economy consists of two companies: one that sells umbrellas and another that sells sunscreen.

a. 4-4-5 Calendar
b. Diversification
c. 7-Eleven
d. 529 plan

16. In statistics, the _____, R^2 is used in the context of statistical models whose main purpose is the prediction of future outcomes on the basis of other related information. It is the proportion of variability in a data set that is accounted for by the statistical model. It provides a measure of how well future outcomes are likely to be predicted by the model.

a. 529 plan
b. 4-4-5 Calendar
c. 7-Eleven
d. Coefficient of determination

Chapter 8. Index Models

17. A scatter plot is a type of display using Cartesian coordinates to display values for two variables for a set of data. The data is displayed as a collection of points, each having the value of one variable determining the position on the horizontal axis and the value of the other variable determining the position on the vertical axis. A scatter plot is also called a scatter chart, _____ and scatter graph.

   a. 7-Eleven
   b. 529 plan
   c. 4-4-5 Calendar
   d. Scatter diagram

18. In statistics, _____ is a collection of statistical models, and their associated procedures, in which the observed variance is partitioned into components due to different explanatory variables. The initial techniques of the _____ were developed by the statistician and geneticist R. A. Fisher in the 1920s and 1930s, and is sometimes known as Fisher's ANOVA or Fisher's _____, due to the use of Fisher's F-distribution as part of the test of statistical significance.

There are three conceptual classes of such models:

1. Fixed-effects models assumes that the data came from normal populations which may differ only in their means. (Model 1)
2. Random effects models assume that the data describe a hierarchy of different populations whose differences are constrained by the hierarchy. (Model 2)
3. Mixed-effect models describe situations where both fixed and random effects are present. (Model 3)

   a. ABN Amro
   b. Analysis of variance
   c. AAB
   d. A Random Walk Down Wall Street

19. _____ mature in one year or less. Like zero-coupon bonds, they do not pay interest prior to maturity; instead they are sold at a discount of the par value to create a positive yield to maturity. Many regard _____ as the least risky investment available to U.S. investors.

   a. 4-4-5 Calendar
   b. Treasury securities
   c. Treasury bills
   d. Treasury Inflation Protected Securities

20. In probability theory and statistics, the _____ of a random variable, probability distribution averaging the squared distance of its possible values from the expected value (mean.) Whereas the mean is a way to describe the location of a distribution, the _____ is a way to capture its scale or degree of being spread out. The unit of _____ is the square of the unit of the original variable.

   a. Harmonic mean
   b. Semivariance
   c. Monte Carlo methods
   d. Variance

21. In statistical hypothesis testing, the _____ is the probability of obtaining a result at least as extreme as the one that was actually observed, given that the null hypothesis is true. The fact that _____s are based on this assumption is crucial to their correct interpretation.

More technically, a _____ of an experiment is a random variable defined over the sample space of the experiment such that its distribution under the null hypothesis is uniform on the interval [0,1].

   a. Standard deviation
   b. P-value
   c. Median
   d. Standard score

22. In statistics and probability theory, the _____ is a matrix of covariances between elements of a vector. It is the natural generalization to higher dimensions of the concept of the variance of a scalar-valued random variable.

If entries in the column vector

$$X = \begin{bmatrix} X_1 \\ \vdots \\ X_n \end{bmatrix}$$

are random variables, each with finite variance, then the _____ Σ is the matrix whose (i, j) entry is the covariance

$$\Sigma_{ij} = \text{cov}(X_i, X_j) = E\big[(X_i - \mu_i)(X_j - \mu_j)\big]$$

where

$$\mu_i = E(X_i)$$

is the expected value of the ith entry in the vector X.

    a. 7-Eleven
    b. 529 plan
    c. 4-4-5 Calendar
    d. Covariance matrix

23. _____, authored by professors Benjamin Graham and David Dodd of Columbia Business School, laid the intellectual foundation for what would later be called value investing. The work was first published in 1934, following unprecedented losses on Wall Street. In summing up lessons learned, Graham and Dodd chided Wall Street for its myopic focus on a company's reported earnings per share, and were particularly harsh on the favored 'earnings trends.' They encouraged investors to take an entirely different approach by gauging the rough value of the operating business that lay behind the security.

    a. Security analysis
    b. 4-4-5 Calendar
    c. Growth stocks
    d. Stock valuation

24. The term _____ or economic cycle refers to the fluctuations of economic activity (business fluctuations) around a long-term growth trend. The cycle involves shifts over time between periods of relatively rapid growth of output (recovery and prosperity), and periods of relative stagnation or decline (contraction or recession.) These fluctuations are often measured using the real gross domestic product.

    a. Business cycle
    b. Deflation
    c. Behavioral finance
    d. Fixed exchange rate

25. In statistics, a _____ is a tabulation of the values that one or more variables take in a sample.

Chapter 8. Index Models

Univariate _____s are often presented as lists ordered by quantity showing the number of times each value appears. For example, if 100 people rate a five-point Likert scale assessing their agreement with a statement on a scale on which 1 denotes strong agreement and 5 strong disagreement, the _____ of their responses might look like:

This simple tabulation has two drawbacks.

a. Random variables
c. Variance
b. Covariance
d. Frequency distribution

26. _____ is a mathematical science pertaining to the collection, analysis, interpretation or explanation, and presentation of data. It also provides tools for prediction and forecasting based on data. It is applicable to a wide variety of academic disciplines, from the natural and social sciences to the humanities, government and business.
   a. Mean
   b. Covariance
   c. Statistics
   d. Sample size

27. _____ refers to a portfolio management strategy where the manager makes specific investments with the goal of outperforming an investment benchmark index. Investors or mutual funds that do not aspire to create a return in excess of a benchmark index will often invest in an index fund that replicates as closely as possible the investment weighting and returns of that index; this is called passive management. _____ is the opposite of passive management, because in passive management the manager does not seek to outperform the benchmark index.
   a. A Random Walk Down Wall Street
   b. Active management
   c. AAB
   d. ABN Amro

28. In business and accounting, _____s are everything of value that is owned by a person or company. The balance sheet of a firm records the monetary value of the _____s owned by the firm. The two major _____ classes are tangible _____s and intangible _____s.
   a. Accounts payable
   b. EBITDA
   c. Asset
   d. Income

29. The _____ is a measure of the excess return (or Risk Premium) per unit of risk in an investment asset or a trading strategy it is defined as:

$$S = \frac{R - R_f}{\sigma} = \frac{E[R - R_f]}{\sqrt{\mathrm{var}[R - R_f]}},$$

where R is the asset return, R_f is the return on a benchmark asset, such as the risk free rate of return, $E[R - R_f]$ is the expected value of the excess of the asset return over the benchmark return, and σ is the standard deviation of the asset excess return.

Chapter 8. Index Models

Note, if R_f is a constant risk free return throughout the period,

$$\sqrt{\text{var}[R - R_f]} = \sqrt{\text{var}[R]}.$$

The _____ is used to characterize how well the return of an asset compensates the investor for the risk taken. When comparing two assets each with the expected return E[R] against the same benchmark with return R_f, the asset with the higher _____ gives more return for the same risk.

a. P/E ratio
b. Current ratio
c. Receivables turnover ratio
d. Sharpe ratio

30. _____ measures the active return of an investment manager divided by the amount of risk the manager takes relative to a benchmark. It is used in the analysis of performance of mutual funds, hedge funds, etc. Specifically, the _____ is defined as active return divided by tracking error.

a. Information ratio
b. Asset turnover
c. Operating leverage
d. Earnings yield

31. In Finance the _____ is a mathematical model for portfolio allocation developed in 1990 at Goldman Sachs by Fischer Black and Robert Litterman, and published in 1992. It seeks to overcome problems that institutional investors have encountered in applying modern portfolio theory in practice. The model starts with the equilibrium assumption that the asset allocation of a representative agent should be proportional to the market values of the available assets, and then modifies that to take into account the 'views' (i.e. the specific opinions about asset returns) of the investor in question to arrive at a bespoke asset allocation.

a. Capital surplus
b. Clientele effect
c. Black-Litterman model
d. Specific risk

32. In Finance the _____ is a mathematical model for security selection published by Fischer Black and Jack Treynor in 1973. The model assumes an investor who considers that most securities are priced efficiently, but who believes he has information that can be used to predict the abnormal performance (Alpha) of a few of them; the model finds the optimum portfolio to hold under such conditions.

In essence the optimal portfolio consists of two parts: an index fund containing all securities in proportion to their market value and an 'active portfolio' containing the securities for which the investor has made a prediction about alpha.

a. Binomial model
b. LIBOR market model
c. Treynor-Black model
d. Modified Internal Rate of Return

33. Modern portfolio theory (MPT) proposes how rational investors will use diversification to optimize their portfolios, and how a risky asset should be priced. The basic concepts of the theory are Markowitz diversification, the _____, capital asset pricing model, the alpha and beta coefficients, the Capital Market Line and the Securities Market Line.

Chapter 8. Index Models

MPT models an asset's return as a random variable, and models a portfolio as a weighted combination of assets so that the return of a portfolio is the weighted combination of the assets' returns.

a. AAB
c. ABN Amro
b. A Random Walk Down Wall Street
d. Efficient frontier

34. In finance, a _____ is a position established in one market in an attempt to offset exposure to the price risk of an equal but opposite obligation or position in another market -- usually, but not always, in the context of one's commercial activity. Hedging is a strategy designed to minimize exposure to such business risks as a sharp contraction in demand for one's inventory, while still allowing the business to profit from producing and maintaining that inventory. A typical hedger might be a farmer with 2000 acres of unharvested wheat in the ground, who would rather tend his crop without the distraction of uncertain prices.

a. 7-Eleven
c. 4-4-5 Calendar
b. 529 plan
d. Hedge

35. A _____ is a private investment fund open to a limited range of investors that is permitted by regulators to undertake a wider range of activities than other investment funds and also pays a performance fee to its investment manager. Each fund will have its own strategy which determines the type of investments and the methods of investment it undertakes. _____s as a class invest in a broad range of investments extending over shares, debt, commodities and beyond.

a. 7-Eleven
c. 4-4-5 Calendar
b. Hedge fund
d. 529 plan

36. An investment strategy or portfolio is considered _____ if it seeks to entirely avoid some form of market risk, typically by hedging. In order to evaluate market neutrality, it is first necessary to specify the risk being avoided. For example, convertible arbitrage attempts to fully hedge fluctuations in the price of the underlying common stock.

a. Flight-to-quality
c. Credit event
b. Black-Litterman model
d. Market neutral

37. In e-business terms, a _____ is an organization that originated and does business purely through the internet, they have no physical store (brick and mortar) where customers can shop. Examples of large _____ companies include Amazon.com and Netflix.com. There are also many smaller, niche oriented _____ mail order companies such as women's travel accessories company Christine Columbus and fashion jewelry merchant Jewels of Denial.

a. Pure play
c. 4-4-5 Calendar
b. The Dogs of the Dow
d. 529 plan

Chapter 9. The Capital Asset Pricing Model

1. The term _____ has three unrelated technical definitions, and is also used in a variety of non-technical ways.

   - In financial economics, it refers to any asset used to make money, as opposed to assets used for personal enjoyment or consumption. This is an important distinction because two people can disagree sharply about the value of personal assets, one person might think a sports car is more valuable than a pickup truck, another person might have the opposite taste. But if an asset is held for the purpose of making money, taste has nothing to do with it, only differences of opinion about how much money the asset will produce. With the further assumption that people agree on the probability distribution of future cash flows, it is possible to have an objective _____ pricing model. Even without the assumption of agreement, it is possible to set rational limits on _____ value.
   - In governmental accounting, it is defined as any asset used in operations with an initial useful life extending beyond one reporting period. Generally, government managers have a 'stewardship' duty to maintain _____s under their control. See International Public Sector Accounting Standards for details.
   - In US tax accounting, it is defined as any property other than a list of exceptions. The main exceptions are anything held for sale, and any real estate or depreciable property used in business. Almost everything you own and use for personal purposes, pleasure or investment is a _____. If something is a _____ for tax purposes, gains or losses on sale or disposition are capital gains or capital losses. For individuals, however, capital losses on property held for personal use are generally not deductible. See the IRS publication Tax Facts about Capital Gains and Losses for details.

   A well-known financial accounting textbook advises that the term be avoided except in tax accounting because it is used in so many different senses, not all of them well-defined. For example it is often used as a synonym for fixed assets or for investments in securities.

   A common non-technical usage occurs when people ask that employees or the environment or something else be treated as a _____.

   a. Settlement date
   c. Solvency
   b. Political risk
   d. Capital asset

2. In finance, the _____ is used to determine a theoretically appropriate required rate of return of an asset, if that asset is to be added to an already well-diversified portfolio, given that asset's non-diversifiable risk. The model takes into account the asset's sensitivity to non-diversifiable risk (also known as systemic risk or market risk), often represented by the quantity beta (β) in the financial industry, as well as the expected return of the market and the expected return of a theoretical risk-free asset.

   The model was introduced by Jack Treynor (1961, 1962), William Sharpe (1964), John Lintner (1965a,b) and Jan Mossin (1966) independently, building on the earlier work of Harry Markowitz on diversification and modern portfolio theory.

   a. Random walk hypothesis
   c. Cox-Ingersoll-Ross model
   b. Hull-White model
   d. Capital asset pricing model

3. In business and accounting, _____s are everything of value that is owned by a person or company. The balance sheet of a firm records the monetary value of the _____s owned by the firm. The two major _____ classes are tangible _____s and intangible _____s.

Chapter 9. The Capital Asset Pricing Model

    a. Income
    b. EBITDA
    c. Accounts payable
    d. Asset

4. In finance, _____ is the process of estimating the potential market value of a financial asset or liability. they can be done on assets (for example, investments in marketable securities such as stocks, options, business enterprises, or intangible assets such as patents and trademarks) or on liabilities (e.g., Bonds issued by a company.) _____s are required in many contexts including investment analysis, capital budgeting, merger and acquisition transactions, financial reporting, taxable events to determine the proper tax liability, and in litigation.
    a. Share
    b. Margin
    c. Procter ' Gamble
    d. Valuation

5. A _____ is a portfolio consisting of a weighted sum of every asset in the market, with weights in the proportions that they exist in the market (with the necessary assumption that these assets are infinitely divisible.)

Neha Tyagi's critique (1977) states that this is only a theoretical concept, as to create a _____ for investment purposes in practice would necessarily include every single possible available asset, including real estate, precious metals, stamp collections, jewelry, and anything with any worth, as the theoretical market being referred to would be the world market. As a result, proxies for the market are used in practice by investors.

    a. Market portfolio
    b. Central Securities Depository
    c. Delta neutral
    d. Market price

6. _____ is a graph created by investors to measure the risk of risky and risk-free assets. The graph displays to the investors on the return they can make by taking on a certain level of risk. It is also known as a 'reward-to-variability ratio'.
    a. Capital allocation line
    b. Divestment
    c. Portfolio investment
    d. Dollar cost averaging

7. The _____ is the market for securities, where companies and governments can raise longterm funds. The _____ includes the stock market and the bond market. Financial regulators, such as the U.S. Securities and Exchange Commission, oversee the _____s in their designated countries to ensure that investors are protected against fraud.
    a. Delta neutral
    b. Spot rate
    c. Capital market
    d. Forward market

8. _____ proposes how rational investors will use diversification to optimize their portfolios, and how a risky asset should be priced. The basic concepts of the theory are Markowitz diversification, the efficient frontier, capital asset pricing model, the alpha and beta coefficients, the Capital Market Line and the Securities Market Line.

_____ models an asset's return as a random variable, and models a portfolio as a weighted combination of assets so that the return of a portfolio is the weighted combination of the assets' returns.

    a. Payback period
    b. Market value
    c. Consumer basket
    d. Modern portfolio theory

9. The _____ is a linear factor model with wealth and state variable that forecast changes in the distribution of future returns or income.

Chapter 9. The Capital Asset Pricing Model

The main difference between _____ and standard CAPM is additing state variables that acknowledge the fact that investors hedge against shortfalls in consumption or against changes in the future investment opportunity set.

a. A Random Walk Down Wall Street
b. AAB
c. ABN Amro
d. Intertemporal Capital Asset Pricing Model

10. Modern portfolio theory (MPT) proposes how rational investors will use diversification to optimize their portfolios, and how a risky asset should be priced. The basic concepts of the theory are Markowitz diversification, the _____, capital asset pricing model, the alpha and beta coefficients, the Capital Market Line and the Securities Market Line.

MPT models an asset's return as a random variable, and models a portfolio as a weighted combination of assets so that the return of a portfolio is the weighted combination of the assets' returns.

a. A Random Walk Down Wall Street
b. AAB
c. ABN Amro
d. Efficient frontier

11. A _____ is a professionally managed type of collective investment scheme that pools money from many investors and invests it in stocks, bonds, short-term money market instruments, and/or other securities. The _____ will have a fund manager that trades the pooled money on a regular basis. Currently, the worldwide value of all _____ s totals more than $26 trillion.

Since 1940, there have been three basic types of investment companies in the United States: open-end funds, also known in the US as _____ s; unit investment trusts (UITs); and closed-end funds.

a. Financial intermediary
b. Trust company
c. Net asset value
d. Mutual fund

12. An _____ or index tracker is a collective investment scheme (usually a mutual fund or exchange-traded fund) that aims to replicate the movements of an index of a specific financial market regardless of market conditions.

Tracking can be achieved by trying to hold all of the securities in the index, in the same proportions as the index. Other methods include statistically sampling the market and holding 'representative' securities.

a. Investment company
b. AAB
c. A Random Walk Down Wall Street
d. Index fund

13. _____ is a financial strategy in which a fund manager makes as few portfolio decisions as possible, in order to minimize transaction costs, including the incidence of capital gains tax. One popular method is to mimic the performance of an externally specified index--called 'index funds'. The ethos of an index fund is aptly summed up in the injunction to an index fund manager: 'Don't just do something, sit there!'

_____ is most common on the equity market, where index funds track a stock market index, but it is becoming more common in other investment types, including bonds, commodities and hedge funds.

a. Net asset value
c. Savings and loan association
b. Trust company
d. Passive management

14.

In finance, the _____ can be the expected rate of return above the risk-free interest rate. When measuring risk, a common sense approach is to compare the risk-free return on T-bills and the very risky return on other investments. The difference between these two returns can be interpreted as a measure of the excess return on the average risky asset. This excess return is known as the _____.

a. Risk adjusted return on capital
c. Risk aversion
b. Risk premium
d. Risk modeling

15. In probability theory and statistics, _____ is a measure of how much two variables change together (variance is a special case of the _____ when the two variables are identical.)

If two variables tend to vary together (that is, when one of them is above its expected value, then the other variable tends to be above its expected value too), then the _____ between the two variables will be positive. On the other hand, when one of them is above its expected value the other variable tends to be below its expected value, then the _____ between the two variables will be negative.

a. Stratified sampling
c. Probability distribution
b. Frequency distribution
d. Covariance

16. In statistics and probability theory, the _____ is a matrix of covariances between elements of a vector. It is the natural generalization to higher dimensions of the concept of the variance of a scalar-valued random variable.

If entries in the column vector

$$X = \begin{bmatrix} X_1 \\ \vdots \\ X_n \end{bmatrix}$$

are random variables, each with finite variance, then the _____ Σ is the matrix whose (i, j) entry is the covariance

$$\Sigma_{ij} = \text{cov}(X_i, X_j) = \text{E}\big[(X_i - \mu_i)(X_j - \mu_j)\big]$$

where

$$\mu_i = \text{E}(X_i)$$

94 Chapter 9. The Capital Asset Pricing Model

is the expected value of the ith entry in the vector X.

a. 529 plan
c. 4-4-5 Calendar
b. 7-Eleven
d. Covariance matrix

17. The _____ is the weighted-average most likely outcome in gambling, probability theory, economics or finance.

In gambling and probability theory, there is usually a discrete set of possible outcomes. In this case, _____ is a measure of the relative balance of win or loss weighted by their chances of occurring.

a. Expected return
c. ABN Amro
b. A Random Walk Down Wall Street
d. AAB

18. A _____ is a fungible, negotiable instrument representing financial value. They are broadly categorized into debt securities (such as banknotes, bonds and debentures), and equity securities; e.g., common stocks. The company or other entity issuing the _____ is called the issuer.

a. Securities lending
c. Book entry
b. Tracking stock
d. Security

19. In probability theory and statistics, the _____ of a random variable, probability distribution averaging the squared distance of its possible values from the expected value (mean.) Whereas the mean is a way to describe the location of a distribution, the _____ is a way to capture its scale or degree of being spread out. The unit of _____ is the square of the unit of the original variable.

a. Monte Carlo methods
c. Semivariance
b. Harmonic mean
d. Variance

20. _____ is an economic concept with commonplace familiarity. It is the price that a good or service is offered at, or will fetch, in the marketplace. It is of interest mainly in the study of microeconomics.

a. Central Securities Depository
c. Convertible arbitrage
b. Delta hedging
d. Market price

21. The term _____ or economic cycle refers to the fluctuations of economic activity (business fluctuations) around a long-term growth trend. The cycle involves shifts over time between periods of relatively rapid growth of output (recovery and prosperity), and periods of relative stagnation or decline (contraction or recession.) These fluctuations are often measured using the real gross domestic product.

a. Fixed exchange rate
c. Behavioral finance
b. Deflation
d. Business cycle

22. In Modern Portfolio Theory, the _____ is the graphical representation of the Capital Asset Pricing Model. It displays the expected rate of return for an overall market as a function of systematic (non-diversifiable) risk (beta.)

The Y-Intercept (beta=0) of the _____ is equal to the risk-free interest rate.

Chapter 9. The Capital Asset Pricing Model

a. Divestment
c. Rebalancing
b. Security market line
d. Certificate in Investment Performance Measurement

23. _____ is a risk-adjusted measure of the so-called active return on an investment. It is the return in excess of the compensation for the risk borne, and thus commonly used to assess active managers' performances. Often, the return of a benchmark is subtracted in order to consider relative performance, which yields Jensen's _____.
   a. Alpha
   b. Option
   c. Amortization
   d. Annuity

24. The _____ is the rate of return that must be met for a company to undertake a particular project. The _____ is usually determined by evaluating existing opportunities in operations expansion, rate of return for investments, and other factors deemed relevant by management. A risk premium can also be attached to the _____ if management feels that specific opportunities inherently contain more risk than others that could be pursued with the same resources.
   a. Gross profit
   b. Capital structure
   c. Hurdle rate
   d. Corporate finance

25. The _____ is a capital budgeting metric used by firms to decide whether they should make investments. It is an indicator of the efficiency or quality of an investment, as opposed to net present value (NPV), which indicates value or magnitude.

The IRR is the annualized effective compounded return rate which can be earned on the invested capital, i.e., the yield on the investment.

   a. A Random Walk Down Wall Street
   b. Internal rate of return
   c. AAB
   d. ABN Amro

26. _____ is the planning process used to determine whether a firm's long term investments such as new machinery, replacement machinery, new plants, new products, and research development projects are worth pursuing. It is budget for major capital, or investment, expenditures.

Many formal methods are used in _____, including the techniques such as

- Net present value
- Profitability index
- Internal rate of return
- Modified Internal Rate of Return
- Equivalent annuity

These methods use the incremental cash flows from each potential investment, or project. Techniques based on accounting earnings and accounting rules are sometimes used - though economists consider this to be improper - such as the accounting rate of return, and 'return on investment.' Simplified and hybrid methods are used as well, such as payback period and discounted payback period.

   a. Capital budgeting
   b. Shareholder value
   c. Preferred stock
   d. Financial distress

Chapter 9. The Capital Asset Pricing Model

27. In finance, _____, also known as return on investment is the ratio of money gained or lost on an investment relative to the amount of money invested. The amount of money gained or lost may be referred to as interest, profit/loss, gain/loss, or net income/loss. The money invested may be referred to as the asset, capital, principal, or the cost basis of the investment.
   a. Rate of return
   b. Composiition of Creditors
   c. Stock or scrip dividends
   d. Doctrine of the Proper Law

28. In accounting, _____ or *Carrying value* is the value of an asset according to its balance sheet account balance. For assets, the value is based on the original cost of the asset less any depreciation, amortization or impairment costs made against the asset. A company's _____ is its total assets minus intangible assets and liabilities.
   a. Current liabilities
   b. Pro forma
   c. Book value
   d. Retained earnings

29. In economics, _____ is a measure of the relative satisfaction from or desirability of consumption of various goods and services. Given this measure, one may speak meaningfully of increasing or decreasing _____, and thereby explain economic behavior in terms of attempts to increase one's _____. For illustrative purposes, changes in _____ are sometimes expressed in units called utils.
   a. Utility function
   b. Utility
   c. AAB
   d. A Random Walk Down Wall Street

30. In statistics, a _____ is a tabulation of the values that one or more variables take in a sample.

Univariate _____s are often presented as lists ordered by quantity showing the number of times each value appears. For example, if 100 people rate a five-point Likert scale assessing their agreement with a statement on a scale on which 1 denotes strong agreement and 5 strong disagreement, the _____ of their responses might look like:

This simple tabulation has two drawbacks.

   a. Covariance
   b. Variance
   c. Random variables
   d. Frequency distribution

31. _____ is an international professional designation offered by the _____ Institute (formerly known as AIMR) to financial analysts who complete a series of three examinations. In order to become a '_____ Charterholder' candidates must pass all three six-hour exams, possess a bachelor's degree (or equivalent, as assessed by the _____ institute) and have 48 months of work experience in an investment decision-making position. _____ charterholders are also obligated to adhere to a strict Code of Ethics and Standards governing their professional conduct.
   a. 4-4-5 Calendar
   b. 529 plan
   c. Chartered Financial Analyst
   d. 7-Eleven

32. _____ is concerned with the tasks of developing and applying quantitative or statistical methods to the study and elucidation of economic principles. _____ combines economic theory with statistics to analyze and test economic relationships. Theoretical _____ considers questions about the statistical properties of estimators and tests, while applied _____ is concerned with the application of econometric methods to assess economic theories.

Chapter 9. The Capital Asset Pricing Model

a. A Random Walk Down Wall Street
b. Econometrics
c. ABN Amro
d. AAB

33. A _____, securities analyst, research analyst, equity analyst, or investment analyst is a person who performs financial analysis for external or internal clients as a core part of the job.

An analyst studies companies and other entities to arrive at the estimate of their financial value. It is normally done by analyzing financial reports, aided by follow-up interviews with company representatives and industry experts.

a. Stockbroker
b. Financial Analyst
c. Purchasing manager
d. Portfolio manager

34. In econometrics, an _____ model considers the variance of the current error term to be a function of the variances of the previous time period's error terms. _____ relates the error variance to the square of a previous period's error. It is employed commonly in modeling financial time series that exhibit time-varying volatility clustering, i.e. periods of swings followed by periods of relative calm.

a. Autoregressive conditional heteroscedasticity
b. A Random Walk Down Wall Street
c. ABN Amro
d. AAB

35. _____ refers to the stock of skills and knowledge embodied in the ability to perform labor so as to produce economic value. Many early economic theories refer to it simply as labor, one of three factors of production, and consider it to be a fungible resource -- homogeneous and easily interchangeable. Other conceptions of labor dispense with these assumptions.

a. Mercantilism
b. Behavioral finance
c. Human capital
d. Market structure

36. _____, refers to consumption opportunity gained by an entity within a specified time frame, which is generally expressed in monetary terms. However, for households and individuals, '_____ is the sum of all the wages, salaries, profits, interests payments, rents and other forms of earnings received... in a given period of time.' For firms, _____ generally refers to net-profit: what remains of revenue after expenses have been subtracted.

a. Annual report
b. Accrual
c. OIBDA
d. Income

37. In finance, a _____ is a position established in one market in an attempt to offset exposure to the price risk of an equal but opposite obligation or position in another market -- usually, but not always, in the context of one's commercial activity. Hedging is a strategy designed to minimize exposure to such business risks as a sharp contraction in demand for one's inventory, while still allowing the business to profit from producing and maintaining that inventory. A typical hedger might be a farmer with 2000 acres of unharvested wheat in the ground, who would rather tend his crop without the distraction of uncertain prices.

a. 529 plan
b. 7-Eleven
c. 4-4-5 Calendar
d. Hedge

38. In the valuation of a life insurance company, the actuary considers a series of future uncertain cashflows (including incoming premiums and outgoing claims, for example) and attempts to put a value on these cashflows. There are many ways of calculating such a value, but these approaches are often arbitrary in that the interest rate chosen for discounting is itself rather arbitrarily chosen.

One possible approach, and one that is gaining increasing attention, is the use of _____ or hedge portfolios. The theory is that we can choose a portfolio of assets (fixed interest bonds, zero coupon bonds, index-linked bonds, etc.) whose cashflows are identical to the magnitude and the timing of the cashflows to be valued.

a. 4-4-5 Calendar
b. 7-Eleven
c. Replicating portfolios
d. 529 plan

39. In economics, _____ is a rise in the general level of prices of goods and services in an economy over a period of time. The term '_____' once referred to increases in the money supply (monetary _____); however, economic debates about the relationship between money supply and price levels have led to its primary use today in describing price _____. _____ can also be described as a decline in the real value of money--a loss of purchasing power in the medium of exchange which is also the monetary unit of account.

a. ABN Amro
b. Inflation
c. A Random Walk Down Wall Street
d. AAB

40. A _____ or market-based mechanism is any of a wide variety of ways to match up buyers and sellers.

An example of a _____ uses announced bid and ask prices. Generally speaking, when two parties wish to engage in a trade, the purchaser will announce a price he is willing to pay (the bid price) and seller will announce a price he is willing to accept (the ask price).

a. 4-4-5 Calendar
b. 7-Eleven
c. 529 plan
d. Price mechanism

41. The _____ for securities is the difference between the price quoted by a market maker for an immediate sale and an immediate purchase The size of the bid-offer spread in a given commodity is a measure of the liquidity of the market.

The trader initiating the transaction is said to demand liquidity, and the other party to the transaction supplies liquidity.

a. Defined contribution plan
b. Bid/offer spread
c. Trade-off
d. Capital outflow

42. _____ is a measure of the ability of a debtor to pay their debts as and when they fall due. It is usually expressed as a ratio or a percentage of current liabilities.

For a corporation with a published balance sheet there are various ratios used to calculate a measure of liquidity.

a. Invested capital
b. Operating leverage
c. Operating profit margin
d. Accounting liquidity

43. In economics and contract theory, _____ deals with the study of decisions in transactions where one party has more or better information than the other. This creates an imbalance of power in transactions which can sometimes cause the transactions to go awry. Examples of this problem are adverse selection and moral hazard.

Chapter 9. The Capital Asset Pricing Model

a. Information asymmetry
b. ABN Amro
c. A Random Walk Down Wall Street
d. AAB

44. A _____ is an order to buy a security at no more (or sell at no less) than a specific price. This gives the customer some control over the price at which the trade is executed, but may prevent the order from being executed ('filled'.)

A buy _____ can only be executed by the broker at the limit price or lower.

a. Block premium
b. Limit order
c. Commercial mortgage-backed securities
d. Common stock

45. In economics, business, and accounting, a _____ is the value of money that has been used up to produce something, and hence is not available for use anymore. In business, the _____ may be one of acquisition, in which case the amount of money expended to acquire it is counted as _____. In this case, money is the input that is gone in order to acquire the thing.

a. Marginal cost
b. Fixed costs
c. Sliding scale fees
d. Cost

46. '_____' is a 1970 paper by the economist George Akerlof. It discusses information asymmetry, which occurs when the seller knows more about a product than the buyer. Akerlof, Michael Spence, and Joseph Stiglitz jointly received the Nobel Memorial Prize in Economic Sciences in 2001 for their research related to asymmetric information.

a. 7-Eleven
b. 529 plan
c. 4-4-5 Calendar
d. The Market for Lemons: Quality Uncertainty and the Market Mechanism

47. _____ represents the impact on the stock price that investors would cause in reaction to a change in policy of a company.

a. Volatility clustering
b. Trade date
c. Clientele effect
d. Bonus share

48. _____ is a fee paid on borrowed assets. It is the price paid for the use of borrowed money, or, money earned by deposited funds. Assets that are sometimes lent with _____ include money, shares, consumer goods through hire purchase, major assets such as aircraft, and even entire factories in finance lease arrangements.

a. Insolvency
b. AAB
c. Interest
d. A Random Walk Down Wall Street

49. An _____ is the price a borrower pays for the use of money they do not own, and the return a lender receives for deferring the use of funds, by lending it to the borrower. _____s are normally expressed as a percentage rate over the period of one year.

_____s targets are also a vital tool of monetary policy and are used to control variables like investment, inflation, and unemployment.

a. A Random Walk Down Wall Street
b. ABN Amro
c. AAB
d. Interest rate

50. _____ is the risk (variability in value) borne by an interest-bearing asset, such as a loan or a bond, due to variability of interest rates. In general, as rates rise, the price of a fixed rate bond will fall, and vice versa. _____ is commonly measured by the bond's duration.

    a. A Random Walk Down Wall Street   b. International Fisher effect
    c. Interest rate risk   d. Official bank rate

51. _____ arises from situations in which a party interested in trading an asset cannot do it because nobody in the market wants to trade that asset. _____ becomes particularly important to parties who are about to hold or currently hold an asset, since it affects their ability to trade.

Manifestation of _____ is very different from a drop of price to zero.

    a. Credit risk   b. Tracking error
    c. Liquidity risk   d. Currency risk

Chapter 10. Arbitrage Pricing Theory and Multifactor Models of Risk and Return

1. In economics and finance, _____ is the practice of taking advantage of a price differential between two or more markets: striking a combination of matching deals that capitalize upon the imbalance, the profit being the difference between the market prices. When used by academics, an _____ is a transaction that involves no negative cash flow at any probabilistic or temporal state and a positive cash flow in at least one state; in simple terms, a risk-free profit.
   - a. Efficient-market hypothesis
   - b. Initial margin
   - c. Issuer
   - d. Arbitrage

2. _____ , in finance, is a general theory of asset pricing, that has become influential in the pricing of stocks.

   _____ holds that the expected return of a financial asset can be modeled as a linear function of various macro-economic factors or theoretical market indices, where sensitivity to changes in each factor is represented by a factor-specific beta coefficient. The model-derived rate of return will then be used to price the asset correctly - the asset price should equal the expected end of period price discounted at the rate implied by model.
   - a. ABN Amro
   - b. A Random Walk Down Wall Street
   - c. AAB
   - d. Arbitrage pricing theory

3. In finance, the _____ is used to determine a theoretically appropriate required rate of return of an asset, if that asset is to be added to an already well-diversified portfolio, given that asset's non-diversifiable risk. The model takes into account the asset's sensitivity to non-diversifiable risk (also known as systemic risk or market risk), often represented by the quantity beta (β) in the financial industry, as well as the expected return of the market and the expected return of a theoretical risk-free asset.

   The model was introduced by Jack Treynor (1961, 1962), William Sharpe (1964), John Lintner (1965a,b) and Jan Mossin (1966) independently, building on the earlier work of Harry Markowitz on diversification and modern portfolio theory.
   - a. Random walk hypothesis
   - b. Cox-Ingersoll-Ross model
   - c. Hull-White model
   - d. Capital asset pricing model

4. A _____ is a fungible, negotiable instrument representing financial value. They are broadly categorized into debt securities (such as banknotes, bonds and debentures), and equity securities; e.g., common stocks. The company or other entity issuing the _____ is called the issuer.
   - a. Securities lending
   - b. Tracking stock
   - c. Security
   - d. Book entry

5. _____ is the discipline of identifying, monitoring and limiting risks. In some cases the acceptable risk may be near zero. Risks can come from accidents, natural causes and disasters as well as deliberate attacks from an adversary.
   - a. Risk management
   - b. 4-4-5 Calendar
   - c. Penny stock
   - d. FIFO

6. In finance, _____ is that risk which is common to an entire market and not to any individual entity or component thereof. It should be distinguished from systemic risk which is the risk that the entire financial system will collapse as a result of some catastrophic event.

   Risks can be reduced in four main ways: Avoidance, Reduction, Retention and Transfer.

Chapter 10. Arbitrage Pricing Theory and Multifactor Models of Risk and Return

    a. Conglomerate merger
    b. Capital surplus
    c. Primary market
    d. Systematic risk

7. A _____ is a financial contract whose value is derived from the value of something else (known as the underlying.) The underlying on which a _____ is based can be an asset, weather conditions bonds or other forms of credit.
   - a. 7-Eleven
   - b. 4-4-5 Calendar
   - c. 529 plan
   - d. Derivative

8. A _____ is a variable associated with an increased risk of disease or infection. They are correlational and not necessarily causal, because correlation does not imply causation. For example, being young cannot be said to cause measles, but young people are more at risk as they are less likely to have developed immunity during a previous epidemic.
   - a. 4-4-5 Calendar
   - b. 7-Eleven
   - c. 529 plan
   - d. Risk factor

9. The term _____ has three unrelated technical definitions, and is also used in a variety of non-technical ways.

   - In financial economics, it refers to any asset used to make money, as opposed to assets used for personal enjoyment or consumption. This is an important distinction because two people can disagree sharply about the value of personal assets, one person might think a sports car is more valuable than a pickup truck, another person might have the opposite taste. But if an asset is held for the purpose of making money, taste has nothing to do with it, only differences of opinion about how much money the asset will produce. With the further assumption that people agree on the probability distribution of future cash flows, it is possible to have an objective _____ pricing model. Even without the assumption of agreement, it is possible to set rational limits on _____ value.
   - In governmental accounting, it is defined as any asset used in operations with an initial useful life extending beyond one reporting period. Generally, government managers have a 'stewardship' duty to maintain _____ s under their control. See International Public Sector Accounting Standards for details.
   - In US tax accounting, it is defined as any property other than a list of exceptions. The main exceptions are anything held for sale, and any real estate or depreciable property used in business. Almost everything you own and use for personal purposes, pleasure or investment is a _____. If something is a _____ for tax purposes, gains or losses on sale or disposition are capital gains or capital losses. For individuals, however, capital losses on property held for personal use are generally not deductible. See the IRS publication Tax Facts about Capital Gains and Losses for details.

   A well-known financial accounting textbook advises that the term be avoided except in tax accounting because it is used in so many different senses, not all of them well-defined. For example it is often used as a synonym for fixed assets or for investments in securities.

   A common non-technical usage occurs when people ask that employees or the environment or something else be treated as a _____.

   - a. Solvency
   - b. Political risk
   - c. Settlement date
   - d. Capital asset

10. In Modern Portfolio Theory, the _____ is the graphical representation of the Capital Asset Pricing Model. It displays the expected rate of return for an overall market as a function of systematic (non-diversifiable) risk (beta.)

Chapter 10. Arbitrage Pricing Theory and Multifactor Models of Risk and Return

The Y-Intercept (beta=0) of the _____ is equal to the risk-free interest rate.

 a. Rebalancing
 b. Certificate in Investment Performance Measurement
 c. Divestment
 d. Security market line

11. In business and accounting, _____s are everything of value that is owned by a person or company. The balance sheet of a firm records the monetary value of the _____s owned by the firm. The two major _____ classes are tangible _____s and intangible _____s.
 a. Income
 b. Accounts payable
 c. Asset
 d. EBITDA

12. In finance, _____ is the process of estimating the potential market value of a financial asset or liability. they can be done on assets (for example, investments in marketable securities such as stocks, options, business enterprises, or intangible assets such as patents and trademarks) or on liabilities (e.g., Bonds issued by a company.) _____s are required in many contexts including investment analysis, capital budgeting, merger and acquisition transactions, financial reporting, taxable events to determine the proper tax liability, and in litigation.
 a. Share
 b. Margin
 c. Procter ' Gamble
 d. Valuation

13. In finance, _____ is the risk involved in using models to value financial securities. Rebonato considers alternative definitions including:

1) After observing a set of prices for the underlying and hedging instruments, different but identically calibrated models might produce different prices for the same exotic product. 2) Losses will be incurred because of an 'incorrect' hedging strategy suggested by a model.

 a. Model risk
 b. Price-to-book ratio
 c. Takeover
 d. Duty of loyalty

14. _____ is a step in a risk management process. _____ is the determination of quantitative or qualitative value of risk related to a concrete situation and a recognized threat (also called hazard.) Quantitative _____ requires calculations of two components of risk: R, the magnitude of the potential loss L, and the probability p that the loss will occur.
 a. 7-Eleven
 b. 529 plan
 c. 4-4-5 Calendar
 d. Risk assessment

15. In e-business terms, a _____ is an organization that originated and does business purely through the internet, they have no physical store (brick and mortar) where customers can shop. Examples of large _____ companies include Amazon.com and Netflix.com. There are also many smaller, niche oriented _____ mail order companies such as women's travel accessories company Christine Columbus and fashion jewelry merchant Jewels of Denial.
 a. 529 plan
 b. Pure play
 c. The Dogs of the Dow
 d. 4-4-5 Calendar

16. The _____ is an economic law stated as: 'In an efficient market all identical goods must have only one price.'

Chapter 10. Arbitrage Pricing Theory and Multifactor Models of Risk and Return

The intuition for this law is that all sellers will flock to the highest prevailing price, and all buyers to the lowest current market price. In an efficient market the convergence on one price is instant.

Commodities can be traded on financial markets, where there will be a single offer price, and bid price.

a. Law of one price
b. Letter of credit
c. Liability
d. Personal property

17. _____ in finance is a risk management technique, related to hedging, that mixes a wide variety of investments within a portfolio. Because the fluctuations of a single security have less impact on a diverse portfolio, _____ minimizes the risk from any one investment.

A simple example of _____ is the following: On a particular island the entire economy consists of two companies: one that sells umbrellas and another that sells sunscreen.

a. 529 plan
b. 4-4-5 Calendar
c. 7-Eleven
d. Diversification

18. The _____ is the weighted-average most likely outcome in gambling, probability theory, economics or finance.

In gambling and probability theory, there is usually a discrete set of possible outcomes. In this case, _____ is a measure of the relative balance of win or loss weighted by their chances of occurring.

a. ABN Amro
b. AAB
c. Expected return
d. A Random Walk Down Wall Street

19. In probability theory and statistics, the _____ of a random variable, probability distribution averaging the squared distance of its possible values from the expected value (mean.) Whereas the mean is a way to describe the location of a distribution, the _____ is a way to capture its scale or degree of being spread out. The unit of _____ is the square of the unit of the original variable.

a. Monte Carlo methods
b. Harmonic mean
c. Semivariance
d. Variance

20. In economics, business, and accounting, a _____ is the value of money that has been used up to produce something, and hence is not available for use anymore. In business, the _____ may be one of acquisition, in which case the amount of money expended to acquire it is counted as _____. In this case, money is the input that is gone in order to acquire the thing.

a. Fixed costs
b. Sliding scale fees
c. Marginal cost
d. Cost

21. The _____ is an expected return that the provider of capital plans to earn on their investment.

Capital (money) used for funding a business should earn returns for the capital providers who risk their capital. For an investment to be worthwhile, the expected return on capital must be greater than the _____.

Chapter 10. Arbitrage Pricing Theory and Multifactor Models of Risk and Return

a. Cost of capital
b. Capital intensity
c. 4-4-5 Calendar
d. Weighted average cost of capital

22. The _____ is a linear factor model with wealth and state variable that forecast changes in the distribution of future returns or income.

The main difference between _____ and standard CAPM is additing state variables that acknowledge the fact that investors hedge against shortfalls in consumption or against changes in the future investment opportunity set.

a. ABN Amro
b. Intertemporal Capital Asset Pricing Model
c. AAB
d. A Random Walk Down Wall Street

23. In economics, _____ is a rise in the general level of prices of goods and services in an economy over a period of time. The term '_____' once referred to increases in the money supply (monetary _____); however, economic debates about the relationship between money supply and price levels have led to its primary use today in describing price _____.
_____ can also be described as a decline in the real value of money--a loss of purchasing power in the medium of exchange which is also the monetary unit of account.

a. A Random Walk Down Wall Street
b. Inflation
c. ABN Amro
d. AAB

Chapter 11. The Efficient Market Hypothesis

1. In finance, the _____ is used to determine a theoretically appropriate required rate of return of an asset, if that asset is to be added to an already well-diversified portfolio, given that asset's non-diversifiable risk. The model takes into account the asset's sensitivity to non-diversifiable risk (also known as systemic risk or market risk), often represented by the quantity beta (β) in the financial industry, as well as the expected return of the market and the expected return of a theoretical risk-free asset.

The model was introduced by Jack Treynor (1961, 1962), William Sharpe (1964), John Lintner (1965a,b) and Jan Mossin (1966) independently, building on the earlier work of Harry Markowitz on diversification and modern portfolio theory.

   a. Random walk hypothesis
   b. Cox-Ingersoll-Ross model
   c. Hull-White model
   d. Capital asset pricing model

2. A _____, is a mathematical formalization of a trajectory that consists of taking successive random steps. The results of _____ analysis have been applied to computer science, physics, ecology, economics and a number of other fields as a fundamental model for random processes in time. For example, the path traced by a molecule as it travels in a liquid or a gas, the search path of a foraging animal, the price of a fluctuating stock and the financial status of a gambler can all be modeled as _____s.

   a. 4-4-5 Calendar
   b. 529 plan
   c. 7-Eleven
   d. Random walk

3. A _____ is the price of a single share of a no. of saleable stocks of the company. Once the stock is purchased, the owner becomes a shareholder of the company that issued the share.

   a. Whisper numbers
   b. Trading curb
   c. Share price
   d. Stock split

4. In business, a _____ is the purchase of one company (the target) by another (the acquirer or bidder). In the UK the term refers to the acquisition of a public company whose shares are listed on a stock exchange, in contrast to the acquisition of a private company.

Before a bidder makes an offer for another company, it usually first informs that company's board of directors.

   a. 4-4-5 Calendar
   b. Stock swap
   c. 529 plan
   d. Takeover

5. In finance, an _____ is the difference between the expected return of a security and the actual return. _____s are sometimes triggered by 'events.' Events can include mergers, dividend announcements, company earning announcements, interest rate increases, lawsuits, etc. all which can contribute to an _____.

   a. ABN Amro
   b. AAB
   c. A Random Walk Down Wall Street
   d. Abnormal return

6. In business and finance, a _____ (also referred to as equity _____) of stock means a _____ of ownership in a corporation (company.) In the plural, stocks is often used as a synonym for _____s especially in the United States, but it is less commonly used that way outside of North America.

In the United Kingdom, South Africa, and Australia, stock can also refer to completely different financial instruments such as government bonds or, less commonly, to all kinds of marketable securities.

a. Procter ' Gamble
c. Bucket shop
b. Margin
d. Share

7. _____ is the trading of a corporation's stock or other securities (e.g. bonds or stock options) by individuals with potential access to non-public information about the company. In most countries, trading by corporate insiders such as officers, key employees, directors, and large shareholders may be legal, if this trading is done in a way that does not take advantage of non-public information. However, the term is frequently used to refer to a practice in which an insider or a related party trades based on material non-public information obtained during the performance of the insider's duties at the corporation, or otherwise in breach of a fiduciary duty or other relationship of trust and confidence or where the non-public information was misappropriated from the company.
   a. Intellidex
   c. Open outcry
   b. Insider trading
   d. Equity investment

8. A _____ is a fungible, negotiable instrument representing financial value. They are broadly categorized into debt securities (such as banknotes, bonds and debentures), and equity securities; e.g., common stocks. The company or other entity issuing the _____ is called the issuer.
   a. Book entry
   c. Securities lending
   b. Tracking stock
   d. Security

9. The _____ of 1934 is a law governing the secondary trading of securities (stocks, bonds, and debentures) in the United States of America. The Act, 48 Stat. 881 (enacted June 6, 1934), codified at 15 U.S.C. Â§ 78a et seq., was a sweeping piece of legislation. The Act and related statutes form the basis of regulation of the financial markets and their participants in the United States.
   a. Securities Exchange Act
   c. 4-4-5 Calendar
   b. 7-Eleven
   d. 529 plan

10. _____ is a security analysis discipline for forecasting the future direction of prices through the study of past market data, primarily price and volume. In its purest form, _____ considers only the actual price and volume behavior of the market or instrument. Technical analysts may employ models and trading rules based on price and volume transformations, such as the relative strength index, moving averages, regressions, inter-market and intra-market price correlations, cycles or, classically, through recognition of chart patterns.
    a. Point and figure
    c. Support and resistance
    b. Technical analysis
    d. Dow theory

11. The _____ is a financial technical analysis momentum oscillator measuring the velocity and magnitude of directional price movement by comparing upward and downward close-to-close movements.

The _____ was developed by J. Welles Wilder and published in Commodities magazine (now called Futures magazine) in June 1978, and in his New Concepts in Technical Trading Systems the same year.

   a. Global depository receipt
   c. Database auditing
   b. Stock or scrip dividends
   d. Relative strength Index

12. _____ is a concept in technical analysis that the movement of the price of a security will tend to stop and reverse at certain predetermined price levels.

108 Chapter 11. The Efficient Market Hypothesis

A support level is a price level where the price tends to find support as it is going down. This means the price is more likely to 'bounce' off this level rather than break through it.

A resistance level is the opposite of a support level. It is where the price tends to find resistance as it is going up. This means the price is more likely to 'bounce' off this level rather than break through it.

- a. Technical analysis
- b. Point and figure
- c. Dow theory
- d. Support and resistance

13. In Finance the _____ is a mathematical model for portfolio allocation developed in 1990 at Goldman Sachs by Fischer Black and Robert Litterman, and published in 1992. It seeks to overcome problems that institutional investors have encountered in applying modern portfolio theory in practice. The model starts with the equilibrium assumption that the asset allocation of a representative agent should be proportional to the market values of the available assets, and then modifies that to take into account the 'views' (i.e. the specific opinions about asset returns) of the investor in question to arrive at a bespoke asset allocation.

- a. Specific risk
- b. Clientele effect
- c. Capital surplus
- d. Black-Litterman model

14. _____ of a business involves analyzing its financial statements and health, its management and competitive advantages, and its competitors and markets. The term is used to distinguish such analysis from other types of investment analysis, such as quantitative analysis and technical analysis.

_____ is performed on historical and present data, but with the goal of making financial forecasts.

- a. Stock valuation
- b. Fundamental analysis
- c. Growth stocks
- d. 4-4-5 Calendar

15. In Finance the _____ is a mathematical model for security selection published by Fischer Black and Jack Treynor in 1973. The model assumes an investor who considers that most securities are priced efficiently, but who believes he has information that can be used to predict the abnormal performance (Alpha) of a few of them; the model finds the optimum portfolio to hold under such conditions.

In essence the optimal portfolio consists of two parts: an index fund containing all securities in proportion to their market value and an 'active portfolio' containing the securities for which the investor has made a prediction about alpha.

- a. Treynor-Black model
- b. LIBOR market model
- c. Binomial model
- d. Modified Internal Rate of Return

16. _____ refers to a portfolio management strategy where the manager makes specific investments with the goal of outperforming an investment benchmark index. Investors or mutual funds that do not aspire to create a return in excess of a benchmark index will often invest in an index fund that replicates as closely as possible the investment weighting and returns of that index; this is called passive management. _____ is the opposite of passive management, because in passive management the manager does not seek to outperform the benchmark index.

Chapter 11. The Efficient Market Hypothesis

a. A Random Walk Down Wall Street
c. AAB
b. ABN Amro
d. Active management

17. _____ measures the active return of an investment manager divided by the amount of risk the manager takes relative to a benchmark. It is used in the analysis of performance of mutual funds, hedge funds, etc. Specifically, the _____ is defined as active return divided by tracking error.
a. Earnings yield
c. Operating leverage
b. Asset turnover
d. Information ratio

18. An _____ is an investment vehicle traded on stock exchanges, much like stocks. An ETF holds assets such as stocks or bonds and trades at approximately the same price as the net asset value of its underlying assets over the course of the trading day. Most ETFs track an index, such as the Dow Jones Industrial Average or the S'P 500.
a. Exchange-traded fund
c. A Random Walk Down Wall Street
b. AAB
d. ABN Amro

19. An _____ or index tracker is a collective investment scheme (usually a mutual fund or exchange-traded fund) that aims to replicate the movements of an index of a specific financial market regardless of market conditions.

Tracking can be achieved by trying to hold all of the securities in the index, in the same proportions as the index. Other methods include statistically sampling the market and holding 'representative' securities.

a. Index fund
c. AAB
b. Investment company
d. A Random Walk Down Wall Street

20. _____ is a financial strategy in which a fund manager makes as few portfolio decisions as possible, in order to minimize transaction costs, including the incidence of capital gains tax. One popular method is to mimic the performance of an externally specified index--called 'index funds'. The ethos of an index fund is aptly summed up in the injunction to an index fund manager: 'Don't just do something, sit there!'

_____ is most common on the equity market, where index funds track a stock market index, but it is becoming more common in other investment types, including bonds, commodities and hedge funds.

a. Passive management
c. Savings and loan association
b. Net asset value
d. Trust company

21. _____ in finance is a risk management technique, related to hedging, that mixes a wide variety of investments within a portfolio. Because the fluctuations of a single security have less impact on a diverse portfolio, _____ minimizes the risk from any one investment.

A simple example of _____ is the following: On a particular island the entire economy consists of two companies: one that sells umbrellas and another that sells sunscreen.

a. 529 plan
c. Diversification
b. 7-Eleven
d. 4-4-5 Calendar

22. _____ is used to assign the available resources in an economic way. It is part of resource management.

Chapter 11. The Efficient Market Hypothesis

In strategic planning, a _____ decision is a plan for using available resources, for example human resources, especially in the near term, to achieve goals for the future.

a. 7-Eleven
b. 4-4-5 Calendar
c. 529 plan
d. Resource allocation

23. In finance, a _____ is a debt security, in which the authorized issuer owes the holders a debt and, depending on the terms of the _____, is obliged to pay interest (the coupon) and/or to repay the principal at a later date, termed maturity.

Thus a _____ is a loan: the issuer is the borrower, the _____ holder is the lender, and the coupon is the interest. _____s provide the borrower with external funds to finance long-term investments, or, in the case of government _____s, to finance current expenditure.

a. Convertible bond
b. Puttable bond
c. Catastrophe bonds
d. Bond

24. A _____ is a portfolio consisting of a weighted sum of every asset in the market, with weights in the proportions that they exist in the market (with the necessary assumption that these assets are infinitely divisible.)

Neha Tyagi's critique (1977) states that this is only a theoretical concept, as to create a _____ for investment purposes in practice would necessarily include every single possible available asset, including real estate, precious metals, stamp collections, jewelry, and anything with any worth, as the theoretical market being referred to would be the world market. As a result, proxies for the market are used in practice by investors.

a. Market Portfolio
b. Market price
c. Central Securities Depository
d. Delta neutral

25. An _____ is a statistical method to assess the impact of an event on the value of a firm. For example, the announcement of a merger between two firms can be analyzed to see whether investors believe the merger will create or destroy value. Event studies have been used in a large variety of studies, including [mergers and acquisitions], earnings announcements, debt or equity issues, corporate reorganisations, investment decisions and corporate social responsibility (MacKinlay 1997; McWilliams ' Siegel, 1997.)

a. Event study
b. AAB
c. ABN Amro
d. A Random Walk Down Wall Street

26. _____ is a distortion of evidence or data that arises from the way that the data are collected. It is sometimes referred to as the selection effect. The term _____ most often refers to the distortion of a statistical analysis, due to the method of collecting samples.

a. 7-Eleven
b. 4-4-5 Calendar
c. 529 plan
d. Selection bias

27. _____ is a measure of the ability of a debtor to pay their debts as and when they fall due. It is usually expressed as a ratio or a percentage of current liabilities.

Chapter 11. The Efficient Market Hypothesis

For a corporation with a published balance sheet there are various ratios used to calculate a measure of liquidity.

   a. Invested capital
   c. Operating leverage
   b. Operating profit margin
   d. Accounting liquidity

28. A _____ is a private or public market for the trading of company stock and derivatives of company stock at an agreed price; these are securities listed on a stock exchange as well as those only traded privately.

The size of the world _____ is estimated at about $36.6 trillion US at the beginning of October 2008 . The world derivatives market has been estimated at about $480 trillion face or nominal value, 12 times the size of the entire world economy.

   a. Adolph Coors
   c. Stock market
   b. Anton Gelonkin
   d. Andrew Tobias

29. In probability theory and statistics, _____ indicates the strength and direction of a linear relationship between two random variables. That is in contrast with the usage of the term in colloquial speech, which denotes any relationship, not necessarily linear. In general statistical usage, _____ or co-relation refers to the departure of two random variables from independence.
   a. Probability distribution
   c. Variance
   b. Geometric mean
   d. Correlation

30. In finance, a _____ is one who attempts to profit by investing in a manner that differs from the conventional wisdom, when the consensus opinion appears to be wrong.

A _____ believes that certain crowd behavior among investors can lead to exploitable mispricings in securities markets. For example, widespread pessimism about a stock can drive a price so low that it overstates the company's risks, and understates its prospects for returning to profitability.

   a. Direct access trading
   c. Day trading
   b. Contrarian
   d. Secured debt

31. The _____ of a stock is a measure of the price paid for a share relative to the annual income or profit earned by the firm per share. It is a financial ratio used for valuation: a higher _____ means that investors are paying more for each unit of income, so the stock is more expensive compared to one with lower _____.

The _____ has units of years, which can be interpreted as 'number of years of earnings to pay back purchase price'.

   a. Sustainable growth rate
   c. P/E ratio
   b. Quick ratio
   d. Return of capital

32. _____, is when a company issues common stock or shares to the public for the first time. They are often issued by smaller, younger companies seeking capital to expand, but can also be done by large privately-owned companies looking to become publicly traded.

In an _____ the issuer may obtain the assistance of an underwriting firm, which helps it determine what type of security to issue (common or preferred), best offering price and time to bring it to market.

a. Asian Financial Crisis
c. Initial public offering
b. Insolvency
d. Interest

33. The _____ is the tendency of the stock market to rise between December 31 and the end of the first week in January. There are many theories for why this happens, the main one being that it occurs because many investors choose to sell some of their stock right before the end of the year in order to claim a capital loss for tax purposes. Once the tax calendar rolls over to a new year on January 1st these same investors quickly reinvest their money in the market, causing stock prices to rise.

a. Revaluation
c. January effect
b. Death spiral financing
d. Sector rotation

34. The _____ is a financial ratio used to compare a company's book value to its current market price. Book value is an accounting term denoting the portion of the company held by the shareholders; in other words, the company's total tangible assets less its total liabilities. The calculation can be performed in two ways, but the result should be the same each way. In the first way, the company's market capitalization can be divided by the company's total book value from its balance sheet. The second way, using per-share values, is to divide the company's current share price by the book value per share (i.e. its book value divided by the number of outstanding shares).

a. Whisper numbers
c. Stop order
b. Stock repurchase
d. Price-to-book ratio

35.

In finance, the _____ can be the expected rate of return above the risk-free interest rate. When measuring risk, a common sense approach is to compare the risk-free return on T-bills and the very risky return on other investments. The difference between these two returns can be interpreted as a measure of the excess return on the average risky asset. This excess return is known as the _____.

a. Risk adjusted return on capital
c. Risk aversion
b. Risk modeling
d. Risk premium

36. A _____ is a professionally managed type of collective investment scheme that pools money from many investors and invests it in stocks, bonds, short-term money market instruments, and/or other securities. The _____ will have a fund manager that trades the pooled money on a regular basis. Currently, the worldwide value of all _____s totals more than $26 trillion.

Since 1940, there have been three basic types of investment companies in the United States: open-end funds, also known in the US as _____s; unit investment trusts (UITs); and closed-end funds.

a. Mutual fund
c. Trust company
b. Net asset value
d. Financial intermediary

Chapter 11. The Efficient Market Hypothesis

37. _____ is the return on an investment portfolio. The investment portfolio can contain a single asset or multiple assets. The _____ is measured over a specific period of time and in a specific currency.
   a. Alternative investment
   b. Investment decisions
   c. Investment performance
   d. Asset allocation

38. In business and accounting, _____s are everything of value that is owned by a person or company. The balance sheet of a firm records the monetary value of the _____s owned by the firm. The two major _____ classes are tangible _____s and intangible _____s.
   a. Income
   b. Asset
   c. EBITDA
   d. Accounts payable

39. _____ is a term used to refer to how an investor distributes his or her investments among various classes of investment vehicles (e.g., stocks and bonds.)

A large part of financial planning is finding an _____ that is appropriate for a given person in terms of their appetite for and ability to shoulder risk. This can depend on various factors; see investor profile.

   a. Alternative investment
   b. Investment performance
   c. Investing online
   d. Asset allocation

40. A _____ is a collective investment scheme that invests in bonds and other debt securities. _____s yield monthly dividends that include interest payments on the fund's underlying securities plus any capital appreciation in the prices of the portfolio's bonds. _____s tend to pay higher dividends than CDs and money market accounts, and they generally pay out dividends more frequently and regularly than individual bonds.
   a. Premium bond
   b. Private activity bond
   c. Gilts
   d. Bond fund

41. In finance, _____ is the tendency for failed companies to be excluded from performance studies because they no longer exist. It often causes the results of studies to skew higher because only companies which were successful enough to survive until the end of the period are included.

For example, a mutual fund company's selection of funds today will include only those that have been successful in the past.

   a. 529 plan
   b. 7-Eleven
   c. Survivorship bias
   d. 4-4-5 Calendar

Chapter 12. Behavioral Finance and Technical Analysis

1. Behavioral economics and _____ are closely related fields that have evolved to be a separate branch of economic and financial analysis which applies scientific research on human and social, cognitive and emotional factors to better understand economic decisions by, say, consumers, borrowers, investors, and how they affect market prices, returns and the allocation of resources.

   The field is primarily concerned with the bounds of rationality (selfishness, self-control) of economic agents. Behavioral models typically integrate insights from psychology with neo-classical economic theory.

   a. Market structure
   b. Behavioral finance
   c. Medium of exchange
   d. Recession

2. In business, investment, and accounting, the principle or convention of _____ has at least two meanings.

   In investment and finance, it is a strategy which aims at long-term capital appreciation with low risk. It can be characterized as moderate or cautious and is the opposite of aggressive behavior.

   a. Debt-snowball method
   b. Duration gap
   c. Barcampbank
   d. Conservatism

3. The _____ of a stock is a measure of the price paid for a share relative to the annual income or profit earned by the firm per share. It is a financial ratio used for valuation: a higher _____ means that investors are paying more for each unit of income, so the stock is more expensive compared to one with lower _____.

   The _____ has units of years, which can be interpreted as 'number of years of earnings to pay back purchase price'.

   a. Quick ratio
   b. Return of capital
   c. Sustainable growth rate
   d. P/E ratio

4. The _____ of a statistical sample is the number of observations that constitute it. It is typically denoted n, a positive integer (natural number.)

   Typically, all else being equal, a larger _____ leads to increased precision in estimates of various properties of the population.

   a. Harmonic mean
   b. Correlation
   c. Frequency distribution
   d. Sample size

5. The _____ is an anomaly discovered in behavioral finance. It relates to the tendency of investors to sell shares whose price has increased, while keeping assets that have dropped in value. Investors are unwilling to recognize losses (which they would be forced to do if they sold assets which had fallen in value), but are more willing to recognize gains.

   a. Psychological level
   b. Herd behavior
   c. Prospect theory
   d. Disposition effect

6. A concept first named by Richard Thaler (1980), _____ attempts to describe the process whereby people code, categorize and evaluate economic outcomes. _____ theorists argue that people group their assets into a number of non-fungible mental accounts.

Chapter 12. Behavioral Finance and Technical Analysis   115

One detailed application of _____, the behavioral life cycle hypothesis (Shefrin ' Thaler, 1988), posits that people mentally frame assets as belonging to either current income, current wealth or future income and this has implications for their behavior as the accounts are largely non-fungible and marginal propensity to consume out of each account is different.

a. Psychological level
b. Disposition effect
c. Mental accounting
d. Quantitative behavioral finance

7. _____ is a theory that describes decisions between alternatives that involve risk, i.e. alternatives with uncertain outcomes, where the probabilities are known. The model is descriptive: it tries to model real-life choices, rather than optimal decisions.

_____ was developed by Daniel Kahneman, professor at Princeton University's Department of Psychology, and Amos Tversky in 1979 as a psychologically realistic alternative to expected utility theory.

a. Prospect theory
b. Herd behavior
c. The equity premium puzzle
d. Dumb agent theory

8. In economics, _____ is a measure of the relative satisfaction from or desirability of consumption of various goods and services. Given this measure, one may speak meaningfully of increasing or decreasing _____, and thereby explain economic behavior in terms of attempts to increase one's _____. For illustrative purposes, changes in _____ are sometimes expressed in units called utils.

a. Utility
b. AAB
c. Utility function
d. A Random Walk Down Wall Street

9. In economics and finance, _____ is the practice of taking advantage of a price differential between two or more markets: striking a combination of matching deals that capitalize upon the imbalance, the profit being the difference between the market prices. When used by academics, an _____ is a transaction that involves no negative cash flow at any probabilistic or temporal state and a positive cash flow in at least one state; in simple terms, a risk-free profit.

a. Issuer
b. Initial margin
c. Efficient-market hypothesis
d. Arbitrage

10. While preferences are the conventional foundation of microeconomics, it is often convenient to represent preferences with a _____ and reason indirectly about preferences with _____s. Let X be the consumption set, the set of all mutually-exclusive packages the consumer could conceivably consume (such as an indifference curve map without the indifference curves.) The consumer's _____ $u : X \to \mathbf{R}$ ranks each package in the consumption set.

a. Utility
b. Utility function
c. AAB
d. A Random Walk Down Wall Street

11. The term _____ or economic cycle refers to the fluctuations of economic activity (business fluctuations) around a long-term growth trend. The cycle involves shifts over time between periods of relatively rapid growth of output (recovery and prosperity), and periods of relative stagnation or decline (contraction or recession.) These fluctuations are often measured using the real gross domestic product.

a. Fixed exchange rate
b. Deflation
c. Business cycle
d. Behavioral finance

12. _____ is a theory which assumes that restrictions placed upon funds, that would ordinarily be used by rational traders to arbitrage away pricing inefficiencies, leave prices in a non-equilibrium state for protracted periods of time.

The efficient market hypothesis assumes that whenever mispricing of a publicly-traded stock occurs as a result of an over-reaction to news, or some similar event, an opportunity for low-risk profit is created for rational traders. The low-risk profit opportunity exists through the tool of arbitrage, which, briefly, is buying and selling differently priced items of the same value, and pocketing the difference.

a. Delta hedging
b. Forward market
c. Market anomaly
d. Limits to arbitrage

13. The _____ of a commodity, a security or a currency is the price that is quoted for immediate (spot) settlement (payment and delivery.) Spot settlement is normally one or two business days from trade date. This is in contrast with the forward price established in a forward contract or futures contract, where contract terms (price) are set now, but delivery and payment will occur at a future date.

a. Market anomaly
b. Spot rate
c. Limits to arbitrage
d. Long position

14. The _____ is an economic law stated as: 'In an efficient market all identical goods must have only one price.'

The intuition for this law is that all sellers will flock to the highest prevailing price, and all buyers to the lowest current market price. In an efficient market the convergence on one price is instant.

Commodities can be traded on financial markets, where there will be a single offer price, and bid price.

a. Personal property
b. Liability
c. Letter of credit
d. Law of one price

15. In finance, _____ is the risk involved in using models to value financial securities. Rebonato considers alternative definitions including:

1) After observing a set of prices for the underlying and hedging instruments, different but identically calibrated models might produce different prices for the same exotic product. 2) Losses will be incurred because of an 'incorrect' hedging strategy suggested by a model.

a. Duty of loyalty
b. Price-to-book ratio
c. Takeover
d. Model risk

16. In economics, business, and accounting, a _____ is the value of money that has been used up to produce something, and hence is not available for use anymore. In business, the _____ may be one of acquisition, in which case the amount of money expended to acquire it is counted as _____. In this case, money is the input that is gone in order to acquire the thing.

Chapter 12. Behavioral Finance and Technical Analysis

a. Cost
b. Sliding scale fees
c. Fixed costs
d. Marginal cost

17. A _____, is a collective investment scheme with a limited number of shares.

New shares are rarely issued after the fund is launched; shares are not normally redeemable for cash or securities until the fund liquidates. Typically an investor can acquire shares in a _____ by buying shares on a secondary market from a broker, market maker, or other investor as opposed to an open-end fund where all transactions eventually involve the fund company creating new shares on the fly (in exchange for either cash or securities) or redeeming shares (for cash or securities.)

a. Money market funds
b. Closed-end fund
c. Stock fund
d. Mutual fund fees and expenses

18. _____ is a heterodox theory on stock price movements that is used as the basis for technical analysis. The theory was derived from 255 Wall Street Journal editorials written by Charles H. Dow (1851-1902), journalist, founder and first editor of the Wall Street Journal and co-founder of Dow Jones and Company. Following Dow's death, William P. Hamilton, Robert Rhea and E. George Schaefer organized and collectively represented '_____,' based on Dow's editorials.

a. Technical analysis
b. Money flow
c. Point and figure
d. Dow theory

19. _____ is a security analysis discipline for forecasting the future direction of prices through the study of past market data, primarily price and volume. In its purest form, _____ considers only the actual price and volume behavior of the market or instrument. Technical analysts may employ models and trading rules based on price and volume transformations, such as the relative strength index, moving averages, regressions, inter-market and intra-market price correlations, cycles or, classically, through recognition of chart patterns.

a. Dow theory
b. Support and resistance
c. Technical analysis
d. Point and figure

20. The _____ is a form of technical analysis that attempts to forecast trends in the financial markets and other collective activities. It is named after Ralph Nelson Elliott (1871-1948), an accountant who developed the concept in the 1930s: he proposed that market prices unfold in specific patterns, which practitioners today call Elliott waves. Elliott published his views of market behavior in the book The Wave Principle (1938), in a series of articles in Financial World magazine in 1939, and most fully in his final major work, Nature's Laws - The Secret of the Universe (1946.)

a. AAB
b. A Random Walk Down Wall Street
c. ABN Amro
d. Elliott wave principle

21. In statistics, a _____, is a type of finite impulse response filter used to analyze a set of data points by creating a series of averages of different subsets of the full data set. A _____ is not a single number, but it is a set of numbers, each of which is the average of the corresponding subset of a larger set of data points. A _____ may also use unequal weights for each data value in the subset to emphasize particular values in the subset.

a. Voluntary Emissions Reductions
b. Gordon growth model
c. Moving average
d. Loans and interest, in Judaism

22. In finance, a _____ is one who attempts to profit by investing in a manner that differs from the conventional wisdom, when the consensus opinion appears to be wrong.

A _____ believes that certain crowd behavior among investors can lead to exploitable mispricings in securities markets. For example, widespread pessimism about a stock can drive a price so low that it overstates the company's risks, and understates its prospects for returning to profitability.

a. Day trading
b. Direct access trading
c. Secured debt
d. Contrarian

Chapter 13. Empirical Evidence on Security Returns

1. In finance, the _____ is used to determine a theoretically appropriate required rate of return of an asset, if that asset is to be added to an already well-diversified portfolio, given that asset's non-diversifiable risk. The model takes into account the asset's sensitivity to non-diversifiable risk (also known as systemic risk or market risk), often represented by the quantity beta (β) in the financial industry, as well as the expected return of the market and the expected return of a theoretical risk-free asset.

   The model was introduced by Jack Treynor (1961, 1962), William Sharpe (1964), John Lintner (1965a,b) and Jan Mossin (1966) independently, building on the earlier work of Harry Markowitz on diversification and modern portfolio theory.

   a. Hull-White model
   b. Random walk hypothesis
   c. Cox-Ingersoll-Ross model
   d. Capital asset pricing model

2. The term _____ has three unrelated technical definitions, and is also used in a variety of non-technical ways.

   - In financial economics, it refers to any asset used to make money, as opposed to assets used for personal enjoyment or consumption. This is an important distinction because two people can disagree sharply about the value of personal assets, one person might think a sports car is more valuable than a pickup truck, another person might have the opposite taste. But if an asset is held for the purpose of making money, taste has nothing to do with it, only differences of opinion about how much money the asset will produce. With the further assumption that people agree on the probability distribution of future cash flows, it is possible to have an objective _____ pricing model. Even without the assumption of agreement, it is possible to set rational limits on _____ value.
   - In governmental accounting, it is defined as any asset used in operations with an initial useful life extending beyond one reporting period. Generally, government managers have a 'stewardship' duty to maintain _____s under their control. See International Public Sector Accounting Standards for details.
   - In US tax accounting, it is defined as any property other than a list of exceptions. The main exceptions are anything held for sale, and any real estate or depreciable property used in business. Almost everything you own and use for personal purposes, pleasure or investment is a _____. If something is a _____ for tax purposes, gains or losses on sale or disposition are capital gains or capital losses. For individuals, however, capital losses on property held for personal use are generally not deductible. See the IRS publication Tax Facts about Capital Gains and Losses for details.

   A well-known financial accounting textbook advises that the term be avoided except in tax accounting because it is used in so many different senses, not all of them well-defined. For example it is often used as a synonym for fixed assets or for investments in securities.

   A common non-technical usage occurs when people ask that employees or the environment or something else be treated as a _____.

   a. Capital asset
   b. Political risk
   c. Solvency
   d. Settlement date

3. In economics, business, and accounting, a _____ is the value of money that has been used up to produce something, and hence is not available for use anymore. In business, the _____ may be one of acquisition, in which case the amount of money expended to acquire it is counted as _____. In this case, money is the input that is gone in order to acquire the thing.

a. Cost
b. Fixed costs
c. Marginal cost
d. Sliding scale fees

4. The _____ is an expected return that the provider of capital plans to earn on their investment.

Capital (money) used for funding a business should earn returns for the capital providers who risk their capital. For an investment to be worthwhile, the expected return on capital must be greater than the _____.

a. Capital intensity
b. 4-4-5 Calendar
c. Cost of capital
d. Weighted average cost of capital

5. The _____ is the rate of return that must be met for a company to undertake a particular project. The _____ is usually determined by evaluating existing opportunities in operations expansion, rate of return for investments, and other factors deemed relevant by management. A risk premium can also be attached to the _____ if management feels that specific opportunities inherently contain more risk than others that could be pursued with the same resources.

a. Hurdle rate
b. Capital structure
c. Gross profit
d. Corporate finance

6. _____ is a graph created by investors to measure the risk of risky and risk-free assets. The graph displays to the investors on the return they can make by taking on a certain level of risk. It is also known as a 'reward-to-variability ratio'.

a. Divestment
b. Portfolio investment
c. Dollar cost averaging
d. Capital allocation line

7. In business and accounting, _____s are everything of value that is owned by a person or company. The balance sheet of a firm records the monetary value of the _____s owned by the firm. The two major _____ classes are tangible _____s and intangible _____s.

a. EBITDA
b. Accounts payable
c. Income
d. Asset

8. In finance, _____ is the process of estimating the potential market value of a financial asset or liability. they can be done on assets (for example, investments in marketable securities such as stocks, options, business enterprises, or intangible assets such as patents and trademarks) or on liabilities (e.g., Bonds issued by a company.) _____s are required in many contexts including investment analysis, capital budgeting, merger and acquisition transactions, financial reporting, taxable events to determine the proper tax liability, and in litigation.

a. Procter ' Gamble
b. Margin
c. Valuation
d. Share

9. The _____ is the weighted-average most likely outcome in gambling, probability theory, economics or finance.

In gambling and probability theory, there is usually a discrete set of possible outcomes. In this case, _____ is a measure of the relative balance of win or loss weighted by their chances of occurring.

a. ABN Amro
b. AAB
c. A Random Walk Down Wall Street
d. Expected return

Chapter 13. Empirical Evidence on Security Returns

10. A _____ is a fungible, negotiable instrument representing financial value. They are broadly categorized into debt securities (such as banknotes, bonds and debentures), and equity securities; e.g., common stocks. The company or other entity issuing the _____ is called the issuer.
   a. Tracking stock
   c. Security
   b. Book entry
   d. Securities lending

11. In Modern Portfolio Theory, the _____ is the graphical representation of the Capital Asset Pricing Model. It displays the expected rate of return for an overall market as a function of systematic (non-diversifiable) risk (beta.)

The Y-Intercept (beta=0) of the _____ is equal to the risk-free interest rate.

   a. Divestment
   c. Rebalancing
   b. Security market line
   d. Certificate in Investment Performance Measurement

12. _____ is the difference between a measured value of quantity and its true value. In statistics, an error is not a 'mistake'. Variability is an inherent part of things being measured and of the measurement process.
   a. A Random Walk Down Wall Street
   c. ABN Amro
   b. AAB
   d. Observational error

13. _____ refers to the stock of skills and knowledge embodied in the ability to perform labor so as to produce economic value. Many early economic theories refer to it simply as labor, one of three factors of production, and consider it to be a fungible resource -- homogeneous and easily interchangeable. Other conceptions of labor dispense with these assumptions.
   a. Mercantilism
   c. Human capital
   b. Market structure
   d. Behavioral finance

14. The _____ is an asset pricing model commonly used in the finance industry to measure risk and return of a stock. Mathematically the SIM is expressed as:

$$\boxed{}>$$

$$\boxed{}>$$

where:

   $r_{it} >- r_f$ is the excess return on the stock
   a_i is the company's alpha
   B_i is the company's beta
   $r_{mt} >- r_f$ is the excess return on the market index
   E_{it} is the residual return

The accuracy of the model is enhanced by the stock return's influence by market (beta) and firm-specific risk factors (alpha), unexpected returns (residual) and the relation to the performance of a market index (such as the All Ordinaries.) Security analysts often use the SIM for such functions as computing stock betas, evaluating stock selection skills, and conducting event studies.

a. Capital asset
b. Country risk
c. Single-index model
d. Political risk

15. The _____ is a linear factor model with wealth and state variable that forecast changes in the distribution of future returns or income.

The main difference between _____ and standard CAPM is additing state variables that acknowledge the fact that investors hedge against shortfalls in consumption or against changes in the future investment opportunity set.

a. A Random Walk Down Wall Street
b. ABN Amro
c. AAB
d. Intertemporal Capital Asset Pricing Model

16. In statistics, the _____, R^2 is used in the context of statistical models whose main purpose is the prediction of future outcomes on the basis of other related information. It is the proportion of variability in a data set that is accounted for by the statistical model. It provides a measure of how well future outcomes are likely to be predicted by the model.

a. 529 plan
b. Coefficient of determination
c. 7-Eleven
d. 4-4-5 Calendar

17. In finance, _____ is that risk which is common to an entire market and not to any individual entity or component thereof. It should be distinguished from systemic risk which is the risk that the entire financial system will collapse as a result of some catastrophic event.

Risks can be reduced in four main ways: Avoidance, Reduction, Retention and Transfer.

a. Primary market
b. Conglomerate merger
c. Capital surplus
d. Systematic risk

18. A _____ is a variable associated with an increased risk of disease or infection. They are correlational and not necessarily causal, because correlation does not imply causation. For example, being young cannot be said to cause measles, but young people are more at risk as they are less likely to have developed immunity during a previous epidemic.

a. 529 plan
b. Risk factor
c. 4-4-5 Calendar
d. 7-Eleven

19. _____ is a system of buying stocks or other securities that have had high returns over the past three to twelve months, and selling those that have had poor returns over the same period. It has been reported that this strategy yields average returns of 1% per month for the following 3-12 months as shown by Narasimhan Jegadeesh and Sheridan Titman.

While no consensus exists about the validity of this claim, economists have trouble reconciling this phenomenon using efficient market theory.

Chapter 13. Empirical Evidence on Security Returns 123

a. 7-Eleven
b. 4-4-5 Calendar
c. 529 plan
d. Momentum investing

20. In economics, _____ is a rise in the general level of prices of goods and services in an economy over a period of time. The term '_____' once referred to increases in the money supply (monetary _____); however, economic debates about the relationship between money supply and price levels have led to its primary use today in describing price _____. _____ can also be described as a decline in the real value of money--a loss of purchasing power in the medium of exchange which is also the monetary unit of account.

a. ABN Amro
b. AAB
c. A Random Walk Down Wall Street
d. Inflation

21. The term _____ or economic cycle refers to the fluctuations of economic activity (business fluctuations) around a long-term growth trend. The cycle involves shifts over time between periods of relatively rapid growth of output (recovery and prosperity), and periods of relative stagnation or decline (contraction or recession.) These fluctuations are often measured using the real gross domestic product.

a. Business cycle
b. Behavioral finance
c. Deflation
d. Fixed exchange rate

22. _____ is the risk that the value of an investment will decrease due to moves in market factors. The five standard _____ factors are:

- Equity risk, the risk that stock prices will change.
- Interest rate risk, the risk that interest rates will change.
- Currency risk, the risk that foreign exchange rates will change.
- Commodity risk, the risk that commodity prices (e.g. grains, metals) will change.

As with other forms of risk, _____ may be measured in a number of ways. Traditionally, this is done using a Value at Risk methodology. Value at risk is well established as a risk management technique, but it contains a number of limiting assumptions that constrain its accuracy.

a. Transaction risk
b. Market risk
c. Currency risk
d. Tracking error

23.

In finance, the _____ can be the expected rate of return above the risk-free interest rate. When measuring risk, a common sense approach is to compare the risk-free return on T-bills and the very risky return on other investments. The difference between these two returns can be interpreted as a measure of the excess return on the average risky asset. This excess return is known as the _____.

a. Risk adjusted return on capital
b. Risk aversion
c. Risk modeling
d. Risk premium

24. The _____ is an anomaly discovered in behavioral finance. It relates to the tendency of investors to sell shares whose price has increased, while keeping assets that have dropped in value. Investors are unwilling to recognize losses (which they would be forced to do if they sold assets which had fallen in value), but are more willing to recognize gains.

a. Psychological level
b. Herd behavior
c. Prospect theory
d. Disposition effect

25. In investing, _____ refers to the greater risk-adjusted return of value stocks over growth stocks. Eugene Fama and K. G. French first identified the premium in 1992, using a measure they called HML (high book-to-market ratio minus low book-to-market ratio) to measure equity returns based on valuation. Other experts, such as John C. Bogle, have argued that no _____ exists, claiming that Fama and French's research is period dependent.
   a. 529 plan
   b. 4-4-5 Calendar
   c. 7-Eleven
   d. Value premium

26. _____ is a measure of the ability of a debtor to pay their debts as and when they fall due. It is usually expressed as a ratio or a percentage of current liabilities.

For a corporation with a published balance sheet there are various ratios used to calculate a measure of liquidity.

   a. Operating leverage
   b. Invested capital
   c. Operating profit margin
   d. Accounting liquidity

27. In econometrics, an _____ model considers the variance of the current error term to be a function of the variances of the previous time period's error terms. _____ relates the error variance to the square of a previous period's error. It is employed commonly in modeling financial time series that exhibit time-varying volatility clustering, i.e. periods of swings followed by periods of relative calm.
   a. A Random Walk Down Wall Street
   b. AAB
   c. ABN Amro
   d. Autoregressive conditional heteroscedasticity

28. The _____ is an American stock exchange. It is the largest electronic screen-based equity securities trading market in the United States. With approximately 3,200 companies, it has more trading volume per day than any other stock exchange in the world.
   a. 7-Eleven
   b. 529 plan
   c. 4-4-5 Calendar
   d. Nasdaq

29. In business and finance, a _____ (also referred to as equity _____) of stock means a _____ of ownership in a corporation (company.) In the plural, stocks is often used as a synonym for _____s especially in the United States, but it is less commonly used that way outside of North America.

In the United Kingdom, South Africa, and Australia, stock can also refer to completely different financial instruments such as government bonds or, less commonly, to all kinds of marketable securities.

   a. Share
   b. Margin
   c. Procter ' Gamble
   d. Bucket shop

30. _____ most frequently refers to the standard deviation of the continuously compounded returns of a financial instrument with a specific time horizon. It is often used to quantify the risk of the instrument over that time period. _____ is typically expressed in annualized terms, and it may either be an absolute number ($5) or a fraction of the mean (5%).

Chapter 13. Empirical Evidence on Security Returns

a. Volatility
c. Currency swap
b. Seasoned equity offering
d. Portfolio insurance

31. In financial mathematics, the _____ of an option contract is the volatility implied by the market price of the option based on an option pricing model. In other words, it is the volatility that, given a particular pricing model, yields a theoretical value for the option equal to the current market price. Non-option financial instruments that have embedded optionality, such as an interest rate cap, can also have an _____.
   a. Interest rate future
   c. Equity derivative
   b. Interest rate derivative
   d. Implied volatility

32. The _____ is a term coined by economists Rajnish Mehra and Edward C. Prescott. It is based on the observation that in order to reconcile the much higher return on equity stock compared to government bonds in the United States, individuals must have implausibly high risk aversion according to standard economics models. Similar situations prevail in many other industrialized countries.
   a. A Random Walk Down Wall Street
   c. ABN Amro
   b. Equity premium puzzle
   d. AAB

33. In finance, _____, also known as return on investment is the ratio of money gained or lost on an investment relative to the amount of money invested. The amount of money gained or lost may be referred to as interest, profit/loss, gain/loss, or net income/loss. The money invested may be referred to as the asset, capital, principal, or the cost basis of the investment.
   a. Composiition of Creditors
   c. Stock or scrip dividends
   b. Doctrine of the Proper Law
   d. Rate of return

34. In the United States, the Financial Industry Regulatory Authority (FINRA) is a self-regulatory organization (SRO) under the Securities Exchange Act of 1934, successor to the _____, Inc.

FINRA is responsible for regulatory oversight of all securities firms that do business with the public; professional training, testing and licensing of registered persons; arbitration and mediation; market regulation by contract for The NASDAQ Stock Market, Inc., the American Stock Exchange LLC, and the International Securities Exchange, LLC; and industry utilities, such as Trade Reporting Facilities and other over-the-counter operations.

   a. 7-Eleven
   c. 4-4-5 Calendar
   b. National Association of Securities Dealers
   d. 529 plan

35. A _____ is a payment made by a corporation to its shareholder members. When a corporation earns a profit or surplus, that money can be put to two uses: it can either be re-invested in the business (called retained earnings), or it can be paid to the shareholders as a _____. Many corporations retain a portion of their earnings and pay the remainder as a _____.
   a. Dividend yield
   c. Dividend
   b. Special dividend
   d. Dividend puzzle

36. A '_____' is a 'Charge' that is paid to obtain the right to delay a payment. Essentially, the payer purchases the right to make a given payment in the future instead of in the Present. The '_____', or 'Charge' that must be paid to delay the payment, is simply the difference between what the payment amount would be if it were paid in the present and what the payment amount would be paid if it were paid in the future.

a. Risk modeling
c. Value at risk
b. Risk aversion
d. Discount

37. The _____ is a measure of the excess return (or Risk Premium) per unit of risk in an investment asset or a trading strategy it is defined as:

$$S = \frac{R - R_f}{\sigma} = \frac{E[R - R_f]}{\sqrt{\text{var}[R - R_f]}},$$

where R is the asset return, R_f is the return on a benchmark asset, such as the risk free rate of return, $E[R - R_f]$ is the expected value of the excess of the asset return over the benchmark return, and σ is the standard deviation of the asset excess return.

Note, if R_f is a constant risk free return throughout the period,

$$\sqrt{\text{var}[R - R_f]} = \sqrt{\text{var}[R]}.$$

The _____ is used to characterize how well the return of an asset compensates the investor for the risk taken. When comparing two assets each with the expected return E[R] against the same benchmark with return R_f, the asset with the higher _____ gives more return for the same risk.

a. P/E ratio
c. Receivables turnover ratio
b. Sharpe ratio
d. Current ratio

38. In finance, _____ is the tendency for failed companies to be excluded from performance studies because they no longer exist. It often causes the results of studies to skew higher because only companies which were successful enough to survive until the end of the period are included.

For example, a mutual fund company's selection of funds today will include only those that have been successful in the past.

a. 529 plan
c. 4-4-5 Calendar
b. Survivorship bias
d. 7-Eleven

39. A _____ is a private or public market for the trading of company stock and derivatives of company stock at an agreed price; these are securities listed on a stock exchange as well as those only traded privately.

The size of the world _____ is estimated at about $36.6 trillion US at the beginning of October 2008. The world derivatives market has been estimated at about $480 trillion face or nominal value, 12 times the size of the entire world economy.

Chapter 13. Empirical Evidence on Security Returns 127

a. Adolph Coors
c. Andrew Tobias

b. Anton Gelonkin
d. Stock market

40. _____ refers to any type of investment that yields a regular (or fixed) return.

For example, if you lend money to a borrower and the borrower has to pay interest once a month, you have been issued a fixed-income security. When a company does this, it is often called a bond or corporate bank debt (although preferred stock is also sometimes considered to be _____).

a. 529 plan
c. Bond market

b. 4-4-5 Calendar
d. Fixed income

41. In finance, the yield curve is the relation between the interest rate (or cost of borrowing) and the time to maturity of the debt for a given borrower in a given currency. For example, the current U.S. dollar interest rates paid on U.S. Treasury securities for various maturities are closely watched by many traders, and are commonly plotted on a graph such as the one on the right which is informally called 'the yield curve.' More formal mathematical descriptions of this relation are often called the _____.

The yield of a debt instrument is the annualized percentage increase in the value of the investment.

a. 529 plan
c. 7-Eleven

b. 4-4-5 Calendar
d. Term structure of interest rates

42. In finance, the term _____ describes the amount in cash that returns to the owners of a security. Normally it does not include the price variations, at the difference of the total return. _____ applies to various stated rates of return on stocks (common and preferred, and convertible), fixed income instruments (bonds, notes, bills, strips, zero coupon), and some other investment type insurance products (e.g. annuities.)

a. Yield to maturity
c. Yield

b. Macaulay duration
d. 4-4-5 Calendar

43. In finance, the _____ is the relation between the interest rate (or cost of borrowing) and the time to maturity of the debt for a given borrower in a given currency. For example, the current U.S. dollar interest rates paid on U.S. Treasury securities for various maturities are closely watched by many traders, and are commonly plotted on a graph such as the one on the right which is informally called 'the _____.' More formal mathematical descriptions of this relation are often called the term structure of interest rates.

The yield of a debt instrument is the annualized percentage increase in the value of the investment.

a. 4-4-5 Calendar
c. 7-Eleven

b. 529 plan
d. Yield curve

44. In finance, _____ is the interest that has accumulated since the principal investment, or since the previous interest payment if there has been one already. For a financial instrument such as a bond, interest is calculated and paid in set intervals.

The primary formula for calculating the interest accrued in a given period is:

Chapter 13. Empirical Evidence on Security Returns

$$I_A = T \times P \times R$$

where I_A is the _____, T is the fraction of the year, P is the principal, and R is the annualized interest rate.

a. AAB
b. ABN Amro
c. A Random Walk Down Wall Street
d. Accrued interest

45. In finance, a _____ is a debt security, in which the authorized issuer owes the holders a debt and, depending on the terms of the _____, is obliged to pay interest (the coupon) and/or to repay the principal at a later date, termed maturity.

Thus a _____ is a loan: the issuer is the borrower, the _____ holder is the lender, and the coupon is the interest. _____s provide the borrower with external funds to finance long-term investments, or, in the case of government _____s, to finance current expenditure.

a. Puttable bond
b. Convertible bond
c. Bond
d. Catastrophe bonds

46. The _____ is the market for securities, where companies and governments can raise longterm funds. The _____ includes the stock market and the bond market. Financial regulators, such as the U.S. Securities and Exchange Commission, oversee the _____s in their designated countries to ensure that investors are protected against fraud.

a. Capital market
b. Delta neutral
c. Spot rate
d. Forward market

47. _____, refers to consumption opportunity gained by an entity within a specified time frame, which is generally expressed in monetary terms. However, for households and individuals, '_____ is the sum of all the wages, salaries, profits, interests payments, rents and other forms of earnings received... in a given period of time.' For firms, _____ generally refers to net-profit: what remains of revenue after expenses have been subtracted.

a. Annual report
b. Income
c. OIBDA
d. Accrual

48. _____ is a fee paid on borrowed assets. It is the price paid for the use of borrowed money, or, money earned by deposited funds. Assets that are sometimes lent with _____ include money, shares, consumer goods through hire purchase, major assets such as aircraft, and even entire factories in finance lease arrangements.

a. AAB
b. A Random Walk Down Wall Street
c. Insolvency
d. Interest

49. An _____ is the price a borrower pays for the use of money they do not own, and the return a lender receives for deferring the use of funds, by lending it to the borrower. _____s are normally expressed as a percentage rate over the period of one year.

_____s targets are also a vital tool of monetary policy and are used to control variables like investment, inflation, and unemployment.

a. AAB
c. A Random Walk Down Wall Street
b. ABN Amro
d. Interest rate

Chapter 14. Bond Prices and Yields

1. _____ is that which is owed; usually referencing assets owed, but the term can cover other obligations. In the case of assets, _____ is a means of using future purchasing power in the present before a summation has been earned. Some companies and corporations use _____ as a part of their overall corporate finance strategy.

   a. Debt
   b. Credit cycle
   c. Partial Payment
   d. Cross-collateralization

2. _____ refers to any type of investment that yields a regular (or fixed) return.

   For example, if you lend money to a borrower and the borrower has to pay interest once a month, you have been issued a fixed-income security. When a company does this, it is often called a bond or corporate bank debt (although preferred stock is also sometimes considered to be _____).

   a. Fixed income
   b. Bond market
   c. 4-4-5 Calendar
   d. 529 plan

3. A _____ is a fungible, negotiable instrument representing financial value. They are broadly categorized into debt securities (such as banknotes, bonds and debentures), and equity securities; e.g., common stocks. The company or other entity issuing the _____ is called the issuer.

   a. Tracking stock
   b. Book entry
   c. Securities lending
   d. Security

4. A _____ is the highest price that a buyer (i.e., bidder) is willing to pay for a good. It is usually referred to simply as the 'bid.'

   In bid and ask, the _____ stands in contrast to the ask price or 'offer', and the difference between the two is called the bid/ask spread.

   An unsolicited bid or offer is when a person or company receives a bid even though they are not looking to sell.

   a. Bid price
   b. Mid price
   c. Political risk
   d. Settlement date

5. In finance, a _____ is a debt security, in which the authorized issuer owes the holders a debt and, depending on the terms of the _____, is obliged to pay interest (the coupon) and/or to repay the principal at a later date, termed maturity.

   Thus a _____ is a loan: the issuer is the borrower, the _____ holder is the lender, and the coupon is the interest. _____s provide the borrower with external funds to finance long-term investments, or, in the case of government _____s, to finance current expenditure.

   a. Convertible bond
   b. Puttable bond
   c. Catastrophe bonds
   d. Bond

6. _____ (also trust indenture or deed of trust) is a legal document issued to lenders and describes key terms such as the interest rate, maturity date, convertibility, pledge, promises, representations, covenants, and other terms of the bond offering. When the Offering Memorandum is prepared in advance of marketing a Bond, the indenture will typically be summarised in the 'Description of Notes' section.

Chapter 14. Bond Prices and Yields

a. McFadden Act
b. Court of Audit of Belgium
c. Fair Labor Standards Act
d. Bond indenture

7. The coupon or _____ of a bond is the amount of interest paid per year expressed as a percentage of the face value of the bond.

For example if you hold $10,000 nominal of a bond described as a 4.5% loan stock, you will receive $450 in interest each year (probably in two installments of $225 each.)

Not all bonds have coupons.

a. Coupon rate
b. Revenue bonds
c. Puttable bond
d. Zero-coupon bond

8. _____ are bonds where the principal is indexed to inflation. They are thus designed to cut out the inflation risk of an investment. _____ pay a periodic coupon that is equal to the product of the inflation index and the nominal coupon rate. The relationship between coupon payments, breakeven inflation and real interest rates is given by the Fisher equation.

a. AAB
b. A Random Walk Down Wall Street
c. ABN Amro
d. Inflation-indexed bonds

9. _____, in finance and accounting, means stated value or face value. From this comes the expressions at par (at the _____), over par (over _____) and under par (under _____.)

The term '_____' has several meanings depending on context and geography.

a. FIDC
b. Par value
c. Sinking fund
d. Global Squeeze

10. In finance, the yield curve is the relation between the interest rate (or cost of borrowing) and the time to maturity of the debt for a given borrower in a given currency. For example, the current U.S. dollar interest rates paid on U.S. Treasury securities for various maturities are closely watched by many traders, and are commonly plotted on a graph such as the one on the right which is informally called 'the yield curve.' More formal mathematical descriptions of this relation are often called the _____.

The yield of a debt instrument is the annualized percentage increase in the value of the investment.

a. 529 plan
b. 4-4-5 Calendar
c. 7-Eleven
d. Term structure of interest rates

11. _____ are government bonds issued by the United States Department of the Treasury through the Bureau of the Public Debt. They are the debt financing instruments of the U.S. Federal government, and they are often referred to simply as Treasuries or Treasurys. There are four types of marketable _____: Treasury bills, Treasury notes, Treasury bonds, and Treasury Inflation Protected Securities (TIPS.)

a. Treasury Inflation-Protected Securities
b. 4-4-5 Calendar
c. Treasury Inflation Protected Securities
d. Treasury securities

12. In finance, the term _____ describes the amount in cash that returns to the owners of a security. Normally it does not include the price variations, at the difference of the total return. _____ applies to various stated rates of return on stocks (common and preferred, and convertible), fixed income instruments (bonds, notes, bills, strips, zero coupon), and some other investment type insurance products (e.g. annuities.)

   a. Yield to maturity   b. 4-4-5 Calendar
   c. Macaulay duration   d. Yield

13. In finance, the _____ is the relation between the interest rate (or cost of borrowing) and the time to maturity of the debt for a given borrower in a given currency. For example, the current U.S. dollar interest rates paid on U.S. Treasury securities for various maturities are closely watched by many traders, and are commonly plotted on a graph such as the one on the right which is informally called 'the _____.' More formal mathematical descriptions of this relation are often called the term structure of interest rates.

The yield of a debt instrument is the annualized percentage increase in the value of the investment.

   a. 529 plan   b. 4-4-5 Calendar
   c. 7-Eleven   d. Yield curve

14. A _____ is a bond bought at a price lower than its face value, with the face value repaid at the time of maturity. It does not make periodic interest payments, or have so-called 'coupons,' hence the term _____. Investors earn return from the compounded interest all paid at maturity plus the difference between the discounted price of the bond and its par value.

   a. Corporate bond   b. Bond fund
   c. Clean price   d. Zero-coupon bond

15. In finance, _____ is the interest that has accumulated since the principal investment, or since the previous interest payment if there has been one already. For a financial instrument such as a bond, interest is calculated and paid in set intervals.

The primary formula for calculating the interest accrued in a given period is:

$$I_A = T \times P \times R$$

where I_A is the _____, T is the fraction of the year, P is the principal, and R is the annualized interest rate.

   a. ABN Amro   b. AAB
   c. A Random Walk Down Wall Street   d. Accrued interest

16. The _____ is the market for securities, where companies and governments can raise longterm funds. The _____ includes the stock market and the bond market. Financial regulators, such as the U.S. Securities and Exchange Commission, oversee the _____s in their designated countries to ensure that investors are protected against fraud.

   a. Capital market   b. Forward market
   c. Spot rate   d. Delta neutral

Chapter 14. Bond Prices and Yields 133

17. _____, refers to consumption opportunity gained by an entity within a specified time frame, which is generally expressed in monetary terms. However, for households and individuals, '_____ is the sum of all the wages, salaries, profits, interests payments, rents and other forms of earnings received... in a given period of time.' For firms, _____ generally refers to net-profit: what remains of revenue after expenses have been subtracted.

   a. Annual report
   b. OIBDA
   c. Income
   d. Accrual

18. _____ is a fee paid on borrowed assets. It is the price paid for the use of borrowed money, or, money earned by deposited funds. Assets that are sometimes lent with _____ include money, shares, consumer goods through hire purchase, major assets such as aircraft, and even entire factories in finance lease arrangements.

   a. A Random Walk Down Wall Street
   b. Insolvency
   c. AAB
   d. Interest

19. An _____ is the price a borrower pays for the use of money they do not own, and the return a lender receives for deferring the use of funds, by lending it to the borrower. _____s are normally expressed as a percentage rate over the period of one year.

   _____s targets are also a vital tool of monetary policy and are used to control variables like investment, inflation, and unemployment.

   a. AAB
   b. A Random Walk Down Wall Street
   c. Interest rate
   d. ABN Amro

20. An _____ or bill is a commercial document issued by a seller to the buyer, indicating the products, quantities, and agreed prices for products or services the seller has provided the buyer. An _____ indicates the buyer must pay the seller, according to the payment terms.

   In the rental industry, an _____ must include a specific reference to the duration of the time being billed, so rather than quantity, price and discount the invoicing amount is based on quantity, price, discount and duration.

   a. AAB
   b. A Random Walk Down Wall Street
   c. Invoice
   d. ABN Amro

21. A _____, in its most general sense, is a solemn promise to engage in or refrain from a specified action.

   More specifically, a _____, in contrast to a contract, is a one-way agreement whereby the _____er is the only party bound by the promise. A _____ may have conditions and prerequisites that qualify the undertaking, including the actions of second or third parties, but there is no inherent agreement by such other parties to fulfill those requirements.

   a. Federal Trade Commission Act
   b. Partnership
   c. Clayton Antitrust Act
   d. Covenant

22. The _____ is a financial market where participants buy and sell debt securities, usually in the form of bonds. As of 2006, the size of the international _____ is an estimated $45 trillion, of which the size of the outstanding U.S. _____ debt was $25.2 trillion.

Nearly all of the $923 billion average daily trading volume in the U.S. _____ takes place between broker-dealers and large institutions in a decentralized, over-the-counter market.

a. Bond market
b. Fixed income
c. 529 plan
d. 4-4-5 Calendar

23. A _____ is a bond issued by a corporation. The term is usually applied to longer-term debt instruments, generally with a maturity date falling at least a year after their issue date. (The term 'commercial paper' is sometimes used for instruments with a shorter maturity.)

a. Corporate bond
b. Brady bonds
c. Serial bond
d. Government bond

24. A _____ is a payment made by a corporation to its shareholder members. When a corporation earns a profit or surplus, that money can be put to two uses: it can either be re-invested in the business (called retained earnings), or it can be paid to the shareholders as a _____. Many corporations retain a portion of their earnings and pay the remainder as a _____.

a. Dividend yield
b. Dividend puzzle
c. Dividend
d. Special dividend

25. In finance, the _____ is the global financial market for short-term borrowing and lending. It provides short-term liquidity funding for the global financial system. The _____ is where short-term obligations such as Treasury bills, commercial paper and bankers' acceptances are bought and sold.

a. Money market
b. Consumer debt
c. Cramdown
d. Debt-for-equity swap

26. A _____ is a document that indicates that the bearer of the document has title to property, such as shares or bonds. They differ from normal registered instruments, in that no records are kept of who owns the underlying property, or of the transactions involving transfer of ownership. Whoever physically holds the bearer bond papers owns the property.

a. Marketable
b. Book entry
c. Securities lending
d. Bearer instrument

27. A _____ is different from normal stock in that it is unregistered - no records are kept of the owner, or the transactions involving ownership. Whoever physically holds the _____ papers owns the stock or corporation. This is useful for investors and corporate officers who wish to retain anonymity.

a. Revenue bonds
b. Clean price
c. Gilts
d. Bearer bond

28. A _____ is a financial contract between two parties, the buyer and the seller of this type of option. Often it is simply labeled a 'call'. The buyer of the option has the right, but not the obligation to buy an agreed quantity of a particular commodity or financial instrument (the underlying instrument) from the seller of the option at a certain time (the expiration date) for a certain price (the strike price.)

a. Bull spread
b. Bear spread
c. Bear call spread
d. Call option

Chapter 14. Bond Prices and Yields

29. _____ is a type of bond that allows the issuer of the bond to retain the privilege of redeeming the bond at some point before the bond reaches the date of maturity. In other words, on the call dates, the issuer has the right, but not the obligation, to buy back the bonds from the bond holders at the call price. Technically speaking, the bonds are not really bought and held by the issuer but cancelled immediately.

   a. Bond fund
   c. Coupon rate
   b. Gilts
   d. Callable bond

30. In finance, a _____ is a type of bond that can be converted into shares of stock in the issuing company, usually at some pre-announced ratio. It is a hybrid security with debt- and equity-like features. Although it typically has a low coupon rate, the holder is compensated with the ability to convert the bond to common stock, usually at a substantial discount to the stock's market value.

   a. Gilts
   c. Corporate bond
   b. Bond fund
   d. Convertible bond

31. _____ is the provision of resources (such as granting a loan) by one party to another party where that second party does not reimburse the first party immediately, thereby generating a debt, and instead arranges either to repay or return those resources (or material(s) of equal value) at a later date. The first party is called a creditor, also known as a lender, while the second party is called a debtor, also known as a borrower.

Movements of financial capital are normally dependent on either _____ or equity transfers.

   a. Clearing house
   c. Warrant
   b. Comparable
   d. Credit

32. _____ is the risk of loss due to a debtor's non-payment of a loan or other line of credit (either the principal or interest (coupon) or both)

Most lenders employ their own models (credit scorecards) to rank potential and existing customers according to risk, and then apply appropriate strategies. With products such as unsecured personal loans or mortgages, lenders charge a higher price for higher risk customers and vice versa. With revolving products such as credit cards and overdrafts, risk is controlled through careful setting of credit limits.

   a. Credit risk
   c. Market risk
   b. Transaction risk
   d. Liquidity risk

33. _____, in accrual accounting, is any account where the asset or liability is not realized until a future date, e.g. annuities, charges, taxes, income, etc. The _____ item may be carried, dependent on type of deferral, as either an asset or liability.See also: accrual

_____ is also used in the university admissions process. It is the action by which a school rejects a student for early admission but still opts to review that student in the general admissions pool.

   a. Net profit
   c. Deferred
   b. Revenue
   d. Current asset

Chapter 14. Bond Prices and Yields

34. _____ is a combination of straight bond and embedded put option. The holder of the _____ has the right, but not the obligation, to demand early repayment of the principal. The put option is usually exercisable on specified dates.
   a. Brady bonds
   b. Convertible bond
   c. Callable bond
   d. Puttable bond

35. _____ occurs when an entity that has issued callable bonds calls those debt securities from the debt holders with the express purpose of reissuing new debt at a lower coupon rate. In essence, the issue of new, lower-interest debt allows the company to prematurely refund the older, higher-interest debt.

On the contrary, NonRefundable Bonds may be callable but they cannot be re-issued with a lower coupon rate.

   a. Refunding
   b. No-arbitrage bounds
   c. Systematic risk
   d. Market neutral

36. An _____ is a contract written by a seller that conveys to the buyer the right -- but not the obligation -- to buy (in the case of a call _____) or to sell (in the case of a put _____) a particular asset, such as a piece of property such as, among others, a futures contract. In return for granting the _____, the seller collects a payment (the premium) from the buyer.

For example, buying a call _____ provides the right to buy a specified quantity of a security at a set strike price at some time on or before expiration, while buying a put _____ provides the right to sell.

   a. Amortization
   b. AT'T Mobility LLC
   c. Annuity
   d. Option

37. In financial accounting, _____s are precautions for which the amount or probability of occurrence are not known. Typical examples are _____s for warranty costs and _____ for taxes the term reserve is used instead of term _____; such a use, however, is inconsistent with the terminology suggested by International Accounting Standards Board.
   a. Momentum Accounting and Triple-Entry Bookkeeping
   b. Petty cash
   c. Money measurement concept
   d. Provision

38. _____ is typically a higher ranking stock than voting shares, and its terms are negotiated between the corporation and the investor.

_____ usually carry no voting rights, but may carry superior priority over common stock in the payment of dividends and upon liquidation. _____ may carry a dividend that is paid out prior to any dividends to common stock holders.

   a. Second lien loan
   b. Trade-off theory
   c. Follow-on offering
   d. Preferred stock

Chapter 14. Bond Prices and Yields

39. _____ is a legal entity that develops, registers and sells securities for the purpose of financing its operations. _____s may be domestic or foreign governments, corporations or investment trusts. _____s are legally responsible for the obligations of the issue and for reporting financial conditions, material developments and any other operational activities as required by the regulations of their jurisdictions.
    a. Arbitrage
    b. Initial margin
    c. Efficient-market hypothesis
    d. Issuer

40. _____ are asset-backed securities of current and future revenues of the first 25 albums (287 songs) of David Bowie's collection recorded before 1990. Issued by David Bowie in 1997, they were bought for $55 million by the Prudential Insurance Company. The 287 included songs also acted as collateral to insure the bond.
    a. Bowie bonds
    b. Corporate bond
    c. Clean price
    d. Revenue bonds

41. _____ are risk-linked securities that transfer a specified set of risks from a sponsor to investors. They are often structured as floating rate corporate bonds whose principal is forgiven if specified trigger conditions are met. They are typically used by insurers as an alternative to traditional catastrophe reinsurance.
    a. Catastrophe bonds
    b. Brady bonds
    c. Clean price
    d. Callable bond

42. The institution most often referenced by the word '_____' is a public or publicly traded _____, the shares of which are traded on a public stock exchange (e.g., the New York Stock Exchange or Nasdaq in the United States) where shares of stock of _____s are bought and sold by and to the general public. Most of the largest businesses in the world are publicly traded _____s. However, the majority of _____s are said to be closely held, privately held or close _____s, meaning that no ready market exists for the trading of shares.
    a. Protect
    b. Corporation
    c. Depository Trust Company
    d. Federal Home Loan Mortgage Corporation

43. A _____ is an international bond that is denominated in a currency not native to the country where it is issued. It can be categorised according to the currency in which it is issued. London is one of the centers of the _____ market, but _____s may be traded throughout the world - for example in Singapore or Tokyo.
    a. Economic entity
    b. Eurobond
    c. Education production function
    d. Interest rate option

44. The _____ (NYSE: FNM), commonly known as Fannie Mae, is a stockholder-owned corporation chartered by Congress in 1968 as a government sponsored enterprise (GSE), but founded in 1938 during the Great Depression. The corporation's purpose is to purchase and securitize mortgages in order to ensure that funds are consistently available to the institutions that lend money to home buyers.

On September 7, 2008, James Lockhart, director of the Federal Housing Finance Agency (FHFA), announced that Fannie Mae and Freddie Mac were being placed into conservatorship of the FHFA.

    a. General partnership
    b. The Depository Trust ' Clearing Corporation
    c. SPDR
    d. Federal National Mortgage Association

Chapter 14. Bond Prices and Yields

45. The _____ provide stable, on-demand, low-cost funding to American financial institutions for home mortgage loans, small business, rural, agricultural, and economic development lending. With their members, the _____ank System represents the largest collective source of home mortgage and community credit in the United States. The banks do not provide loans directly to individuals, only to other banks.
    a. 529 plan
    b. 7-Eleven
    c. 4-4-5 Calendar
    d. Federal Home Loan Banks

46. The _____ (NYSE: FRE) is an insolvent government sponsored enterprise (GSE) of the United States federal government.

    The _____ was created in 1970 to expand the secondary market for mortgages in the US. Along with other GSEs, Freddie Mac buys mortgages on the secondary market, pools them, and sells them as mortgage-backed securities to investors on the open market.

    a. Public company
    b. Governmental Accounting Standards Board
    c. The Depository Trust ' Clearing Corporation
    d. Federal Home Loan Mortgage Corporation

47. The _____ is a U.S. government-owned corporation within the Department of Housing and Urban Development

    Ginnie Mae provides guarantees on mortgage-backed securities backed by federally insured or guaranteed loans, mainly loans issued by the Federal Housing Administration, Department of Veterans Affairs, Rural Housing Service, and Office of Public and Indian Housing. Ginnie Mae securities are the only MBS that are guaranteed by the United States government.

    a. Certified Emission Reductions
    b. Cash budget
    c. Case-Shiller Home Price Indices
    d. GNMA

48. The _____ is a U.S. government-owned corporation within the Department of Housing and Urban Development

    Ginnie Mae provides guarantees on mortgage-backed securities backed by federally insured or guaranteed loans, mainly loans issued by the Federal Housing Administration, Department of Veterans Affairs, Rural Housing Service, and Office of Public and Indian Housing. Ginnie Mae securities are the only MBS that are guaranteed by the United States government.

    a. 4-4-5 Calendar
    b. Jumbo mortgage
    c. Graduated payment mortgage
    d. Government National Mortgage Association

49. An _____ is a type of bond or other type of debt instrument used in finance whose coupon rate has an inverse relationship to short-term interest rates (or its reference rate.) With an _____, as interest rates rise the coupon rate falls. The basic structure is the same as an ordinary floating rate note except for the direction in which the coupon rate is adjusted.
    a. ABN Amro
    b. Inverse floater
    c. A Random Walk Down Wall Street
    d. AAB

Chapter 14. Bond Prices and Yields

50. The U.S. _____ is an independent agency of the United States government which holds primary responsibility for enforcing the federal securities laws and regulating the securities industry, the nation's stock and options exchanges, and other electronic securities markets. The SEC was created by section 4 of the SEC of 1934 (now codified as 15 U.S.C. § 78d and commonly referred to as the 1934 Act.)
   a. 529 plan
   b. 7-Eleven
   c. Securities and Exchange Commission
   d. 4-4-5 Calendar

51. _____ are bonds that have a variable coupon, equal to a money market reference rate, like LIBOR or federal funds rate, plus a spread. The spread is a rate that remains constant. Almost all _____ have quarterly coupons, i.e. they pay out interest every three months, though counter examples do exist.
   a. CVECAs
   b. Gordon growth model
   c. Loan participation
   d. Floating rate notes

52. In economics, _____ is a rise in the general level of prices of goods and services in an economy over a period of time. The term '_____' once referred to increases in the money supply (monetary _____); however, economic debates about the relationship between money supply and price levels have led to its primary use today in describing price _____. _____ can also be described as a decline in the real value of money--a loss of purchasing power in the medium of exchange which is also the monetary unit of account.
   a. AAB
   b. ABN Amro
   c. A Random Walk Down Wall Street
   d. Inflation

53. Treasury securities are government bonds issued by the United States Department of the Treasury through the Bureau of the Public Debt. They are the debt financing instruments of the U.S. Federal government, and they are often referred to simply as Treasuries or Treasurys. There are four types of marketable treasury securities: Treasury bills, Treasury notes, Treasury bonds, and _____ (_____.)
   a. Treasury Inflation Protected Securities
   b. Treasury Inflation-Protected Securities
   c. Treasury securities
   d. 4-4-5 Calendar

54. In finance, _____, also known as return on investment is the ratio of money gained or lost on an investment relative to the amount of money invested. The amount of money gained or lost may be referred to as interest, profit/loss, gain/loss, or net income/loss. The money invested may be referred to as the asset, capital, principal, or the cost basis of the investment.
   a. Doctrine of the Proper Law
   b. Composiition of Creditors
   c. Stock or scrip dividends
   d. Rate of return

55. An _____ can be defined as a contract which provides an income stream in return for an initial payment.

An immediate _____ is an _____ for which the time between the contract date and the date of the first payment is not longer than the time interval between payments. A common use for an immediate _____ is to provide a pension to a retired person or persons.

   a. Amortization
   b. Intrinsic value
   c. AT'T Inc.
   d. Annuity

Chapter 14. Bond Prices and Yields

56. The _____ or redemption yield is the yield promised to the bondholder on the assumption that the bond or other fixed-interest security such as gilts will be held to maturity, that all coupon and principal payments will be made and coupon payments are reinvested at the bond's promised yield at the same rate as invested. It is a measure of the return of the bond. This technique in theory allows investors to calculate the fair value of different financial instruments.

   a. 4-4-5 Calendar   b. Macaulay duration
   c. Yield   d. Yield to maturity

57. _____ is a life of security. It may also refer to the final payment date of a loan or other financial instrument, at which point all remaining interest and principal is due to be paid.

1, 3, 6 months _____ band can be calculated by using 30-day per month periods.

   a. Maturity   b. Primary market
   c. False billing   d. Replacement cost

58. _____ is a securities industry term describing the date on which a trade (bonds, equities, foreign exchange, commodities etc) settles. That is, the actual day on which transfer of cash or assets is completed.

It is not necessarily the same as value date (when the settlement amount is calculated.)

   a. Single-index model   b. Political risk
   c. Mid price   d. Settlement date

59. The _____ for an investment is a calculated annual yield for an investment, which may not pay out yearly. This allows investments which payout with different frequencies to be compared.

   a. 7-Eleven   b. 4-4-5 Calendar
   c. Bond equivalent yield   d. 529 plan

60. The _____, interest yield, income yield, flat yield or running yield is a financial term used in reference to bonds and other fixed-interest securities such as gilts. It is the ratio of the annual interest payment and the bond's current price.

The _____ only therefore refers to the yield of the bond at the current moment. It does not reflect the total return over the life of the bond. In particular, it takes no account of reinvestment risk (the uncertainty about the rate at which future cashflows can be reinvested) or the fact that bonds usually mature at par value, which can be an important component of a bond's return.

   a. Modified Internal Rate of Return   b. Stochastic volatility
   c. Perpetuity   d. Current yield

61. A '_____' is a 'Charge' that is paid to obtain the right to delay a payment. Essentially, the payer purchases the right to make a given payment in the future instead of in the Present. The '_____', or 'Charge' that must be paid to delay the payment, is simply the difference between what the payment amount would be if it were paid in the present and what the payment amount would be paid if it were paid in the future.

   a. Risk modeling   b. Discount
   c. Risk aversion   d. Value at risk

62. A _____ is a bond bought at a price lower than its face value, with the face value repaid at the time of maturity. It does not make periodic interest payments, or so-called 'coupons,' hence the term zero-coupon bond. Investors earn return from the compounded interest all paid at maturity plus the difference between the discounted price of the bond and its par value.
   a. Callable bond
   b. Municipal bond
   c. Zero coupon bond
   d. Bowie bonds

63. The _____ is a term coined by economists Rajnish Mehra and Edward C. Prescott. It is based on the observation that in order to reconcile the much higher return on equity stock compared to government bonds in the United States, individuals must have implausibly high risk aversion according to standard economics models. Similar situations prevail in many other industrialized countries.
   a. AAB
   b. A Random Walk Down Wall Street
   c. ABN Amro
   d. Equity premium puzzle

64. A _____ is a generic term for any bond selling for more than 100% of par value, i.e., at a price greater than 100.00, which typically occurs for high coupon bonds in a falling interest rate climate.
   a. Premium bond
   b. Revenue bonds
   c. Municipal bond
   d. Nominal yield

65.

In finance, the _____ can be the expected rate of return above the risk-free interest rate. When measuring risk, a common sense approach is to compare the risk-free return on T-bills and the very risky return on other investments. The difference between these two returns can be interpreted as a measure of the excess return on the average risky asset. This excess return is known as the _____.

   a. Risk modeling
   b. Risk adjusted return on capital
   c. Risk aversion
   d. Risk premium

66. In finance, _____ is a measurement of return on an asset or portfolio. It is one of the simplest measures of investment performance.

_____ is the percentage by which the value of a portfolio (or asset) has grown for a particular period.

   a. Market integration
   b. Holding period return
   c. Creditor
   d. Stock market index option

67. _____ mature in one year or less. Like zero-coupon bonds, they do not pay interest prior to maturity; instead they are sold at a discount of the par value to create a positive yield to maturity. Many regard _____ as the least risky investment available to U.S. investors.
   a. Treasury securities
   b. Treasury Inflation Protected Securities
   c. 4-4-5 Calendar
   d. Treasury bills

68. In finance, _____ occurs when a debtor has not met its legal obligations according to the debt contract, e.g. it has not made a scheduled payment, or has violated a loan covenant (condition) of the debt contract. _____ may occur if the debtor is either unwilling or unable to pay their debt. This can occur with all debt obligations including bonds, mortgages, loans, and promissory notes.

a. Vendor finance
b. Credit crunch
c. Debt validation
d. Default

69. The value of speculative bonds is affected to a higher degree than investment grade bonds by the possibility of default. For example, in a recession interest rates may drop, and the drop in interest rates tends to increase the value of investment grade bonds; however, a recession tends to increase the possibility of default in speculative-grade bonds.

The original speculative grade bonds were bonds that once had been investment grade at time of issue, but where the credit rating of the issuer had slipped and the possibility of default increased significantly. These bonds are called '_____'.

a. Return on capital employed
b. Sharpe ratio
c. Seed round
d. Fallen angels

70. In finance, a _____ (non-investment grade bond, speculative grade bond or junk bond) is a bond that is rated below investment grade at the time of purchase. These bonds have a higher risk of default or other adverse credit events, but typically pay higher yields than better quality bonds in order to make them attractive to investors.

a. Sharpe ratio
b. Private equity
c. Volatility
d. High yield bond

71. _____ is a legally declared inability or impairment of ability of an individual or organization to pay their creditors. Creditors may file a _____ petition against a debtor ('involuntary _____') in an effort to recoup a portion of what they are owed or initiate a restructuring. In the majority of cases, however, _____ is initiated by the debtor (a 'voluntary _____' that is filed by the bankrupt individual or organization.)

a. 529 plan
b. 4-4-5 Calendar
c. Bankruptcy
d. Debt settlement

72. The _____ is a financial ratio that measures whether or not a firm has enough resources to pay its debts over the next 12 months. It compares a firm's current assets to its current liabilities. It is expressed as follows:

$$\text{Current ratio} = \frac{\text{Current Assets}}{\text{Current Liabilities}}$$

For example, if WXY Company's current assets are $50,000,000 and its current liabilities are $40,000,000, then its _____ would be $50,000,000 divided by $40,000,000, which equals 1.25.

a. Current ratio
b. PEG ratio
c. Sustainable growth rate
d. Debt service coverage ratio

73. _____ and the related Fisher's linear discriminant are methods used in statistics and machine learning to find the linear combination of features which best separate two or more classes of objects or events. The resulting combination may be used as a linear classifier, or, more commonly, for dimensionality reduction before later classification.

_____ is closely related to ANOVA (analysis of variance) and regression analysis, which also attempt to express one dependent variable as a linear combination of other features or measurements.

a. 7-Eleven
b. 4-4-5 Calendar
c. 529 plan
d. Linear discriminant analysis

74. In finance, _____ (or gearing) is borrowing money to supplement existing funds for investment in such a way that the potential positive or negative outcome is magnified and/or enhanced. It generally refers to using borrowed funds, or debt, so as to attempt to increase the returns to equity. Deleveraging is the action of reducing borrowings.

a. Pension fund
b. Limited partnership
c. Leverage
d. Financial endowment

75. _____ is a measure of the ability of a debtor to pay their debts as and when they fall due. It is usually expressed as a ratio or a percentage of current liabilities.

For a corporation with a published balance sheet there are various ratios used to calculate a measure of liquidity.

a. Operating profit margin
b. Operating leverage
c. Invested capital
d. Accounting liquidity

76. In finance, the Acid-test or _____ or liquid ratio measures the ability of a company to use its near cash or quick assets to immediately extinguish or retire its current liabilities. Quick assets include those current assets that presumably can be quickly converted to cash at close to their book values.

Generally, the acid test ratio should be 1:1 or better, however this varies widely by industry.

a. Financial ratio
b. P/E ratio
c. Net assets
d. Quick ratio

77. The _____ percentage shows how profitable a company's assets are in generating revenue.

_____ can be computed as:

$$ROA = \frac{\text{Net Income}}{\text{Total Assets}}$$

This number tells you 'what the company can do with what it's got', i.e. how many dollars of earnings they derive from each dollar of assets they control. It's a useful number for comparing competing companies in the same industry.

a. Receivables turnover ratio
b. Return on assets
c. Return on sales
d. P/E ratio

78. In business and accounting, _____s are everything of value that is owned by a person or company. The balance sheet of a firm records the monetary value of the _____s owned by the firm. The two major _____ classes are tangible _____s and intangible _____s.
a. Accounts payable
b. Income
c. EBITDA
d. Asset

79. In finance, a _____ or accounting ratio is a ratio of two selected numerical values taken from an enterprise's financial statements. There are many standard ratios used to try to evaluate the overall financial condition of a corporation or other organization. They may be used by managers within a firm, by current and potential shareholders (owners) of a firm, and by a firm's creditors. Security analysts use these to compare the strengths and weaknesses in various companies.
a. Sustainable growth rate
b. Return on capital employed
c. Price/cash flow ratio
d. Financial ratio

80. In statistics, a _____ is a dimensionless quantity derived by subtracting the population mean from an individual raw score and then dividing the difference by the population standard deviation. This conversion process is called standardizing or normalizing; however, 'normalizing' can refer to many types of ratios; see normalization (statistics) for more.

_____s are also called z-values, z-scores, normal scores, and standardized variables; the use of 'Z' is because the normal distribution is also known as the 'Z distribution'.

a. Normal distribution
b. Monte Carlo methods
c. Semivariance
d. Standard score

81. _____s are financial bonds that mature in installments over a period of time. In effect, a $100,000, 5-year _____ would mature in a $20,000 annuity over a 5-year interval. Bond issues consisting of a series of blocks of securities maturing in sequence, the coupon rate can be different.
a. Brady bonds
b. Serial bond
c. Callable bond
d. Bond fund

82. A _____ is a fund established by a government agency or business for the purpose of reducing debt.

The _____ was first used in Great Britain in the 18th century to reduce national debt. While used by Robert Walpole in 1716 and effectively in the 1720s and early 1730s, it originated in the commercial tax syndicates of the Italian peninsula of the 14th century to retire redeemable public debt of those cities.

a. Debtor
b. Modern portfolio theory
c. Security interest
d. Sinking fund

Chapter 14. Bond Prices and Yields   145

83. In lending agreements, _____ is a borrower's pledge of specific property to a lender, to secure repayment of a loan. The _____ serves as protection for a lender against a borrower's risk of default - that is, a borrower failing to pay the principal and interest under the terms of a loan obligation. If a borrower does default on a loan (due to insolvency or other event), that borrower forfeits (gives up) the property pledged as _____ *ollateral* - and the lender then becomes the owner of the _____.
- a. Future-oriented
- b. Collateral
- c. Refinancing risk
- d. Nominal value

84. A _____ is defined as a certificate of agreement of loans which is given under the company's stamp and carries an undertaking that the _____ holder will get a fixed return (fixed on the basis of interest rates) and the principal amount whenever the _____ matures.

In finance, a _____ is a long-term debt instrument used by governments and large companies to obtain funds. It is defined as 'a debt secured only by the debtor's earning power, not by a lien on any specific asset.' It is similar to a bond except the securitization conditions are different.

- a. Collection agency
- b. Partial Payment
- c. Collateral Management
- d. Debenture

85. A _____ is a stock market phenomenon occurring when investors sell what they perceive to be higher-risk investments and purchase safer investments, such as US Treasuries, gold or land. This is considered a sign of fear in the marketplace, as investors seek less risk in exchange for lower profits.
- a. Volatility clustering
- b. Specific risk
- c. Flight-to-quality
- d. Stock market index option

86. In economic models, the _____ time frame assumes no fixed factors of production. Firms can enter or leave the marketplace, and the cost (and availability) of land, labor, raw materials, and capital goods can be assumed to vary. In contrast, in the short-run time frame, certain factors are assumed to be fixed, because there is not sufficient time for them to change.
- a. 529 plan
- b. 4-4-5 Calendar
- c. Short-run
- d. Long-run

Chapter 15. The Term Structure of Interest Rates

1. In finance, the yield curve is the relation between the interest rate (or cost of borrowing) and the time to maturity of the debt for a given borrower in a given currency. For example, the current U.S. dollar interest rates paid on U.S. Treasury securities for various maturities are closely watched by many traders, and are commonly plotted on a graph such as the one on the right which is informally called 'the yield curve.' More formal mathematical descriptions of this relation are often called the _____.

The yield of a debt instrument is the annualized percentage increase in the value of the investment.

- a. 529 plan
- b. Term structure of interest rates
- c. 4-4-5 Calendar
- d. 7-Eleven

2. In finance, the term _____ describes the amount in cash that returns to the owners of a security. Normally it does not include the price variations, at the difference of the total return. _____ applies to various stated rates of return on stocks (common and preferred, and convertible), fixed income instruments (bonds, notes, bills, strips, zero coupon), and some other investment type insurance products (e.g. annuities.)
    - a. Yield
    - b. 4-4-5 Calendar
    - c. Macaulay duration
    - d. Yield to maturity

3. In finance, the _____ is the relation between the interest rate (or cost of borrowing) and the time to maturity of the debt for a given borrower in a given currency. For example, the current U.S. dollar interest rates paid on U.S. Treasury securities for various maturities are closely watched by many traders, and are commonly plotted on a graph such as the one on the right which is informally called 'the _____.' More formal mathematical descriptions of this relation are often called the term structure of interest rates.

The yield of a debt instrument is the annualized percentage increase in the value of the investment.

- a. 7-Eleven
- b. Yield curve
- c. 4-4-5 Calendar
- d. 529 plan

4. _____ is a fee paid on borrowed assets. It is the price paid for the use of borrowed money , or, money earned by deposited funds . Assets that are sometimes lent with _____ include money, shares, consumer goods through hire purchase, major assets such as aircraft, and even entire factories in finance lease arrangements.
    - a. A Random Walk Down Wall Street
    - b. Insolvency
    - c. AAB
    - d. Interest

5. An _____ is the price a borrower pays for the use of money they do not own, and the return a lender receives for deferring the use of funds, by lending it to the borrower. _____s are normally expressed as a percentage rate over the period of one year.

_____s targets are also a vital tool of monetary policy and are used to control variables like investment, inflation, and unemployment.

- a. A Random Walk Down Wall Street
- b. ABN Amro
- c. AAB
- d. Interest rate

Chapter 15. The Term Structure of Interest Rates

6. In finance, a _____ is a debt security, in which the authorized issuer owes the holders a debt and, depending on the terms of the _____, is obliged to pay interest (the coupon) and/or to repay the principal at a later date, termed maturity.

Thus a _____ is a loan: the issuer is the borrower, the _____ holder is the lender, and the coupon is the interest. _____s provide the borrower with external funds to finance long-term investments, or, in the case of government _____s, to finance current expenditure.

   a. Convertible bond
   c. Catastrophe bonds

   b. Puttable bond
   d. Bond

7. A _____ is a fungible, negotiable instrument representing financial value. They are broadly categorized into debt securities (such as banknotes, bonds and debentures), and equity securities; e.g., common stocks. The company or other entity issuing the _____ is called the issuer.

   a. Tracking stock
   c. Book entry

   b. Securities lending
   d. Security

8. The coupon or _____ of a bond is the amount of interest paid per year expressed as a percentage of the face value of the bond.

For example if you hold $10,000 nominal of a bond described as a 4.5% loan stock, you will receive $450 in interest each year (probably in two installments of $225 each.)

Not all bonds have coupons.

   a. Coupon rate
   c. Zero-coupon bond

   b. Puttable bond
   d. Revenue bonds

9. In economics and finance, _____ is the practice of taking advantage of a price differential between two or more markets: striking a combination of matching deals that capitalize upon the imbalance, the profit being the difference between the market prices. When used by academics, an _____ is a transaction that involves no negative cash flow at any probabilistic or temporal state and a positive cash flow in at least one state; in simple terms, a risk-free profit.

   a. Initial margin
   c. Issuer

   b. Arbitrage
   d. Efficient-market hypothesis

10. The _____ is an economic law stated as: 'In an efficient market all identical goods must have only one price.'

The intuition for this law is that all sellers will flock to the highest prevailing price, and all buyers to the lowest current market price. In an efficient market the convergence on one price is instant.

Commodities can be traded on financial markets, where there will be a single offer price, and bid price.

   a. Personal property
   c. Letter of credit

   b. Liability
   d. Law of one price

Chapter 15. The Term Structure of Interest Rates

11. The _____ or redemption yield is the yield promised to the bondholder on the assumption that the bond or other fixed-interest security such as gilts will be held to maturity, that all coupon and principal payments will be made and coupon payments are reinvested at the bond's promised yield at the same rate as invested. It is a measure of the return of the bond. This technique in theory allows investors to calculate the fair value of different financial instruments.

   a. Yield
   b. Macaulay duration
   c. 4-4-5 Calendar
   d. Yield to maturity

12. _____ is a life of security. It may also refer to the final payment date of a loan or other financial instrument, at which point all remaining interest and principal is due to be paid.

1, 3, 6 months _____ band can be calculated by using 30-day per month periods.

   a. Replacement cost
   b. Primary market
   c. False billing
   d. Maturity

13. The _____ of a commodity, a security or a currency is the price that is quoted for immediate (spot) settlement (payment and delivery.) Spot settlement is normally one or two business days from trade date. This is in contrast with the forward price established in a forward contract or futures contract, where contract terms (price) are set now, but delivery and payment will occur at a future date.

   a. Long position
   b. Limits to arbitrage
   c. Market anomaly
   d. Spot rate

14. A _____ is a bond bought at a price lower than its face value, with the face value repaid at the time of maturity. It does not make periodic interest payments, or have so-called 'coupons,' hence the term _____. Investors earn return from the compounded interest all paid at maturity plus the difference between the discounted price of the bond and its par value.

   a. Clean price
   b. Corporate bond
   c. Zero-coupon bond
   d. Bond fund

15. In finance, _____ is a measurement of return on an asset or portfolio. It is one of the simplest measures of investment performance.

_____ is the percentage by which the value of a portfolio (or asset) has grown for a particular period.

   a. Creditor
   b. Holding period return
   c. Market integration
   d. Stock market index option

16. The _____ or forward rate is the agreed upon price of an asset in a forward contract. Using the rational pricing assumption, we can express the _____ in terms of the spot price and any dividends etc., so that there is no possibility for arbitrage.

The _____ is given by:

Chapter 15. The Term Structure of Interest Rates 149

where

F is the _____ to be paid at time T
e^x is the exponential function
r is the risk-free interest rate
q is the cost-of-carry
S_0 is the spot price of the asset (i.e. what it would sell for at time 0)
D_i is a dividend which is guaranteed to be paid at time t_i where $0 < t_i < T$.

The two questions here are what price the short position (the seller of the asset) should offer to maximize his gain, and what price the long position (the buyer of the asset) should accept to maximize his gain?

At the very least we know that both do not want to lose any money in the deal.

a. Biweekly Mortgage
b. Financial Gerontology
c. Security interest
d. Forward price

17. _____ is a measure of the ability of a debtor to pay their debts as and when they fall due. It is usually expressed as a ratio or a percentage of current liabilities.

For a corporation with a published balance sheet there are various ratios used to calculate a measure of liquidity.

a. Operating leverage
b. Invested capital
c. Operating profit margin
d. Accounting liquidity

18. _____ is a term used to explain a difference between two types of financial securities (e.g. stocks), that have all the same qualities except liquidity. For example:

_____ is a segment of a three-part theory that works to explain the behavior of yield curves for interest rates. The upwards-curving component of the interest yield can be explained by the _____.

a. 4-4-5 Calendar
b. 529 plan
c. Liquidity premium
d. 7-Eleven

19. _____ is the risk (variability in value) borne by an interest-bearing asset, such as a loan or a bond, due to variability of interest rates. In general, as rates rise, the price of a fixed rate bond will fall, and vice versa. _____ is commonly measured by the bond's duration.

a. Interest rate risk
b. Official bank rate
c. A Random Walk Down Wall Street
d. International Fisher effect

20. John Maynard Keynes developed the _____ of Interest in the General Theory of Employment Interest and Money. The primary consideration of the _____ is the demand for money as an asset, as a means for holding wealth. Interest rates, he argues, cannot be a reward for savings as such because, if a person hoards his savings in cash, keeping it under his mattress say, he will receive no interest, although he has nevertheless, refrained from consuming all his current income.

a. 7-Eleven
b. 529 plan
c. Liquidity preference
d. 4-4-5 Calendar

21. In finance and economics _____ refers to the rate of interest before adjustment for inflation (in contrast with the real interest rate); or, for interest balls stated' without adjustment for the full effect of compounding (also referred to as the nominal annual rate.) An interest rate is called nominal if the frequency of compounding (e.g. a month) is not identical to the basic time unit (normally a year.)

The real interest rate includes compensation for the lender's lost value due to inflation, whereas the _____ excludes inflation.

a. Nominal interest rate
b. SIBOR
c. Cash accumulation equation
d. Shanghai Interbank Offered Rate

22. A _____ is an agreement between two parties to buy or sell an asset at a specified point of time in the future. The price of the underlying instrument, in whatever form, is paid before control of the instrument changes. This is one of the many forms of buy/sell orders where the time of trade is not the time where the securities themselves are exchanged.

a. Constant maturity credit default swap
b. Loan Credit Default Swap Index
c. Derivatives markets
d. Forward contract

23. A _____ is an exchange of promises between two or more parties to do an act which is enforceable in a court of law. It is where an unqualified offer meets a qualified acceptance and the parties reach Consensus ad Idem. The parties must have the necessary capacity to _____ and the _____ must not be either trifling, indeterminate, impossible or illegal.

a. 7-Eleven
b. 4-4-5 Calendar
c. 529 plan
d. Contract

Chapter 16. Managing Bond Portfolios

1. _____ refers to a portfolio management strategy where the manager makes specific investments with the goal of outperforming an investment benchmark index. Investors or mutual funds that do not aspire to create a return in excess of a benchmark index will often invest in an index fund that replicates as closely as possible the investment weighting and returns of that index; this is called passive management. _____ is the opposite of passive management, because in passive management the manager does not seek to outperform the benchmark index.
   a. ABN Amro
   b. A Random Walk Down Wall Street
   c. AAB
   d. Active management

2. In finance, the _____ of a financial asset measures the sensitivity of the asset's price to interest rate movements, expressed as a number of years. The reason for expressing this sensitivity in years is that the time that will elapse until a cash flow is received allows more interest to accumulate. Therefore the price of an asset with long term cashflows has more interest rate sensitivity than an asset with cashflows in the near future.
   a. Duration
   b. 4-4-5 Calendar
   c. Macaulay duration
   d. Yield to maturity

3. _____ is a fee paid on borrowed assets. It is the price paid for the use of borrowed money , or, money earned by deposited funds . Assets that are sometimes lent with _____ include money, shares, consumer goods through hire purchase, major assets such as aircraft, and even entire factories in finance lease arrangements.
   a. Interest
   b. Insolvency
   c. AAB
   d. A Random Walk Down Wall Street

4. An _____ is the price a borrower pays for the use of money they do not own, and the return a lender receives for deferring the use of funds, by lending it to the borrower. _____s are normally expressed as a percentage rate over the period of one year.

   _____s targets are also a vital tool of monetary policy and are used to control variables like investment, inflation, and unemployment.

   a. AAB
   b. ABN Amro
   c. Interest rate
   d. A Random Walk Down Wall Street

5. _____ is the risk (variability in value) borne by an interest-bearing asset, such as a loan or a bond, due to variability of interest rates. In general, as rates rise, the price of a fixed rate bond will fall, and vice versa. _____ is commonly measured by the bond's duration.
   a. A Random Walk Down Wall Street
   b. International Fisher effect
   c. Interest rate risk
   d. Official bank rate

6. In finance, the term _____ describes the amount in cash that returns to the owners of a security. Normally it does not include the price variations, at the difference of the total return. _____ applies to various stated rates of return on stocks (common and preferred, and convertible), fixed income instruments (bonds, notes, bills, strips, zero coupon), and some other investment type insurance products (e.g. annuities.)
   a. Macaulay duration
   b. 4-4-5 Calendar
   c. Yield to maturity
   d. Yield

152 Chapter 16. Managing Bond Portfolios

7. In finance, the _____ is the relation between the interest rate (or cost of borrowing) and the time to maturity of the debt for a given borrower in a given currency. For example, the current U.S. dollar interest rates paid on U.S. Treasury securities for various maturities are closely watched by many traders, and are commonly plotted on a graph such as the one on the right which is informally called 'the _____.' More formal mathematical descriptions of this relation are often called the term structure of interest rates.

The yield of a debt instrument is the annualized percentage increase in the value of the investment.

a. 529 plan
c. 4-4-5 Calendar
b. Yield curve
d. 7-Eleven

8. In finance, a _____ is a debt security, in which the authorized issuer owes the holders a debt and, depending on the terms of the _____, is obliged to pay interest (the coupon) and/or to repay the principal at a later date, termed maturity.

Thus a _____ is a loan: the issuer is the borrower, the _____ holder is the lender, and the coupon is the interest. _____s provide the borrower with external funds to finance long-term investments, or, in the case of government _____s, to finance current expenditure.

a. Catastrophe bonds
c. Puttable bond
b. Convertible bond
d. Bond

9. _____ is a life of security. It may also refer to the final payment date of a loan or other financial instrument, at which point all remaining interest and principal is due to be paid.

1, 3, 6 months _____ band can be calculated by using 30-day per month periods.

a. Primary market
c. False billing
b. Maturity
d. Replacement cost

10. A _____ is an asset-backed security whose cash flows are backed by the principal and interest payments of a set of mortgage loans. Payments are typically made monthly over the lifetime of the underlying loans.

a. Home equity line of credit
c. Mortgage-backed security
b. Shared appreciation mortgage
d. Conforming loan

11. A _____ is a fungible, negotiable instrument representing financial value. They are broadly categorized into debt securities (such as banknotes, bonds and debentures), and equity securities; e.g., common stocks. The company or other entity issuing the _____ is called the issuer.

a. Tracking stock
c. Securities lending
b. Security
d. Book entry

12. A _____ is a bond bought at a price lower than its face value, with the face value repaid at the time of maturity. It does not make periodic interest payments, or have so-called 'coupons,' hence the term _____. Investors earn return from the compounded interest all paid at maturity plus the difference between the discounted price of the bond and its par value.

a. Clean price
c. Corporate bond
b. Bond fund
d. Zero-coupon bond

13. _____ is the process whereby an organization establishes the parameters within which programs, investments, and acquisitions are reaching the desired results. Performance Reference Model of the Federal Enterprise Architecture, 2005.

This process of measuring performance ofter requires the use of statistical evidence to determine progress toward specific defined organizational objectives.

There are many types of measurements.

a. Performance measurement
c. Cash cow
b. Corporate Transparency
d. Decentralization

14. _____ refers to any type of investment that yields a regular (or fixed) return.

For example, if you lend money to a borrower and the borrower has to pay interest once a month, you have been issued a fixed-income security. When a company does this, it is often called a bond or corporate bank debt (although preferred stock is also sometimes considered to be _____).

a. 4-4-5 Calendar
c. 529 plan
b. Fixed income
d. Bond market

15. In finance, the yield curve is the relation between the interest rate (or cost of borrowing) and the time to maturity of the debt for a given borrower in a given currency. For example, the current U.S. dollar interest rates paid on U.S. Treasury securities for various maturities are closely watched by many traders, and are commonly plotted on a graph such as the one on the right which is informally called 'the yield curve.' More formal mathematical descriptions of this relation are often called the _____.

The yield of a debt instrument is the annualized percentage increase in the value of the investment.

a. 4-4-5 Calendar
c. 7-Eleven
b. 529 plan
d. Term structure of interest rates

16. In finance, _____ is the interest that has accumulated since the principal investment, or since the previous interest payment if there has been one already. For a financial instrument such as a bond, interest is calculated and paid in set intervals.

The primary formula for calculating the interest accrued in a given period is:

$$I_A = T \times P \times R$$

where I_A is the _____, T is the fraction of the year, P is the principal, and R is the annualized interest rate.

Chapter 16. Managing Bond Portfolios

   a. Accrued interest
   c. ABN Amro
   b. A Random Walk Down Wall Street
   d. AAB

17. The _____ is the market for securities, where companies and governments can raise longterm funds. The _____ includes the stock market and the bond market. Financial regulators, such as the U.S. Securities and Exchange Commission, oversee the _____s in their designated countries to ensure that investors are protected against fraud.
   a. Capital market
   c. Delta neutral
   b. Forward market
   d. Spot rate

18. _____, refers to consumption opportunity gained by an entity within a specified time frame, which is generally expressed in monetary terms. However, for households and individuals, '_____ is the sum of all the wages, salaries, profits, interests payments, rents and other forms of earnings received... in a given period of time.' For firms, _____ generally refers to net-profit: what remains of revenue after expenses have been subtracted.
   a. Annual report
   c. OIBDA
   b. Income
   d. Accrual

19. _____ is a type of bond that allows the issuer of the bond to retain the privilege of redeeming the bond at some point before the bond reaches the date of maturity. In other words, on the call dates, the issuer has the right, but not the obligation, to buy back the bonds from the bond holders at the call price. Technically speaking, the bonds are not really bought and held by the issuer but cancelled immediately.
   a. Callable bond
   c. Bond fund
   b. Coupon rate
   d. Gilts

20. An _____ is a contract written by a seller that conveys to the buyer the right -- but not the obligation -- to buy (in the case of a call _____) or to sell (in the case of a put _____) a particular asset, such as a piece of property such as, among others, a futures contract. In return for granting the _____, the seller collects a payment (the premium) from the buyer.

For example, buying a call _____ provides the right to buy a specified quantity of a security at a set strike price at some time on or before expiration, while buying a put _____ provides the right to sell.

   a. AT'T Mobility LLC
   c. Annuity
   b. Amortization
   d. Option

21. The institution most often referenced by the word '_____' is a public or publicly traded _____, the shares of which are traded on a public stock exchange (e.g., the New York Stock Exchange or Nasdaq in the United States) where shares of stock of _____s are bought and sold by and to the general public. Most of the largest businesses in the world are publicly traded _____s. However, the majority of _____s are said to be closely held, privately held or close _____s, meaning that no ready market exists for the trading of shares.
   a. Depository Trust Company
   c. Corporation
   b. Protect
   d. Federal Home Loan Mortgage Corporation

22. The _____ (NYSE: FNM), commonly known as Fannie Mae, is a stockholder-owned corporation chartered by Congress in 1968 as a government sponsored enterprise (GSE), but founded in 1938 during the Great Depression. The corporation's purpose is to purchase and securitize mortgages in order to ensure that funds are consistently available to the institutions that lend money to home buyers.

Chapter 16. Managing Bond Portfolios 155

On September 7, 2008, James Lockhart, director of the Federal Housing Finance Agency (FHFA), announced that Fannie Mae and Freddie Mac were being placed into conservatorship of the FHFA.

    a. SPDR
    c. General partnership
    b. The Depository Trust ' Clearing Corporation
    d. Federal National Mortgage Association

23. The _____ (NYSE: FRE) is an insolvent government sponsored enterprise (GSE) of the United States federal government.

The _____ was created in 1970 to expand the secondary market for mortgages in the US. Along with other GSEs, Freddie Mac buys mortgages on the secondary market, pools them, and sells them as mortgage-backed securities to investors on the open market.

    a. Governmental Accounting Standards Board
    c. Public company
    b. The Depository Trust ' Clearing Corporation
    d. Federal Home Loan Mortgage Corporation

24. A _____ is a financial debt vehicle that was first created in June 1983 by investment banks Salomon Brothers and First Boston for Freddie Mac. (The First Boston team was led by Dexter Senft.) Legally, a _____ is a special purpose entity that is wholly separate from the institution(s) that create it.

    a. Collateralized mortgage obligation
    c. Tranche
    b. 4-4-5 Calendar
    d. Yield curve spread

25. _____ is the provision of resources (such as granting a loan) by one party to another party where that second party does not reimburse the first party immediately, thereby generating a debt, and instead arranges either to repay or return those resources (or material(s) of equal value) at a later date. The first party is called a creditor, also known as a lender, while the second party is called a debtor, also known as a borrower.

Movements of financial capital are normally dependent on either _____ or equity transfers.

    a. Credit
    c. Comparable
    b. Warrant
    d. Clearing house

26. _____ is a key part of the securitization transaction in structured finance, and is important for credit rating agencies when rating a securitization. The credit crisis of 2007-2008 has discredited the process of _____ of structured securities as a legitimate financial practice.

There are two primary types of _____: Internal and External.

    a. 4-4-5 Calendar
    c. Credit enhancement
    b. Tranche
    d. Yield curve spread

27. In structured finance, a _____ is one of a number of related securities offered as part of the same transaction. The word _____ is French for slice, section, series, or portion. In the financial sense of the word, each bond is a different slice of the deal's risk.

Chapter 16. Managing Bond Portfolios

a. 4-4-5 Calendar
c. Yield curve spread
b. Credit enhancement
d. Tranche

28. A bond is considered _____ if its credit rating is BBB- or higher by Standard and Poor's or Baa3 or higher by Moody's or BBB(low) or higher by DBRS. Generally they are bonds that are judged by the rating agency as likely enough to meet payment obligations that banks are allowed to invest in them.

Ratings play a critical role in determining how much companies and other entities that issue debt, including sovereign governments, have to pay to access credit markets, i.e., the amount of interest they pay on their issued debt.

a. AAB
c. A Random Walk Down Wall Street
b. ABN Amro
d. Investment Grade

29. The _____ is a broad base index, maintained by Lehman Brothers, often used to represent investment grade bonds being traded in United States. Index funds and exchange-traded funds are available that track this bond index.

The _____ is a market capitalization-weighted index, meaning the securities in the index are weighted according to the market size of each bond type.

a. 529 plan
c. Lehman Aggregate Bond Index
b. 4-4-5 Calendar
d. 7-Eleven

30. In statistics, _____ is a method of sampling from a population.

When sub-populations vary considerably, it is advantageous to sample each subpopulation (stratum) independently. Stratification is the process of grouping members of the population into relatively homogeneous subgroups before sampling.

a. Correlation
c. Mean
b. Kurtosis
d. Stratified sampling

31. _____ are similar to certificates of deposit that can be purchased at banks; however, they are sold by insurance companies. Like money market funds, they're very safe investments; and like all investments that are considered to be 'very safe', they won't make you very much money. Also known by other names - fixed-income fund, stable value fund, capital-preservation fund, or guaranteed fund, for example -- they generally pay interest from one- to five years.

a. Guaranteed investment contracts
c. Vati-Con
b. Reputational risk
d. CODA plc

32. A _____ is a pool of assets forming an independent legal entity that are bought with the contributions to a pension plan for the exclusive purpose of financing pension plan benefits.

_____s are important shareholders of listed and private companies. They are especially important to the stock market where large institutional investors like the Ontario Teachers' Pension Plan dominate.

Chapter 16. Managing Bond Portfolios 157

    a. Leverage
    b. Leveraged buyout
    c. Limited liability company
    d. Pension fund

33. A _____ is an exchange of promises between two or more parties to do an act which is enforceable in a court of law. It is where an unqualified offer meets a qualified acceptance and the parties reach Consensus ad Idem. The parties must have the necessary capacity to _____ and the _____ must not be either trifling, indeterminate, impossible or illegal.
    a. Contract
    b. 4-4-5 Calendar
    c. 529 plan
    d. 7-Eleven

34. _____ is the action of bringing a portfolio of investments that has deviated away from one's target asset allocation back into line. Under-weighted securities can be purchased with newly saved money; alternatively, over-weighted securities can be sold to purchase under-weighted securities.

The investments in a portfolio will perform according to the market.

    a. Market timing
    b. Divestment
    c. Security market line
    d. Rebalancing

35. _____ is the balance of the amounts of cash being received and paid by a business during a defined period of time, sometimes tied to a specific project. Measurement of _____ can be used

- to evaluate the state or performance of a business or project.
- to determine problems with liquidity. Being profitable does not necessarily mean being liquid. A company can fail because of a shortage of cash, even while profitable.
- to generate project rate of returns. The time of _____s into and out of projects are used as inputs to financial models such as internal rate of return, and net present value.
- to examine income or growth of a business when it is believed that accrual accounting concepts do not represent economic realities. Alternately, _____ can be used to 'validate' the net income generated by accrual accounting.

_____ as a generic term may be used differently depending on context, and certain _____ definitions may be adapted by analysts and users for their own uses. Common terms include operating _____ and free _____.

_____s can be classified into:

1. Operational _____s: Cash received or expended as a result of the company's core business activities.
2. Investment _____s: Cash received or expended through capital expenditure, investments or acquisitions.
3. Financing _____s: Cash received or expended as a result of financial activities, such as interests and dividends.

All three together - the net _____ - are necessary to reconcile the beginning cash balance to the ending cash balance. Loan draw downs or equity injections, that is just shifting of capital but no expenditure as such, are not considered in the net _____.

158　　　　　　　　　　　　　*Chapter 16. Managing Bond Portfolios*

a. Corporate finance
b. Real option
c. Cash flow
d. Shareholder value

36. An _____ is an exchange of tangible assets for intangible assets or vice versa. Since it is a swap of assets, the procedure takes place on the active side of the balance sheet and has no impact on the latter in regards to volume. As an example, a company may sell equity and receive the value in cash thus increasing liquidity.
  a. ABN Amro
  b. AAB
  c. A Random Walk Down Wall Street
  d. Asset swap

37. _____ is the difference between price and the costs of bringing to market whatever it is that is accounted as an enterprise (whether by harvest, extraction, manufacture, or purchase) in terms of the component costs of delivered goods and/or services and any operating or other expenses.

A key difficulty in measuring profit is in defining costs. Pure economic monetary profits can be zero or negative even in competitive equilibrium when accounted monetized costs exceed monetized price.

  a. Accounting profit
  b. A Random Walk Down Wall Street
  c. AAB
  d. Economic profit

38. In finance, a _____ is a derivative in which two counterparties agree to exchange one stream of cash flows against another stream. These streams are called the legs of the _____.

The cash flows are calculated over a notional principal amount, which is usually not exchanged between counterparties.

  a. Volatility arbitrage
  b. Volatility swap
  c. Local volatility
  d. Swap

39. A _____ is a financial contract whose value is derived from the value of something else (known as the underlying.) The underlying on which a _____ is based can be an asset, weather conditions bonds or other forms of credit.
  a. 529 plan
  b. 7-Eleven
  c. 4-4-5 Calendar
  d. Derivative

40. An _____ is a derivative where the underlying asset is the right to pay or receive a (usually notional) amount of money at a given interest rate.

The _____s market is the largest derivatives market in the world. Market observers estimate that $60 trillion dollars by notional value of _____s contract had been exchanged by May 2004.

  a. International Swaps and Derivatives Association
  b. Interest rate derivative
  c. Equity derivative
  d. Open interest

41. An _____ is a type of bond or other type of debt instrument used in finance whose coupon rate has an inverse relationship to short-term interest rates (or its reference rate.) With an _____, as interest rates rise the coupon rate falls. The basic structure is the same as an ordinary floating rate note except for the direction in which the coupon rate is adjusted.

Chapter 16. Managing Bond Portfolios

a. A Random Walk Down Wall Street
c. ABN Amro
b. AAB
d. Inverse floater

42. _____ are bonds that have a variable coupon, equal to a money market reference rate, like LIBOR or federal funds rate, plus a spread. The spread is a rate that remains constant. Almost all _____ have quarterly coupons, i.e. they pay out interest every three months, though counter examples do exist.

a. Loan participation
c. CVECAs
b. Gordon growth model
d. Floating rate notes

43. An _____ is a derivative in which one party exchanges a stream of interest payments for another party's stream of cash flows. _____s can be used by hedgers to manage their fixed or floating assets and liabilities. They can also be used by speculators to replicate unfunded bond exposures to profit from changes in interest rates.

a. Equity swap
c. Interest rate swap
b. Implied volatility
d. International Swaps and Derivatives Association

44. Procter is a surname, and may also refer to:

- Bryan Waller Procter (pseud. Barry Cornwall), English poet
- Goodwin Procter, American law firm
- _____, consumer products multinational

a. Clearing house
c. Bucket shop
b. Procter ' Gamble
d. Valuation

Chapter 17. Macroeconomic and Industry Analysis

1. _____ of a business involves analyzing its financial statements and health, its management and competitive advantages, and its competitors and markets. The term is used to distinguish such analysis from other types of investment analysis, such as quantitative analysis and technical analysis.

_____ is performed on historical and present data, but with the goal of making financial forecasts.

   a. Growth stocks
   c. Stock valuation
   b. 4-4-5 Calendar
   d. Fundamental analysis

2. The term _____ is used to describe a nation's social, or business activity in the process of rapid industrialization. _____ are generally less-wealthy than the developed world, and are wealthier (or the wealthiest of) the developing world. According to The Economist many people find the term dated, but a new term has yet to gain much traction.
   a. ABN Amro
   c. Emerging markets
   b. A Random Walk Down Wall Street
   d. AAB

3. _____ is the branch of economics that studies the dynamics of exchange rates, foreign investment, and how these affect international trade. It also studies international projects, international investments and capital flows, and trade deficits. It includes the study of futures, options and currency swaps.
   a. International finance
   c. AAB
   b. ABN Amro
   d. A Random Walk Down Wall Street

4. In finance, the _____ between two currencies specifies how much one currency is worth in terms of the other. For example an _____ of 102 Japanese yen to the United States dollar means that JPY 102 is worth the same as USD 1. The foreign exchange market is one of the largest markets in the world.
   a. A Random Walk Down Wall Street
   c. ABN Amro
   b. Exchange rate
   d. AAB

5. _____ is the economic policy of restraining trade between nations, through methods such as tariffs on imported goods, restrictive quotas, and a variety of other restrictive government regulations designed to discourage imports, and prevent foreign take-over of local markets and companies. This policy is closely aligned with anti-globalization, and contrasts with free trade, where government barriers to trade are kept to a minimum. The term is mostly used in the context of economics, where _____ refers to policies or doctrines which 'protect' businesses and workers within a country by restricting or regulating trade between foreign nations.
   a. 529 plan
   c. 7-Eleven
   b. 4-4-5 Calendar
   d. Protectionism

6. _____ refers to a business or organization attempting to acquire goods or services to accomplish the goals of the enterprise. Though there are several organizations that attempt to set standards in the _____ process, processes can vary greatly between organizations. Typically the word '_____' is not used interchangeably with the word 'procurement', since procurement typically includes Expediting, Supplier Quality, and Traffic and Logistics (T'L) in addition to _____.
   a. 529 plan
   c. 7-Eleven
   b. 4-4-5 Calendar
   d. Purchasing

7. _____ is the value of goods/services compared to the amount paid with a currency. Currency can be either a commodity money, like gold or silver, or fiat currency like US dollars which are the world reserve currency. As Adam Smith noted, having money gives one the ability to 'command' others' labor, so _____ to some extent is power over other people, to the extent that they are willing to trade their labor or goods for money or currency.

Chapter 17. Macroeconomic and Industry Analysis

a. 4-4-5 Calendar
b. 7-Eleven
c. 529 plan
d. Purchasing power

8. The _____ is one of the measures of national income and input for a given country's economy. _____ is defined as the total cost of all finished goods and services produced within the country in a stipulated period of time (usually a 365-day year.) It is sometimes regarded as the sum of profits added at every level of production (the intermediate stages) of all final goods and services produced within a country in a stipulated timeframe, and it is rarely given a monetary value.

a. Macroeconomics
b. Recession
c. Behavioral finance
d. Gross domestic product

9. Unemployment occurs when a person is available to work and currently seeking work, but the person is without work. The prevalence of unemployment is usually measured using the _____, which is defined as the percentage of those in the labor force who are unemployed. The _____ is also used in economic studies and economic indexes such as the United States' Conference Board's Index of Leading Indicators as a measure of the state of the macroeconomics.

a. ABN Amro
b. A Random Walk Down Wall Street
c. Unemployment rate
d. AAB

10. _____ is a branch of economics that deals with the performance, structure, and behavior of a national or regional economy as a whole. Along with microeconomics, _____ is one of the two most general fields in economics. Macroeconomists study aggregated indicators such as GDP, unemployment rates, and price indices to understand how the whole economy functions.

a. Behavioral finance
b. Recession
c. Human capital
d. Macroeconomics

11. _____ is the amount by which a government, private company, or individual's spending exceeds income over a particular period of time, the opposite of budget surplus.

When the expenditures of a government to individuals and corporations) are greater than its tax revenues, it creates a deficit in the government budget; such a deficit is known as _____. This causes the government to borrow capital from the 'world market', increasing further debt, debt service and interest rates

a. 7-Eleven
b. Deficit spending
c. 529 plan
d. 4-4-5 Calendar

12. _____ is a concept in economics which refers to the extent to which an enterprise or a nation actually uses its installed productive capacity. Thus, it refers to the relationship between actual output that 'is' produced with the installed equipment and the potential output which 'could' be produced with it, if capacity was fully used.

If market demand grows, _____ will rise.

a. 4-4-5 Calendar
b. 529 plan
c. Long-run
d. Capacity utilization

13. In economics, a _____ is a sudden event that increases or decreases demand for goods or services temporarily. A positive _____ increases demand and a negative _____ decreases demand. Prices of goods and services are affected in both cases.

Chapter 17. Macroeconomic and Industry Analysis

a. Demand shock
b. Supply shock
c. Value added
d. Deregulation

14. In economics, _____ is a rise in the general level of prices of goods and services in an economy over a period of time. The term '_____' once referred to increases in the money supply (monetary _____); however, economic debates about the relationship between money supply and price levels have led to its primary use today in describing price _____. _____ can also be described as a decline in the real value of money--a loss of purchasing power in the medium of exchange which is also the monetary unit of account.

a. AAB
b. Inflation
c. A Random Walk Down Wall Street
d. ABN Amro

15. _____ is a fee paid on borrowed assets. It is the price paid for the use of borrowed money , or, money earned by deposited funds . Assets that are sometimes lent with _____ include money, shares, consumer goods through hire purchase, major assets such as aircraft, and even entire factories in finance lease arrangements.

a. AAB
b. Interest
c. Insolvency
d. A Random Walk Down Wall Street

16. An _____ is the price a borrower pays for the use of money they do not own, and the return a lender receives for deferring the use of funds, by lending it to the borrower. _____s are normally expressed as a percentage rate over the period of one year.

_____s targets are also a vital tool of monetary policy and are used to control variables like investment, inflation, and unemployment.

a. A Random Walk Down Wall Street
b. ABN Amro
c. AAB
d. Interest rate

17. A _____ is an event that suddenly changes the price of a commodity or service. It may be caused by a sudden increase or decrease in the supply of a particular good. This sudden change affects the equilibrium price.

a. Value added
b. Demand shock
c. Deregulation
d. Supply shock

18. In finance, the yield curve is the relation between the interest rate (or cost of borrowing) and the time to maturity of the debt for a given borrower in a given currency. For example, the current U.S. dollar interest rates paid on U.S. Treasury securities for various maturities are closely watched by many traders, and are commonly plotted on a graph such as the one on the right which is informally called 'the yield curve.' More formal mathematical descriptions of this relation are often called the _____.

The yield of a debt instrument is the annualized percentage increase in the value of the investment.

a. 7-Eleven
b. 529 plan
c. Term structure of interest rates
d. 4-4-5 Calendar

19. _____ refers to government attempts to influence the direction of the economy through changes in government taxes, or through some spending (fiscal allowances.)

Chapter 17. Macroeconomic and Industry Analysis 163

_____ can be contrasted with the other main type of economic policy, monetary policy, which attempts to stabilize the economy by controlling interest rates and the supply of money. The two main instruments of _____ are government spending and taxation.

a. Tax exemption
c. Qualified residence interest
b. Tax incidence
d. Fiscal policy

20. _____ is monetary policy that seeks to increase the size of the money supply. In most nations, monetary policy is controlled by either a central bank or a finance ministry.

Neoclassical and Keynesian economics significantly differ on the effects and effectiveness of monetary policy on influencing the real economy; there is no clear consensus on how monetary policy affects real economic variables (aggregate output or income, employment.)

a. ABN Amro
c. Expansionary monetary policy
b. A Random Walk Down Wall Street
d. AAB

21. _____ is the process by which the government, or monetary authority of a country controls (i) the supply of money central bank (ii) availability of money, and (iii) cost of money or rate of interest, in order to attain a set of objectives oriented towards the growth and stability of the economy. Monetary theory provides insight into how to craft optimal _____.

_____ is referred to as either being an expansionary policy where an expansionary policy increases the total supply of money in the economy, and a contractionary policy decreases the total money supply.

a. Federal Open Market Committee
c. Natural resources consumption tax
b. Tax exemption
d. Monetary policy

22. _____ are the means of implementing monetary policy by which a central bank controls its national money supply by buying and selling government securities, or other financial instruments. Monetary targets, such as interest rates or exchange rates, are used to guide this implementation.

Since most money is now in the form of electronic records, rather than paper records such as banknotes, _____ are conducted simply by electronically increasing or decreasing ('crediting' or 'debiting') the amount of money that a bank has, e.g., in its reserve account at the central bank, in exchange for a bank selling or buying a financial instrument.

a. A Random Walk Down Wall Street
c. Open market operations
b. ABN Amro
d. AAB

23. In financial accounting, the term _____ is most commonly used to describe any part of shareholders' equity, except for basic share capital. Sometimes, the term is used instead of the term provision; such a use, however, is inconsistent with the terminology suggested by International Accounting Standards Board. For more information about provisions, see provision (accounting.)

Chapter 17. Macroeconomic and Industry Analysis

a. Closing entries
b. FIFO and LIFO accounting
c. Treasury stock
d. Reserve

24. The term _____ or economic cycle refers to the fluctuations of economic activity (business fluctuations) around a long-term growth trend. The cycle involves shifts over time between periods of relatively rapid growth of output (recovery and prosperity), and periods of relative stagnation or decline (contraction or recession.) These fluctuations are often measured using the real gross domestic product.
   a. Behavioral finance
   b. Deflation
   c. Business cycle
   d. Fixed exchange rate

25. A '_____' is a 'Charge' that is paid to obtain the right to delay a payment. Essentially, the payer purchases the right to make a given payment in the future instead of in the Present. The '_____', or 'Charge' that must be paid to delay the payment, is simply the difference between what the payment amount would be if it were paid in the present and what the payment amount would be paid if it were paid in the future.
   a. Discount
   b. Value at risk
   c. Risk aversion
   d. Risk modeling

26. The _____ is an interest rate a central bank charges depository institutions that borrow reserves from it.

The term _____ has two meanings:

- the same as interest rate; the term 'discount' does not refer to the meaning of the word, but to the purpose of using the quantity, such as computations of present value, e.g. net present value / discounted cash flow

- the annual effective _____, which is the annual interest divided by the capital including that interest; this rate is lower than the interest rate; it corresponds to using the value after a year as the nominal value, and seeing the initial value as the nominal value minus a discount; it is used for Treasury Bills and similar financial instruments

The annual effective _____ is the annual interest divided by the capital including that interest, which is the interest rate divided by 100% plus the interest rate. It is the annual discount factor to be applied to the future cash flow, to find the discount, subtracted from a future value to find the value one year earlier.

For example, suppose there is a government bond that sells for $95 and pays $100 in a year's time.

   a. Discount rate
   b. Stochastic volatility
   c. Fisher equation
   d. Black-Scholes

27. In the United States, _____ are overnight borrowings by banks to maintain their bank reserves at the Federal Reserve. Banks keep reserves at Federal Reserve Banks to meet their reserve requirements and to clear financial transactions. Transactions in the _____ market enable depository institutions with reserve balances in excess of reserve requirements to lend reserves to institutions with reserve deficiencies.
   a. 4-4-5 Calendar
   b. Federal funds rate
   c. Federal funds
   d. Regulation T

Chapter 17. Macroeconomic and Industry Analysis

28. An _____ (or business indicator) is a statistic about the economy. _____s allow analysis of economic performance and predictions of future performance.

_____s include various indices, earnings reports, and economic summaries, such as unemployment, housing starts, Consumer Price Index (a measure for inflation), industrial production, bankruptcies, Gross Domestic Product, broadband internet penetration, retail sales, stock market prices, and money supply changes.

a. ABN Amro
c. AAB
b. A Random Walk Down Wall Street
d. Economic indicator

29. _____ is an economic concept with commonplace familiarity. It is the price that a good or service is offered at, or will fetch, in the marketplace. It is of interest mainly in the study of microeconomics.
a. Convertible arbitrage
c. Delta hedging
b. Market price
d. Central Securities Depository

30. A _____ is a normalized average (typically a weighted average) of prices for a given class of goods or services in a given region, during a given interval of time. It is a statistic designed to help to compare how these prices, taken as a whole, differ between time periods or geographical locations.
a. Price discrimination
c. Discounts and allowances
b. Transfer pricing
d. Price index

31. A _____ is a private or public market for the trading of company stock and derivatives of company stock at an agreed price; these are securities listed on a stock exchange as well as those only traded privately.

The size of the world _____ is estimated at about $36.6 trillion US at the beginning of October 2008 . The world derivatives market has been estimated at about $480 trillion face or nominal value, 12 times the size of the entire world economy.

a. Anton Gelonkin
c. Andrew Tobias
b. Adolph Coors
d. Stock market

32. _____ is a type of calendar that is intended to inform financiers and traders about the scheduled major economic numbers (like CPI, PMI, Jobless Claims), government reports and speeches of the most influential persons of the financial world. _____s are usually issued on a hourly basis.
a. AAB
c. A Random Walk Down Wall Street
b. ABN Amro
d. Economic calendar

33. In economics, _____ is the total amount of money available in an economy at a particular point in time. There are several ways to define 'money', but each includes currency in circulation and demand deposits.

_____ data are recorded and published.

a. 7-Eleven
c. Money supply
b. 529 plan
d. 4-4-5 Calendar

Chapter 17. Macroeconomic and Industry Analysis

34. The _____ is a private, nonprofit research organization dedicated to studying the science and empirics of economics, especially the American economy. It is 'committed to undertaking and disseminating unbiased economic research among public policymakers, business professionals, and the academic community.' It publishes NBER Working Papers and books. The NBER is located in Cambridge, Massachusetts with branch offices in Palo Alto, California, and New York City.
   a. National Association of State Boards of Accountancy
   b. Microfinance
   c. General partnership
   d. National Bureau of Economic Research

35. _____ measures the rate of return on the ownership interest (shareholders' equity) of the common stock owners. _____ is viewed as one of the most important financial ratios. It measures a firm's efficiency at generating profits from every dollar of shareholders' equity (also known as net assets or assets minus liabilities.)
   a. Return on equity
   b. Diluted Earnings Per Share
   c. Return of capital
   d. Return on sales

36. The _____ is used by business and government to classify and measure economic activity in Canada, Mexico and the United States. It has largely replaced the older Standard Industrial Classification (SIC) system; however, certain government departments and agencies, such as the U.S. Securities and Exchange Commission (SEC), still use the SIC codes.

    The _____ numbering system is a six-digit code.

    a. 529 plan
    b. 4-4-5 Calendar
    c. NAICS
    d. 7-Eleven

37. The _____ or _____ is used by business and government to classify and measure economic activity in Canada, Mexico and the United States. It has largely replaced the older Standard Industrial Classification (SIC) system; however, certain government departments and agencies, such as the U.S. Securities and Exchange Commission (SEC), still use the SIC codes.

    The _____ numbering system is a six-digit code.

    a. 7-Eleven
    b. 4-4-5 Calendar
    c. North American Industry Classification System
    d. 529 plan

38. A _____ or bank is a financial institution whose primary activity is to act as a payment agent for customers and to borrow and lend money.

    The first modern bank was founded in Italy in Genoa in 1406, its name was Banco di San Giorgio (Bank of St. George.)

    Many other financial activities were added over time.

    a. 4-4-5 Calendar
    b. Bought deal
    c. Black Sea Trade and Development Bank
    d. Banker

Chapter 17. Macroeconomic and Industry Analysis 167

39. _____ are business expenses that are not dependent on the level of production or sales. They tend to be time-related, such as salaries or rents being paid per month. This is in contrast to Variable costs, which are volume-related (and are paid per quantity.)
   a. Transaction cost
   b. Sliding scale fees
   c. Marginal cost
   d. Fixed costs

40. In finance, _____ (or gearing) is borrowing money to supplement existing funds for investment in such a way that the potential positive or negative outcome is magnified and/or enhanced. It generally refers to using borrowed funds, or debt, so as to attempt to increase the returns to equity. Deleveraging is the action of reducing borrowings.
   a. Financial endowment
   b. Limited partnership
   c. Pension fund
   d. Leverage

41. The _____ is a measure of how revenue growth translates into growth in operating income. It is a measure of leverage, and of how risky (volatile) a company's operating income is.

There are various measures of _____, which can be interpreted analogously to financial leverage.

   a. Invested capital
   b. Average accounting return
   c. Operating leverage
   d. Asset turnover

42. _____ are expenses that change in proportion to the activity of a business. In other words, _____ are the sum of marginal costs. It can also be considered normal costs. Along with fixed costs, _____ make up the two components of total cost. Direct Costs, however, are costs that can be associated with a particular cost object.
   a. Fixed costs
   b. Transaction cost
   c. Cost accounting
   d. Variable costs

43. In economics, business, and accounting, a _____ is the value of money that has been used up to produce something, and hence is not available for use anymore. In business, the _____ may be one of acquisition, in which case the amount of money expended to acquire it is counted as _____. In this case, money is the input that is gone in order to acquire the thing.
   a. Marginal cost
   b. Fixed costs
   c. Sliding scale fees
   d. Cost

44. _____ is a term normally applied to stock market trading patterns. In this context, a sector is understood to mean a group of stocks representing companies in similar lines of business.

For example, an investor or trader may describe the current market movements as favoring basic material stocks over semiconductor stocks by calling the environment a _____ from semiconductors to basic materials.

   a. Conglomerate merger
   b. Commercial finance
   c. Refunding
   d. Sector rotation

45. In business, a _____ is a product or a business unit that generates unusually high profit margins: so high that it is responsible for a large amount of a company's operating profit. This profit far exceeds the amount necessary to maintain the _____ business, and the excess is used by the business for other purposes.

Chapter 17. Macroeconomic and Industry Analysis

A firm is said to be acting as a _____ when its earnings per share (EPS) is equal to its dividends per share (DPS), or in other words, when a firm pays out 100% of its free cash flow (FCF) to its shareholders as dividends at the end of each accounting term.

    a. Cash cow
    c. Management by exception
    b. Performance measurement
    d. Corporate Transparency

46. _____ is a life of security. It may also refer to the final payment date of a loan or other financial instrument, at which point all remaining interest and principal is due to be paid.

1, 3, 6 months _____ band can be calculated by using 30-day per month periods.

    a. False billing
    c. Primary market
    b. Replacement cost
    d. Maturity

47. _____ or amalgamation is the act of merging many things into one. In business, it often refers to the mergers or acquisitions of many smaller companies into much larger ones. The financial accounting term of _____ refers to the aggregated financial statements of a group company as consolidated account.

    a. Retained earnings
    c. Cost of goods sold
    b. Write-off
    d. Consolidation

48. In business and accounting, _____s are everything of value that is owned by a person or company. The balance sheet of a firm records the monetary value of the _____s owned by the firm. The two major _____ classes are tangible _____s and intangible _____s.

    a. EBITDA
    c. Accounts payable
    b. Income
    d. Asset

49. _____, in marketing, consists of a consumer's commitment to repurchase the brand and can be demonstrated by repeated buying of a product or service or other positive behaviors such as word of mouth advocacy. True _____ implies that the consumer is willing, at least on occasion, to put aside their own desires in the interest of the brand. _____ has been proclaimed by some to be the ultimate goal of marketing.

    a. 529 plan
    c. 4-4-5 Calendar
    b. 7-Eleven
    d. Brand loyalty

50. A _____ is a set of exclusive rights granted by a state to an inventor or his assignee for a limited period of time in exchange for a disclosure of an invention.

The procedure for granting _____s, the requirements placed on the _____ee and the extent of the exclusive rights vary widely between countries according to national laws and international agreements. Typically, however, a _____ application must include one or more claims defining the invention which must be new, inventive, and useful or industrially applicable.

a. National Securities Markets Improvement Act of 1996   b. Patent
c. Vesting   d. Foreclosure

Chapter 18. Equity Valuation Models

1. _____s is a real estate appraisal term referring to properties with characteristics that are similar to a subject property whose value is being sought. This can be accomplished either by a real estate agent who attempts to establish the value of a potential client's home or property through market analysis or, by a licensed or certified appraiser or surveyor using more defined methods, when performing a real estate appraisal.

Five factors are usually considered when determining _____s:

- Conditions of Sale -- Did the _____ recently transact under conditions (e.g. -- arms length, distress sale, estate settlement) which are consistent with the standard of value under which the appraisal is being performed?
- Financing Conditions -- Was the _____ transaction influenced by non-market or other favorable (or even unfavorable) financing terms? For example, if the _____ sold with a below-market interest rate provided by the seller, and if the standard of value (e.g. -- market value) assumes no such abnormal financing, then the appraiser may need to adjust the _____ price by an amount equal to the estimated impact of the favorable financing.
- Market Conditions -- This is often referred to as the time adjustment and accounts for changing prices over time.
- Locational Comparability -- Are the _____ and the subject property influenced by the same locational characteristics? For example, even two houses in the same neighborhood may have different views which cause one to be more valuable than the other.
- Physical Comparability -- This includes such factors as size, condition, quality, and age.

A real estate appraisal is like any other statistical sampling process. The _____s are the samples drawn and measured, and the outcome is an estimate of value -- called an 'opinion of value' in the terminology of real estate appraisal.

a. Comparable
b. Procter ' Gamble
c. Bucket shop
d. Margin

2. A _____ is a payment made by a corporation to its shareholder members. When a corporation earns a profit or surplus, that money can be put to two uses: it can either be re-invested in the business (called retained earnings), or it can be paid to the shareholders as a _____. Many corporations retain a portion of their earnings and pay the remainder as a _____.

a. Special dividend
b. Dividend puzzle
c. Dividend yield
d. Dividend

3. _____ of a business involves analyzing its financial statements and health, its management and competitive advantages, and its competitors and markets. The term is used to distinguish such analysis from other types of investment analysis, such as quantitative analysis and technical analysis.

_____ is performed on historical and present data, but with the goal of making financial forecasts.

a. 4-4-5 Calendar
b. Growth stocks
c. Stock valuation
d. Fundamental analysis

Chapter 18. Equity Valuation Models

4. A '_____' is a 'Charge' that is paid to obtain the right to delay a payment. Essentially, the payer purchases the right to make a given payment in the future instead of in the Present. The '_____', or 'Charge' that must be paid to delay the payment, is simply the difference between what the payment amount would be if it were paid in the present and what the payment amount would be paid if it were paid in the future.
   a. Risk aversion
   b. Value at risk
   c. Risk modeling
   d. Discount

5. A _____ is a private or public market for the trading of company stock and derivatives of company stock at an agreed price; these are securities listed on a stock exchange as well as those only traded privately.

   The size of the world _____ is estimated at about $36.6 trillion US at the beginning of October 2008. The world derivatives market has been estimated at about $480 trillion face or nominal value, 12 times the size of the entire world economy.

   a. Andrew Tobias
   b. Anton Gelonkin
   c. Stock market
   d. Adolph Coors

6. In finance, _____ is the process of estimating the potential market value of a financial asset or liability. they can be done on assets (for example, investments in marketable securities such as stocks, options, business enterprises, or intangible assets such as patents and trademarks) or on liabilities (e.g., Bonds issued by a company.) _____s are required in many contexts including investment analysis, capital budgeting, merger and acquisition transactions, financial reporting, taxable events to determine the proper tax liability, and in litigation.
   a. Procter ' Gamble
   b. Margin
   c. Share
   d. Valuation

7. In accounting, _____ or *Carrying value* is the value of an asset according to its balance sheet account balance. For assets, the value is based on the original cost of the asset less any depreciation, amortization or impairment costs made against the asset. A company's _____ is its total assets minus intangible assets and liabilities.
   a. Current liabilities
   b. Retained earnings
   c. Pro forma
   d. Book value

8. In finance, _____ refers to the value of a security which is intrinsic to or contained in the security itself. It is also frequently called fundamental value. It is ordinarily calculated by summing the future income generated by the asset, and discounting it to the present value.
   a. Accretion
   b. Amortization
   c. Alpha
   d. Intrinsic value

9. In law, _____ refers to the process by which a company (or part of a company) is brought to an end, and the assets and property of the company redistributed. _____ can also be referred to as winding-up or dissolution, although dissolution technically refers to the last stage of _____. The process of _____ also arises when customs, an authority or agency in a country responsible for collecting and safeguarding customs duties, determines the final computation or ascertainment of the duties or drawback accruing on an entry.
   a. 4-4-5 Calendar
   b. 529 plan
   c. Liquidation
   d. Debt settlement

10. _____ is the likely price of an asset when it is allowed insufficient time to sell on the open market, thereby reducing its exposure to potential buyers. _____ is typically lower than fair market value. Unlike cash or securities, certain illiquid assets, like real estate, often require a period of several months in order to obtain their fair market value in a sale, and will generally sell for a significantly lower price if a sale is forced to occur in a shorter time period.

a. Tenancy
b. Real estate investing
c. REIT
d. Liquidation value

11. _____ is an economic concept with commonplace familiarity. It is the price that a good or service is offered at, or will fetch, in the marketplace. It is of interest mainly in the study of microeconomics.

a. Delta hedging
b. Convertible arbitrage
c. Market price
d. Central Securities Depository

12. The term _____ or replacement value refers to the amount that an entity would have to pay, at the present time, to replace any one of its assets.

In the insurance industry, '_____' is a method of computing the value of an item insured. _____ is not market value, but is instead the cost to replace an item or structure at its pre-loss condition.

a. Replacement cost
b. False billing
c. January effect
d. Bonus share

13. In economics, business, and accounting, a _____ is the value of money that has been used up to produce something, and hence is not available for use anymore. In business, the _____ may be one of acquisition, in which case the amount of money expended to acquire it is counted as _____. In this case, money is the input that is gone in order to acquire the thing.

a. Marginal cost
b. Fixed costs
c. Sliding scale fees
d. Cost

14. _____ is a measurement of corporate or economic size equal to the share price times the number of shares outstanding of a public company. As owning stock represents owning the company, including all its equity, capitalization could represent the public opinion of a company's net worth and is a determining factor in stock valuation. Likewise, the capitalization of stock markets or economic regions may be compared to other economic indicators.

a. Just-in-time
b. Synthetic CDO
c. Proxy fight
d. Market capitalization

15. _____ is a measure of the ratio between the net operating income produced by an asset (usually real estate) and its capital cost (the original price paid to buy the asset) or alternatively its current market value. The rate is calculated in a simple fashion as follows:

- annual net operating income / cost (or value) = _____

Chapter 18. Equity Valuation Models

For example, if a building is purchased for $1,000,000 sale price and it produces $100,000 in positive net operating income (the amount left over after fixed costs and variable costs are subtracted from gross lease income) during one year, then:

- $100,000 / $1,000,000 = 0.10 = 10%

The asset's _____ is ten percent.

_____s are an indirect measure of how fast an investment will pay for itself. In the example above, the purchased building will be fully capitalized (pay for itself) after ten years (100% divided by 10%.)

a. Profitability index
b. Cash concentration
c. Conditional prepayment rate
d. Capitalization rate

16. _____ is a variant of the Discounted cash flow model, a method for valuing a stock or business. Often used to provide difficult-to-resolve valuation issues for litigation, tax planning, and business transactions that are currently off market.

It assumes that the company issues a dividend that has a current value of D that grows at a constant rate g. It also assumes that the required rate of return for the stock remains constant at k which is equal to the cost of equity for that company. It involves summing the infinite series which gives the value of price current P.

a. Securitization
b. Special journals
c. Stock or scrip dividends
d. Gordon growth model

17. The _____ of a stock is a measure of the price paid for a share relative to the annual income or profit earned by the firm per share. It is a financial ratio used for valuation: a higher _____ means that investors are paying more for each unit of income, so the stock is more expensive compared to one with lower _____.

The _____ has units of years, which can be interpreted as 'number of years of earnings to pay back purchase price'.

a. Return of capital
b. P/E ratio
c. Quick ratio
d. Sustainable growth rate

18. _____ is typically a higher ranking stock than voting shares, and its terms are negotiated between the corporation and the investor.

_____ usually carry no voting rights, but may carry superior priority over common stock in the payment of dividends and upon liquidation. _____ may carry a dividend that is paid out prior to any dividends to common stock holders.

a. Follow-on offering
b. Trade-off theory
c. Second lien loan
d. Preferred stock

Chapter 18. Equity Valuation Models

19. In finance, the _____ approach describes a method of valuing a project, company, or asset using the concepts of the time value of money. All future cash flows are estimated and discounted to give their present values. The discount rate used is generally the appropriate cost of capital and may incorporate judgments of the uncertainty (riskiness) of the future cash flows.
   a. Present value of benefits
   b. Net present value
   c. Future-oriented
   d. Discounted cash flow

20. _____ is the balance of the amounts of cash being received and paid by a business during a defined period of time, sometimes tied to a specific project. Measurement of _____ can be used

   - to evaluate the state or performance of a business or project.
   - to determine problems with liquidity. Being profitable does not necessarily mean being liquid. A company can fail because of a shortage of cash, even while profitable.
   - to generate project rate of returns. The time of _____s into and out of projects are used as inputs to financial models such as internal rate of return, and net present value.
   - to examine income or growth of a business when it is believed that accrual accounting concepts do not represent economic realities. Alternately, _____ can be used to 'validate' the net income generated by accrual accounting.

   _____ as a generic term may be used differently depending on context, and certain _____ definitions may be adapted by analysts and users for their own uses. Common terms include operating _____ and free _____.

   _____s can be classified into:

   1. Operational _____s: Cash received or expended as a result of the company's core business activities.
   2. Investment _____s: Cash received or expended through capital expenditure, investments or acquisitions.
   3. Financing _____s: Cash received or expended as a result of financial activities, such as interests and dividends.

   All three together - the net _____ - are necessary to reconcile the beginning cash balance to the ending cash balance. Loan draw downs or equity injections, that is just shifting of capital but no expenditure as such, are not considered in the net _____.

   a. Corporate finance
   b. Real option
   c. Shareholder value
   d. Cash flow

21. A _____ is the price of a single share of a no. of saleable stocks of the company. Once the stock is purchased, the owner becomes a shareholder of the company that issued the share.
   a. Trading curb
   b. Whisper numbers
   c. Share price
   d. Stock split

22. The _____ is a financial ratio used to compare a company's book value to its current market price. Book value is an accounting term denoting the portion of the company held by the shareholders; in other words, the company's total tangible assets less its total liabilities. The calculation can be performed in two ways, but the result should be the same each way. In the first way, the company's market capitalization can be divided by the company's total book value from its balance sheet. The second way, using per-share values, is to divide the company's current share price by the book value per share (i.e. its book value divided by the number of outstanding shares).

a. Stock repurchase
b. Whisper numbers
c. Stop order
d. Price-to-book ratio

23. _____ is the fraction of net income a firm pays to its stockholders in dividends:

The part of the earnings not paid to investors is left for investment to provide for future earnings growth. Investors seeking high current income and limited capital growth prefer companies with high _____. However investors seeking capital growth may prefer lower payout ratio because capital gains are taxed at a lower rate.

a. Dividend puzzle
b. Dividend yield
c. Dividend imputation
d. Dividend payout ratio

24. _____ indicates the percentage of a company's earnings that are not paid out in dividends but credited to retained earnings. It is the opposite of the dividend payout ratio, so that also called the retention rate.

_____ = 1 - Dividend Payout Ratio

a. Dow Jones Indexes
b. Fair market value
c. Retention ratio
d. Bankassurer

25. _____ is the value on a given date of a future payment or series of future payments, discounted to reflect the time value of money and other factors such as investment risk. _____ calculations are widely used in business and economics to provide a means to compare cash flows at different times on a meaningful 'like to like' basis.

The most commonly applied model of the time value of money is compound interest.

a. Net present value
b. Negative gearing
c. Present value of benefits
d. Present value

26. A _____ rocket is a rocket that uses two or more stages, each of which contains its own engines and propellant. A tandem or serial stage is mounted on top of another stage; a parallel stage is attached alongside another stage. The result is effectively two or more rockets stacked on top of or attached next to each other.

a. 7-Eleven
b. 529 plan
c. 4-4-5 Calendar
d. Multistage

Chapter 18. Equity Valuation Models

27. _____ measures the rate of return on the ownership interest (shareholders' equity) of the common stock owners. _____ is viewed as one of the most important financial ratios. It measures a firm's efficiency at generating profits from every dollar of shareholders' equity (also known as net assets or assets minus liabilities.)

   a. Return of capital
   b. Return on sales
   c. Diluted Earnings Per Share
   d. Return on equity

28. The _____ (Price/Earnings To Growth ratio) is a valuation metric for determining the relative trade-off between the price of a stock, the earnings generated per share (EPS), and the company's expected growth.

In general, the P/E ratio is higher for a company with a higher growth rate. Thus using just the P/E ratio would make high-growth companies overvalued relative to others.

   a. Return on assets
   b. Current ratio
   c. Return on equity
   d. PEG ratio

29. _____ and earnings management are euphemisms referring to accounting practices that may follow the letter of the rules of standard accounting practices, but certainly deviate from the spirit of those rules. They are characterized by excessive complication and the use of novel ways of characterizing income, assets, or liabilities and the intent to influence readers towards the interpretations desired by the authors. The terms 'innovative' or 'aggressive' are also sometimes used.

   a. Controlling account
   b. Debit and credit
   c. Non Performing Asset
   d. Creative accounting

30. The term _____ is a term applied to practices that are perfunctory, or seek to satisfy the minimum requirements or to conform to a convention or doctrine. It has different meanings in different fields.

In accounting, _____ earnings are those earnings of companies in addition to actual earnings calculated under the Generally Accepted Accounting Principles (GAAP) in their quarterly and yearly financial reports.

   a. Deferred financing costs
   b. Long-term liabilities
   c. Deferred income
   d. Pro forma

31. In economics and accounting, _____ is seen as the change in the market value of capital over a given period. It is calculated as the market price of the capital at the beginning of the period minus its market price at the end of the period.

Such a method in calculating depreciation differs from other methods, such as straight-line depreciation in that it is included in the calculation of implicit cost, and thus economic profit.

   a. Index number
   b. A Random Walk Down Wall Street
   c. AAB
   d. Economic depreciation

32. _____ is the corporate management term for the act of reorganizing the legal, ownership, operational, or other structures of a company for the purpose of making it more profitable or better organized for its present needs. Alternate reasons for restructing include a change of ownership or ownership structure, demerger repositioning debt _____ and financial _____.

Chapter 18. Equity Valuation Models

a. Concentrated stock
b. Day trading
c. Cross-border leasing
d. Restructuring

33. The term _____ or economic cycle refers to the fluctuations of economic activity (business fluctuations) around a long-term growth trend. The cycle involves shifts over time between periods of relatively rapid growth of output (recovery and prosperity), and periods of relative stagnation or decline (contraction or recession.) These fluctuations are often measured using the real gross domestic product.
   a. Business cycle
   b. Fixed exchange rate
   c. Behavioral finance
   d. Deflation

34. _____ is a term used in accounting, economics and finance to spread the cost of an asset over the span of several years.

In simple words we can say that _____ is the reduction in the value of an asset due to usage, passage of time, wear and tear, technological outdating or obsolescence, depletion or other such factors.

In accounting, _____ is a term used to describe any method of attributing the historical or purchase cost of an asset across its useful life, roughly corresponding to normal wear and tear.

   a. Deferred financing costs
   b. Bottom line
   c. Matching principle
   d. Depreciation

35. In economics, _____ is a rise in the general level of prices of goods and services in an economy over a period of time. The term '_____' once referred to increases in the money supply (monetary _____); however, economic debates about the relationship between money supply and price levels have led to its primary use today in describing price _____. _____ can also be described as a decline in the real value of money--a loss of purchasing power in the medium of exchange which is also the monetary unit of account.
   a. AAB
   b. Inflation
   c. A Random Walk Down Wall Street
   d. ABN Amro

36. In corporate finance, _____ is a cash flow available for distribution among all the security holders of a company. They include equity holders, debt holders, preferred stock holders, convertible security holders, and so on.

Note that the first three lines above are calculated for you on the standard Statement of Cash Flows.

   a. Free cash flow
   b. Funding
   c. Safety stock
   d. Forfaiting

37. _____ is the price at which an asset would trade in a competitive Walrasian auction setting. _____ is often used interchangeably with open _____, fair value or fair _____, although these terms have distinct definitions in different standards, and may differ in some circumstances.

International Valuation Standards defines _____ as 'the estimated amount for which a property should exchange on the date of valuation between a willing buyer and a willing seller in an arm'e;s-length transaction after proper marketing wherein the parties had each acted knowledgeably, prudently, and without compulsion.'

Chapter 18. Equity Valuation Models

_____ is a concept distinct from market price, which is 'e;the price at which one can transact'e;, while _____ is 'e;the true underlying value'e; according to theoretical standards.

a. Debt restructuring
b. Wrap account
c. Market value
d. T-Model

38. _____ is the quotient of earnings per share divided by the share price. It is the reciprocal of the P/E ratio--the E/P or the EPS.

The _____ is quoted as a percentage, allowing an easy comparison to going bond rates.

a. Asset turnover
b. Assets turnover
c. Average accounting return
d. Earnings yield

39. In finance, the term _____ describes the amount in cash that returns to the owners of a security. Normally it does not include the price variations, at the difference of the total return. _____ applies to various stated rates of return on stocks (common and preferred, and convertible), fixed income instruments (bonds, notes, bills, strips, zero coupon), and some other investment type insurance products (e.g. annuities.)

a. 4-4-5 Calendar
b. Macaulay duration
c. Yield to maturity
d. Yield

Chapter 19. Financial Statement Analysis

1. In finance, a _____ or accounting ratio is a ratio of two selected numerical values taken from an enterprise's financial statements. There are many standard ratios used to try to evaluate the overall financial condition of a corporation or other organization. They may be used by managers within a firm, by current and potential shareholders (owners) of a firm, and by a firm's creditors. Security analysts use these to compare the strengths and weaknesses in various companies.
   a. Financial ratio
   b. Return on capital employed
   c. Sustainable growth rate
   d. Price/cash flow ratio

2. _____, refers to consumption opportunity gained by an entity within a specified time frame, which is generally expressed in monetary terms. However, for households and individuals, '_____ is the sum of all the wages, salaries, profits, interests payments, rents and other forms of earnings received... in a given period of time.' For firms, _____ generally refers to net-profit: what remains of revenue after expenses have been subtracted.
   a. Accrual
   b. Annual report
   c. OIBDA
   d. Income

3. An _____ is a financial statement for companies that indicates how Revenue is transformed into net income The purpose of the _____ is to show managers and investors whether the company made or lost money during the period being reported.

The important thing to remember about an _____ is that it represents a period of time.

   a. Income statement
   b. AAB
   c. A Random Walk Down Wall Street
   d. ABN Amro

4. In economics, business, and accounting, a _____ is the value of money that has been used up to produce something, and hence is not available for use anymore. In business, the _____ may be one of acquisition, in which case the amount of money expended to acquire it is counted as _____. In this case, money is the input that is gone in order to acquire the thing.
   a. Sliding scale fees
   b. Marginal cost
   c. Cost
   d. Fixed costs

5. _____, _____ includes the direct costs attributable to the production of the goods sold by a company. This amount includes the materials cost used in creating the goods along with the direct labor costs used to produce the good. It excludes indirect expenses such as distribution costs and sales force costs.
   a. Net profit
   b. Goodwill
   c. Cost of goods sold
   d. Deferred financing costs

6. In financial and business accounting, _____ is a measure of a firm's profitability that excludes interest and income tax expenses.

EBIT = Operating Revenue - Operating Expenses (OPEX) + Non-operating Income

Operating Income = Operating Revenue - Operating Expenses

Operating income is the difference between operating revenues and operating expenses, but it is also sometimes used as a synonym for EBIT and operating profit. This is true if the firm has no non-operating income.

a. Earnings before interest and taxes
b. AAB
c. ABN Amro
d. A Random Walk Down Wall Street

7. _____ is a fee paid on borrowed assets. It is the price paid for the use of borrowed money, or, money earned by deposited funds. Assets that are sometimes lent with _____ include money, shares, consumer goods through hire purchase, major assets such as aircraft, and even entire factories in finance lease arrangements.
a. A Random Walk Down Wall Street
b. AAB
c. Insolvency
d. Interest

8. _____ relates to the cost of borrowing money. It is the price that a lender charges a borrower for the use of the lender's money. _____ is different from OPEX and CAPEX, for it relates to the capital structure of a company.
a. ABN Amro
b. AAB
c. A Random Walk Down Wall Street
d. Interest expense

9. _____ is the difference between operating revenues and operating expenses, but it is also sometimes used as a synonym for EBIT and operating profit. This is true if the firm has no non-_____.

A professional investor contemplating a change to the capital structure of a firm (e.g., through a leveraged buyout) first evaluates a firm's fundamental earnings potential (reflected by Earnings Before Interest, Taxes, Depreciation and Amortization EBITDA and EBIT), and then determines the optimal use of debt vs. equity.

a. Operating income
b. AAB
c. A Random Walk Down Wall Street
d. ABN Amro

10. _____, in bookkeeping, refers to assets, liabilities, income, and expenses recorded on individual pages of the so called book of final entry or ledger. Changes in _____ value are made by chronologically posting debit (DR) and credit (CR) entries to its page. Examples of _____s are cash, _____s receivable, mortgages, loans, land and buildings, common stock, sales, services provided, wages, and payroll overhead.
a. Option
b. Alpha
c. Accretion
d. Account

11. _____ is one of a series of accounting transactions dealing with the billing of customers who owe money to a person, company or organization for goods and services that have been provided to the customer. In most business entities this is typically done by generating an invoice and mailing or electronically delivering it to the customer, who in turn must pay it within an established timeframe called credit or payment terms.

An example of a common payment term is Net 30, meaning payment is due in the amount of the invoice 30 days from the date of invoice.

a. Income
b. Impaired asset
c. Accounting methods
d. Accounts receivable

12. In financial accounting, a _____ or statement of financial position is a summary of a person's or organization's balances. Assets, liabilities and ownership equity are listed as of a specific date, such as the end of its financial year. A _____ is often described as a snapshot of a company's financial condition.

Chapter 19. Financial Statement Analysis 181

a. Balance sheet
b. Statement of retained earnings
c. Statement on Auditing Standards No. 70: Service Organizations
d. Financial statements

13. _____ plant, and equipment, is a term used in accountancy for assets and property which cannot easily be converted into cash. This can be compared with current assets such as cash or bank accounts, which are described as liquid assets. In most cases, only tangible assets are referred to as fixed.
   a. Fixed asset
   b. Remittance advice
   c. Petty cash
   d. Percentage of Completion

14. _____ is an accounting term used to reflect the portion of the book value of a business entity not directly attributable to its assets and liabilities; it normally arises only in case of an acquisition. It reflects the ability of the entity to make a higher profit than would be derived from selling the tangible assets. _____ is also known as an intangible asset.
   a. Cost of goods sold
   b. Consolidation
   c. Net profit
   d. Goodwill

15. In financial accounting, a _____ or statement of cash flows is a financial statement that shows a company's flow of cash. The money coming into the business is called cash inflow, and money going out from the business is called cash outflow. The statement shows how changes in balance sheet and income accounts affect cash and cash equivalents, and breaks the analysis down to operating, investing, and financing activities.
   a. Cash flow statement
   b. 7-Eleven
   c. 4-4-5 Calendar
   d. 529 plan

16. In business and accounting, _____s are everything of value that is owned by a person or company. The balance sheet of a firm records the monetary value of the _____s owned by the firm. The two major _____ classes are tangible _____s and intangible _____s.
   a. EBITDA
   b. Income
   c. Asset
   d. Accounts payable

17. _____ is the balance of the amounts of cash being received and paid by a business during a defined period of time, sometimes tied to a specific project. Measurement of _____ can be used

   - to evaluate the state or performance of a business or project.
   - to determine problems with liquidity. Being profitable does not necessarily mean being liquid. A company can fail because of a shortage of cash, even while profitable.
   - to generate project rate of returns. The time of _____s into and out of projects are used as inputs to financial models such as internal rate of return, and net present value.
   - to examine income or growth of a business when it is believed that accrual accounting concepts do not represent economic realities. Alternately, _____ can be used to 'validate' the net income generated by accrual accounting.

   _____ as a generic term may be used differently depending on context, and certain _____ definitions may be adapted by analysts and users for their own uses. Common terms include operating _____ and free _____.

_____s can be classified into:

1. Operational _____s: Cash received or expended as a result of the company's core business activities.
2. Investment _____s: Cash received or expended through capital expenditure, investments or acquisitions.
3. Financing _____s: Cash received or expended as a result of financial activities, such as interests and dividends.

All three together - the net _____ - are necessary to reconcile the beginning cash balance to the ending cash balance. Loan draw downs or equity injections, that is just shifting of capital but no expenditure as such, are not considered in the net _____.

a. Real option
c. Corporate finance
b. Shareholder value
d. Cash flow

18. _____ is a term used in accounting, economics and finance to spread the cost of an asset over the span of several years.

In simple words we can say that _____ is the reduction in the value of an asset due to usage, passage of time, wear and tear, technological outdating or obsolescence, depletion or other such factors.

In accounting, _____ is a term used to describe any method of attributing the historical or purchase cost of an asset across its useful life, roughly corresponding to normal wear and tear.

a. Bottom line
c. Deferred financing costs
b. Depreciation
d. Matching principle

19. The _____ percentage shows how profitable a company's assets are in generating revenue.

_____ can be computed as:

$$ROA = \frac{\text{Net Income}}{\text{Total Assets}}$$

This number tells you 'what the company can do with what it's got', i.e. how many dollars of earnings they derive from each dollar of assets they control. It's a useful number for comparing competing companies in the same industry.

a. P/E ratio
c. Return on sales
b. Receivables turnover ratio
d. Return on assets

Chapter 19. Financial Statement Analysis

20. _____ measures the rate of return on the ownership interest (shareholders' equity) of the common stock owners. _____ is viewed as one of the most important financial ratios. It measures a firm's efficiency at generating profits from every dollar of shareholders' equity (also known as net assets or assets minus liabilities.)
    a. Return on sales
    b. Return of capital
    c. Return on equity
    d. Diluted Earnings Per Share

21. In finance, _____ (or gearing) is borrowing money to supplement existing funds for investment in such a way that the potential positive or negative outcome is magnified and/or enhanced. It generally refers to using borrowed funds, or debt, so as to attempt to increase the returns to equity. Deleveraging is the action of reducing borrowings.
    a. Pension fund
    b. Limited partnership
    c. Financial endowment
    d. Leverage

22. The term _____ or economic cycle refers to the fluctuations of economic activity (business fluctuations) around a long-term growth trend. The cycle involves shifts over time between periods of relatively rapid growth of output (recovery and prosperity), and periods of relative stagnation or decline (contraction or recession.) These fluctuations are often measured using the real gross domestic product.
    a. Fixed exchange rate
    b. Business cycle
    c. Deflation
    d. Behavioral finance

23. _____ (or spoilage) refers to the process by which tissues of dead organisms break down into simpler forms of matter. Such a breakdown of dead organisms is essential for new growth and development of living organisms because it recycles the finite chemical constituents and frees up the limited physical space in the biome. Bodies of living organisms begin to decompose shortly after death.
    a. 7-Eleven
    b. 529 plan
    c. 4-4-5 Calendar
    d. Decomposition

24. In economics and finance, _____ is the practice of taking advantage of a price differential between two or more markets: striking a combination of matching deals that capitalize upon the imbalance, the profit being the difference between the market prices. When used by academics, an _____ is a transaction that involves no negative cash flow at any probabilistic or temporal state and a positive cash flow in at least one state; in simple terms, a risk-free profit.
    a. Arbitrage
    b. Efficient-market hypothesis
    c. Initial margin
    d. Issuer

25. _____ , in finance, is a general theory of asset pricing, that has become influential in the pricing of stocks.

    _____ holds that the expected return of a financial asset can be modeled as a linear function of various macro-economic factors or theoretical market indices, where sensitivity to changes in each factor is represented by a factor-specific beta coefficient. The model-derived rate of return will then be used to price the asset correctly - the asset price should equal the expected end of period price discounted at the rate implied by model.

    a. ABN Amro
    b. A Random Walk Down Wall Street
    c. AAB
    d. Arbitrage pricing theory

26. _____ is a financial ratio that measures the efficiency of a company's use of its assets in generating sales revenue or sales income to the company.

$$Asset\ Turnover = \frac{Sales}{Average Total Assets}$$

- 'Sales' is the value of 'Net Sales' or 'Sales' from the company's income statement
- 'Average Total Assets' is the value of 'Total assets' from the company's balance sheet in the beginning and the end of the fiscal period divided by 2.

- Assets turnover

a. Inventory turnover
c. Earnings yield
b. Average accounting return
d. Asset turnover

27. The term _____ has three unrelated technical definitions, and is also used in a variety of non-technical ways.

- In financial economics, it refers to any asset used to make money, as opposed to assets used for personal enjoyment or consumption. This is an important distinction because two people can disagree sharply about the value of personal assets, one person might think a sports car is more valuable than a pickup truck, another person might have the opposite taste. But if an asset is held for the purpose of making money, taste has nothing to do with it, only differences of opinion about how much money the asset will produce. With the further assumption that people agree on the probability distribution of future cash flows, it is possible to have an objective _____ pricing model. Even without the assumption of agreement, it is possible to set rational limits on _____ value.
- In governmental accounting, it is defined as any asset used in operations with an initial useful life extending beyond one reporting period. Generally, government managers have a 'stewardship' duty to maintain _____ s under their control. See International Public Sector Accounting Standards for details.
- In US tax accounting, it is defined as any property other than a list of exceptions. The main exceptions are anything held for sale, and any real estate or depreciable property used in business. Almost everything you own and use for personal purposes, pleasure or investment is a _____. If something is a _____ for tax purposes, gains or losses on sale or disposition are capital gains or capital losses. For individuals, however, capital losses on property held for personal use are generally not deductible. See the IRS publication Tax Facts about Capital Gains and Losses for details.

A well-known financial accounting textbook advises that the term be avoided except in tax accounting because it is used in so many different senses, not all of them well-defined. For example it is often used as a synonym for fixed assets or for investments in securities.

A common non-technical usage occurs when people ask that employees or the environment or something else be treated as a _____.

a. Political risk
c. Solvency
b. Settlement date
d. Capital asset

Chapter 19. Financial Statement Analysis

28. In finance, the _____ is used to determine a theoretically appropriate required rate of return of an asset, if that asset is to be added to an already well-diversified portfolio, given that asset's non-diversifiable risk. The model takes into account the asset's sensitivity to non-diversifiable risk (also known as systemic risk or market risk), often represented by the quantity beta (β) in the financial industry, as well as the expected return of the market and the expected return of a theoretical risk-free asset.

The model was introduced by Jack Treynor (1961, 1962), William Sharpe (1964), John Lintner (1965a,b) and Jan Mossin (1966) independently, building on the earlier work of Harry Markowitz on diversification and modern portfolio theory.

a. Random walk hypothesis
c. Capital asset pricing model
b. Hull-White model
d. Cox-Ingersoll-Ross model

29. Times interest earned (TIE) or _____ is a measure of a company's ability to honor its debt payments. It may be calculated as either EBIT or EBITDA divided by the total interest payable.

$$\text{Times-Interest-Earned} = \frac{\text{EBIT or EBITDA}}{\text{Interest Charges}}$$

- Financial ratio
- Financial leverage
- EBIT
- EBITDA
- Debt service coverage ratio

Interest Charges = Traditionally 'charges' refers to interest expense found on the income statement.

Times Interest Earned or Interest Coverage is a great tool when measuring a company's ability to meet its debt obligations.

a. Earnings per share
c. Assets turnover
b. Interest coverage ratio
d. Information ratio

30. _____ is the difference between price and the costs of bringing to market whatever it is that is accounted as an enterprise (whether by harvest, extraction, manufacture, or purchase) in terms of the component costs of delivered goods and/or services and any operating or other expenses.

A key difficulty in measuring profit is in defining costs. Pure economic monetary profits can be zero or negative even in competitive equilibrium when accounted monetized costs exceed monetized price.

a. Economic profit
c. Accounting profit
b. AAB
d. A Random Walk Down Wall Street

31. _____, Net Margin, Net _____ or Net Profit Ratio all refer to a measure of profitability. It is calculated using a formula and written as a percentage or a number.

$$\text{Net profit margin} = \frac{\text{Net profit after taxes}}{\text{Net Sales}}$$

The _____ is mostly used for internal comparison.

a. Net profit margin
c. 4-4-5 Calendar

b. Profit margin
d. Profit maximization

32. In business, operating margin, Operating Income Margin, Operating profit margin or _____ is the ratio of operating income (operating profit in the UK) divided by net sales, usually presented in percent.

$$\text{Operating margin} = \left(\frac{\text{Operating income}}{\text{Revenue}}\right)$$

(Relevant figures in italics)

$$\text{Operating margin} = \left(\frac{6,318}{24,088}\right) = \underline{\underline{26.23\%}}$$

It is a measurement of what proportion of a company's revenue is left over, before taxes and other indirect costs (such as rent, bonus, interest etc.), after paying for variable costs of production as wages, raw materials, etc. A good operating margin is needed for a company to be able to pay for its fixed costs, such as interest on debt.

a. Current ratio
c. Return on assets

b. Return on equity
d. Return on sales

33. In finance, _____ is the process of estimating the potential market value of a financial asset or liability. they can be done on assets (for example, investments in marketable securities such as stocks, options, business enterprises, or intangible assets such as patents and trademarks) or on liabilities (e.g., Bonds issued by a company.) _____s are required in many contexts including investment analysis, capital budgeting, merger and acquisition transactions, financial reporting, taxable events to determine the proper tax liability, and in litigation.

a. Margin
c. Share

b. Procter ' Gamble
d. Valuation

34. _____ is the amount by which a reference rate is multiplied to determine the floating interest rate payable by an inverse floater. Some debt instruments leverage the particular effects of interest rate changes, most commonly in inverse floaters.

As an example, an inverse floater with a multiple may pay interest at the rate of 22 percent minus the product of 2 times the 1-month London Interbank Offered Rate (LIBOR.)

Chapter 19. Financial Statement Analysis

a. Systematic risk
c. Gross spread

b. Trade date
d. Coupon leverage

35. In finance, a _____ is collateral that the holder of a position in securities, options, or futures contracts has to deposit to cover the credit risk of his counterparty (most often his broker.) This risk can arise if the holder has done any of the following:

- borrowed cash from the counterparty to buy securities or options,
- sold securities or options short, or
- entered into a futures contract.

The collateral can be in the form of cash or securities, and it is deposited in a _____ account. On U.S. futures exchanges, '_____' was formally called performance bond.

_____ buying is buying securities with cash borrowed from a broker, using other securities as collateral.

a. Margin
c. Credit

b. Procter ' Gamble
d. Share

36. In finance, the Acid-test or _____ or liquid ratio measures the ability of a company to use its near cash or quick assets to immediately extinguish or retire its current liabilities. Quick assets include those current assets that presumably can be quickly converted to cash at close to their book values.

Generally, the acid test ratio should be 1:1 or better, however this varies widely by industry.

a. Net assets
c. Financial ratio

b. P/E ratio
d. Quick ratio

37. The _____ is a financial ratio that measures whether or not a firm has enough resources to pay its debts over the next 12 months. It compares a firm's current assets to its current liabilities. It is expressed as follows:

$$\text{Current ratio} = \frac{\text{Current Assets}}{\text{Current Liabilities}}$$

For example, if WXY Company's current assets are $50,000,000 and its current liabilities are $40,000,000, then its _____ would be $50,000,000 divided by $40,000,000, which equals 1.25.

a. Sustainable growth rate
c. PEG ratio

b. Debt service coverage ratio
d. Current ratio

Chapter 19. Financial Statement Analysis

38. _____ is a list for goods and materials held available in stock by a business. It is also used for a list of the contents of a household and for a list for testamentary purposes of the possessions of someone who has died. In accounting _____ is considered an asset.

 a. ABN Amro
 b. A Random Walk Down Wall Street
 c. AAB
 d. Inventory

39. The _____ is an equation that equals the cost of goods sold divided by the average inventory. Average inventory equals beginning inventory plus ending inventory divided by 2.

The formula for _____:

$$\text{Inventory Turnover} = \frac{\text{Cost of Goods Sold}}{\text{Average Inventory}}$$

The formula for average inventory:

$$\text{Average Inventory} = \frac{\text{Beginning inventory} + \text{Ending inventory}}{2}$$

A low turnover rate may point to overstocking, obsolescence, or deficiencies in the product line or marketing effort.

 a. Earnings yield
 b. Operating leverage
 c. Information ratio
 d. Inventory turnover

40. _____ is a measure of the ability of a debtor to pay their debts as and when they fall due. It is usually expressed as a ratio or a percentage of current liabilities.

For a corporation with a published balance sheet there are various ratios used to calculate a measure of liquidity.

 a. Operating profit margin
 b. Invested capital
 c. Operating leverage
 d. Accounting liquidity

41. The _____ is a bank regulation that sets the minimum reserves each bank must hold to customer deposits and notes. These reserves are designed to satisfy withdrawal demands, and would normally be in the form of fiat currency stored in a bank vault (vault cash), or with a central bank.

The reserve ratio is sometimes used as a tool in the monetary policy, influencing the country's economy, borrowing, and interest rates.

 a. Reserve requirement
 b. Variable rate mortgage
 c. Wall Street Journal prime rate
 d. Prime rate

Chapter 19. Financial Statement Analysis

42. _____ is an economic concept with commonplace familiarity. It is the price that a good or service is offered at, or will fetch, in the marketplace. It is of interest mainly in the study of microeconomics.
   a. Central Securities Depository
   b. Delta hedging
   c. Convertible arbitrage
   d. Market price

43. The _____ is a financial ratio used to compare a company's book value to its current market price. Book value is an accounting term denoting the portion of the company held by the shareholders; in other words, the company's total tangible assets less its total liabilities. The calculation can be performed in two ways, but the result should be the same each way. In the first way, the company's market capitalization can be divided by the company's total book value from its balance sheet. The second way, using per-share values, is to divide the company's current share price by the book value per share (i.e. its book value divided by the number of outstanding shares).
   a. Stock repurchase
   b. Whisper numbers
   c. Price-to-book ratio
   d. Stop order

44. The _____ of a stock is a measure of the price paid for a share relative to the annual income or profit earned by the firm per share. It is a financial ratio used for valuation: a higher _____ means that investors are paying more for each unit of income, so the stock is more expensive compared to one with lower _____.

The _____ has units of years, which can be interpreted as 'number of years of earnings to pay back purchase price'.

   a. Quick ratio
   b. Sustainable growth rate
   c. Return of capital
   d. P/E ratio

45. _____ is the quotient of earnings per share divided by the share price. It is the reciprocal of the P/E ratio--the E/P or the EPS.

The _____ is quoted as a percentage, allowing an easy comparison to going bond rates.

   a. Asset turnover
   b. Assets turnover
   c. Average accounting return
   d. Earnings yield

46. In finance, the term _____ describes the amount in cash that returns to the owners of a security. Normally it does not include the price variations, at the difference of the total return. _____ applies to various stated rates of return on stocks (common and preferred, and convertible), fixed income instruments (bonds, notes, bills, strips, zero coupon), and some other investment type insurance products (e.g. annuities.)
   a. Yield to maturity
   b. Yield
   c. 4-4-5 Calendar
   d. Macaulay duration

47. In corporate finance, _____ is an estimate of true economic profit after making corrective adjustments to GAAP accounting, including deducting the opportunity cost of equity capital. GAAP is estimated to ignore US$300 billion in shareholder opportunity costs. _____ can be measured as Net Operating Profit After Taxes(or NOPAT) less the money cost of capital.
   a. AAB
   b. ABN Amro
   c. A Random Walk Down Wall Street
   d. Economic value added

Chapter 19. Financial Statement Analysis

48. _____ (or PwC) is one of the world's largest professional services firms. It was formed in 1998 from a merger between Price Waterhouse and Coopers ' Lybrand, both formed in London.

_____ earned aggregated worldwide revenues of $28 billion for fiscal 2008, and employed over 146,000 people in 150 countries.

a. Lending Club
c. Texas ratio
b. PricewaterhouseCoopers
d. Credit karma

49. _____ is the discipline of identifying, monitoring and limiting risks. In some cases the acceptable risk may be near zero. Risks can come from accidents, natural causes and disasters as well as deliberate attacks from an adversary.

a. Penny stock
c. FIFO
b. 4-4-5 Calendar
d. Risk Management

50. _____ refers to the additional value of a commodity over the cost of commodities used to produce it from the previous stage of production. An example is the price of gasoline at the pump over the price of the oil in it. In national accounts used in macroeconomics, it refers to the contribution of the factors of production, i.e., land, labor, and capital goods, to raising the value of a product and corresponds to the incomes received by the owners of these factors.

a. Supply shock
c. Demand shock
b. Deregulation
d. Value added

51. _____ is a rent received on a regular basis, with little effort required to maintain it. It is advocated by some authors, especially by Robert Kiyosaki.

Some examples of _____ are:

- Repeated regular income, earned by a sales person, generated from the payment of a product or service that must be renewed on a regular basis, in order to continue receiving its benefits - also called residual income.
- Rental from property;
- Royalties from publishing a book or from licensing a patent or other form of intellectual property;
- Earnings from internet advertisement on your websites;
- Earnings from a business that does not require direct involvement from the owner or merchant;
- Dividend and interest income from owning securities, such as stocks and bonds, are usually referred to as portfolio income, which can be considered a form of _____;
- Pensions.

_____ is usually taxable. The American Internal Revenue Service defines _____ as 'any activity...

a. Passive income
c. 4-4-5 Calendar
b. Horizontal merger
d. Fixed exchange rate system

Chapter 19. Financial Statement Analysis

52. _____ or First In, First Out, is an abstraction in ways of organizing and manipulation of data relative to time and prioritization. This expression describes the principle of a queue processing technique or servicing conflicting demands by ordering process by first-come, first-served (FCFS) behaviour: what comes in first is handled first, what comes in next waits until the first is finished, etc.

Thus it is analogous to the behaviour of persons queueing (or 'standing in line', in common American parlance), where the persons leave the queue in the order they arrive, or waiting one's turn at a traffic control signal.

a. Risk management
b. 4-4-5 Calendar
c. Penny stock
d. FIFO

53. _____ is the standard framework of guidelines for financial accounting used in the United States of America. It includes the standards, conventions, and rules accountants follow in recording and summarizing transactions, and in the preparation of financial statements. _____ are now issued by the Financial Accounting Standards Board (FASB).

a. Net income
b. Generally accepted accounting principles
c. Revenue
d. Depreciation

54. In economics, _____ is a rise in the general level of prices of goods and services in an economy over a period of time. The term '_____' once referred to increases in the money supply (monetary _____); however, economic debates about the relationship between money supply and price levels have led to its primary use today in describing price _____. _____ can also be described as a decline in the real value of money--a loss of purchasing power in the medium of exchange which is also the monetary unit of account.

a. A Random Walk Down Wall Street
b. AAB
c. ABN Amro
d. Inflation

55. An _____ allows a company to provide a monetary value for items that make up their inventory. Inventories are usually the largest current asset of a business, and proper measurement of them is necessary to assure accurate financial statements. If inventory is not properly measured, expenses and revenues cannot be properly matched and a company could make poor business decisions.

a. AAB
b. ABN Amro
c. A Random Walk Down Wall Street
d. Inventory valuation

56. _____ is an acronym which stands for last in, first out. In computer science and queueing theory this refers to the way items stored in some types of data structures are processed. By definition, in a _____ structured linear list, elements can be added or taken off from only one end, called the 'top'.

a. 4-4-5 Calendar
b. 529 plan
c. LIFO
d. 7-Eleven

57. Gross domestic product (GDP) is defined as the 'value of all final goods and services produced in a country in one year'. On the other hand, _____ is defined as the 'value of all (final) goods and services produced in a country in one year, plus income earned by its citizens abroad, minus income earned by foreigners in the country'. The key difference between the two is that GDP is the total output of a region, eg.

a. Gross national product
b. TED spread
c. 4-4-5 Calendar
d. Purchasing power parity

58. _____ means regulating, adapting or settling in a variety of contexts:

Chapter 19. Financial Statement Analysis

In commercial law, _____ means the settlement of a loss incurred on insured goods. The calculation of the amounts of compensation to be paid by or to the several interests is a complicated matter. It involves much detail and arithmetic, and requires a full and accurate knowledge of the principles of the subject.

a. Equity method
b. Intelligent investor
c. Adjustment
d. Asset recovery

59. The role of the _____ is to issue accounting standards in the United Kingdom. It is recognised for that purpose under the Companies Act 1985. It took over the task of setting accounting standards from the Accounting Standards Committee (ASC) in 1990.

a. A Random Walk Down Wall Street
b. AAB
c. ABN Amro
d. Accounting Standards Board

60. _____ is the field of accountancy concerned with the preparation of financial statements for decision makers, such as stockholders, suppliers, banks, employees, government agencies, owners, and other stakeholders. The fundamental need for _____ is to reduce principal-agent problem by measuring and monitoring agents' performance and reporting the results to interested users.

_____ is used to prepare accounting information for people outside the organization or not involved in the day to day running of the company.

a. 7-Eleven
b. 529 plan
c. 4-4-5 Calendar
d. Financial Accounting

61. The _____ is a private, not-for-profit organization whose primary purpose is to develop generally accepted accounting principles (GAAP) within the United States in the public's interest. The Securities and Exchange Commission (SEC) designated the _____ as the organization responsible for setting accounting standards for public companies in the U.S. It was created in 1973, replacing the Accounting Principles Board and the Committee on Accounting Procedure of the American Institute of Certified Public Accountants. The _____'s mission is 'to establish and improve standards of financial accounting and reporting for the guidance and education of the public, including issuers, auditors, and users of financial information.'

The _____ is not a governmental body.

a. Federal Deposit Insurance Corporation
b. KPMG
c. World Congress of Accountants
d. Financial Accounting Standards Board

62. _____ is the income of individuals or nations after adjusting for inflation. It is calculated by subtracting inflation from the nominal income. Real variables, such as _____, real GDP, and real interest rate are variables that are measured in physical units, while nominal variables such as nominal income, nominal GDP, and nominal interest rate are measured in monetary units.

a. 4-4-5 Calendar
b. 529 plan
c. 7-Eleven
d. Real income

Chapter 19. Financial Statement Analysis

63. _____, in accounting, refers to the overall reasonableness of reported earnings. It is an assessment criterion for how 'repeatable, controllable and bankable' a firm's earnings are, amongst other factors. It recognizes the fact that the economic impact of a given transaction will vary across firms as a function of their fundamental business characteristics, and has variously been defined as the degree to which earnings reflect underlying economic effects, are better estimates of cash flows, are conservative, or are predictable.

    a. Installment Sales Method
    b. Unified Ledger Accounting
    c. Earnings quality
    d. Imprest system

64. _____ is the business practice where a company, or a sales force within a company, inflates its sales figures by forcing more products through a distribution channel than the channel is capable of selling to the world at large. Also known as 'trade loading', this can be the result of a company attempting to inflate its sales figures. Alternatively, it can be a consequence of a poorly managed sales force attempting to meet short term objectives and quotas in a way that is detrimental to the company in the long term.

    a. Peer group analysis
    b. Systematic risk
    c. False billing
    d. Channel stuffing

65. _____ are liabilities that may or may not be incurred by an entity depending on the outcome of a future event such as a court case. These liabilities are recorded in a company's accounts and shown in the balance sheet when both probable and reasonably estimable. A footnote to the balance sheet describes the nature and extent of the _____.

    a. 4-4-5 Calendar
    b. 529 plan
    c. Due-on-sale clause
    d. Contingent liabilities

66. In business, _____ is income that a company receives from its normal business activities, usually from the sale of goods and services to customers. Some companies also receive _____ from interest, dividends or royalties paid to them by other companies. _____ may refer to business income in general, or it may refer to the amount, in a monetary unit, received during a period of time, as in 'Last year, Company X had _____ of $32 million.'

In many countries, including the UK, _____ is referred to as turnover.

    a. Bottom line
    b. Matching principle
    c. Revenue
    d. Furniture, Fixtures and Equipment

67. The _____ principle is a cornerstone of accrual accounting together with matching principle. They both determine the accounting period, in which revenues and expenses are recognized. According to the principle, revenues are recognized when they are (1) realized or realizable, and are (2) earned (usually when goods are transferred or services rendered), no matter when cash is received.

    a. Regulation FD
    b. Tail risk
    c. Commodity Pool Operator
    d. Revenue recognition

68. In accounting and finance, _____ is the portion of receivables that can no longer be collected, typically from accounts receivable or loans. _____ in accounting is considered an expense.

There are two methods to account for _____:

1. Direct write off method (Non - GAAP)

A receivable which is not considered collectible is charged directly to the income statement.

1. Allowance method (GAAP)

An estimate is made at the end of each fiscal year of the amount of _____. This is then accumulated in a provision which is then used to reduce specific receivable accounts as and when necessary.

- a. 529 plan
- b. 4-4-5 Calendar
- c. Tax expense
- d. Bad debt

69. _____ is that which is owed; usually referencing assets owed, but the term can cover other obligations. In the case of assets, _____ is a means of using future purchasing power in the present before a summation has been earned. Some companies and corporations use _____ as a part of their overall corporate finance strategy.
- a. Credit cycle
- b. Cross-collateralization
- c. Partial Payment
- d. Debt

70. In the most general sense, a _____ is anything that is a hindrance, or puts individuals at a disadvantage.

Before we discuss the financial terms, we should note that a _____ can also have a much more important slang meaning.

This is best described in an example.

- a. Covenant
- b. McFadden Act
- c. Liability
- d. Limited liability

71. An _____ is a contract written by a seller that conveys to the buyer the right -- but not the obligation -- to buy (in the case of a call _____) or to sell (in the case of a put _____) a particular asset, such as a piece of property such as, among others, a futures contract. In return for granting the _____, the seller collects a payment (the premium) from the buyer.

For example, buying a call _____ provides the right to buy a specified quantity of a security at a set strike price at some time on or before expiration, while buying a put _____ provides the right to sell.

- a. Amortization
- b. Annuity
- c. Option
- d. AT'T Mobility LLC

72. _____ are defined as identifiable non-monetary assets that cannot be seen, touched or physically measured, which are created through time and/or effort and that are identifiable as a separate asset. There are two primary forms of intangibles - legal intangibles (such as trade secrets (e.g., customer lists), copyrights, patents, trademarks, and goodwill) and competitive intangibles (such as knowledge activities (know-how, knowledge), collaboration activities, leverage activities, and structural activities.) Legal intangibles generate legal property rights defensible in a court of law.
- a. Intangible assets
- b. A Random Walk Down Wall Street
- c. AAB
- d. ABN Amro

Chapter 19. Financial Statement Analysis

73. _____ of a business involves analyzing its financial statements and health, its management and competitive advantages, and its competitors and markets. The term is used to distinguish such analysis from other types of investment analysis, such as quantitative analysis and technical analysis.

_____ is performed on historical and present data, but with the goal of making financial forecasts.

a. Stock valuation
b. Fundamental analysis
c. Growth stocks
d. 4-4-5 Calendar

74. A _____ is a fungible, negotiable instrument representing financial value. They are broadly categorized into debt securities (such as banknotes, bonds and debentures), and equity securities; e.g., common stocks. The company or other entity issuing the _____ is called the issuer.

a. Securities lending
b. Book entry
c. Tracking stock
d. Security

75. The U.S. _____ is an independent agency of the United States government which holds primary responsibility for enforcing the federal securities laws and regulating the securities industry, the nation's stock and options exchanges, and other electronic securities markets. The SEC was created by section 4 of the SEC of 1934 (now codified as 15 U.S.C. Â§ 78d and commonly referred to as the 1934 Act.)

a. 7-Eleven
b. 529 plan
c. 4-4-5 Calendar
d. Securities and Exchange Commission

76. _____, authored by professors Benjamin Graham and David Dodd of Columbia Business School, laid the intellectual foundation for what would later be called value investing. The work was first published in 1934, following unprecedented losses on Wall Street. In summing up lessons learned, Graham and Dodd chided Wall Street for its myopic focus on a company's reported earnings per share, and were particularly harsh on the favored 'earnings trends.' They encouraged investors to take an entirely different approach by gauging the rough value of the operating business that lay behind the security.

a. 4-4-5 Calendar
b. Growth stocks
c. Stock valuation
d. Security Analysis

77. _____ is an investment paradigm that derives from the ideas on investment and speculation that Ben Graham ' David Dodd began teaching at Columbia Business School in 1928 and subsequently developed in their 1934 text Security Analysis. Although _____ has taken many forms since its inception, it generally involves buying securities whose shares appear underpriced by some form(s) of fundamental analysis. As examples, such securities may be stock in public companies that trade at discounts to book value or tangible book value, have high dividend yields, have low price-to-earning multiples or have low price-to-book ratios.

a. 4-4-5 Calendar
b. Value investing
c. 529 plan
d. Quality investing

Chapter 20. Options Markets: Introduction

1. A _____ is a financial contract whose value is derived from the value of something else (known as the underlying.) The underlying on which a _____ is based can be an asset, weather conditions bonds or other forms of credit.
    a. 7-Eleven
    b. 4-4-5 Calendar
    c. Derivative
    d. 529 plan

2. An _____ is a contract written by a seller that conveys to the buyer the right -- but not the obligation -- to buy (in the case of a call _____) or to sell (in the case of a put _____) a particular asset, such as a piece of property such as, among others, a futures contract. In return for granting the _____, the seller collects a payment (the premium) from the buyer.

    For example, buying a call _____ provides the right to buy a specified quantity of a security at a set strike price at some time on or before expiration, while buying a put _____ provides the right to sell.

    a. Amortization
    b. AT'T Mobility LLC
    c. Option
    d. Annuity

3. A _____ is a fungible, negotiable instrument representing financial value. They are broadly categorized into debt securities (such as banknotes, bonds and debentures), and equity securities; e.g., common stocks. The company or other entity issuing the _____ is called the issuer.
    a. Security
    b. Securities lending
    c. Book entry
    d. Tracking stock

4. A _____ is a financial contract between two parties, the buyer and the seller of this type of option. Often it is simply labeled a 'call'. The buyer of the option has the right, but not the obligation to buy an agreed quantity of a particular commodity or financial instrument (the underlying instrument) from the seller of the option at a certain time (the expiration date) for a certain price (the strike price.)
    a. Bear call spread
    b. Bull spread
    c. Call option
    d. Bear spread

5. In options, the _____ is a key variable in a derivatives contract between two parties. Where the contract requires delivery of the underlying instrument, the trade will be at the _____, regardless of the spot price (market price) of the underlying instrument at that time.

    Definition - The fixed price at which the owner of an option can purchase, in the case of a call in the case of a put, the underlying security or commodity.

    a. Moneyness
    b. Naked put
    c. Strike price
    d. Swaption

6. In business and finance accounting, _____ is equal to the gross profit minus overheads minus interest payable plus/minus one off items for a given time period (usually: accounting period.)

    A common synonym for '_____' when discussing financial statements (which include a balance sheet and an income statement) is the bottom line. This term results from the traditional appearance of an income statement which shows all allocated revenues and expenses over a specified time period with the resulting summation on the bottom line of the report.

Chapter 20. Options Markets: Introduction

a. Deferred
b. Salvage value
c. Gross sales
d. Net profit

7. In finance, a _____ is a position established in one market in an attempt to offset exposure to the price risk of an equal but opposite obligation or position in another market -- usually, but not always, in the context of one's commercial activity. Hedging is a strategy designed to minimize exposure to such business risks as a sharp contraction in demand for one's inventory, while still allowing the business to profit from producing and maintaining that inventory. A typical hedger might be a farmer with 2000 acres of unharvested wheat in the ground, who would rather tend his crop without the distraction of uncertain prices.

a. 4-4-5 Calendar
b. 7-Eleven
c. 529 plan
d. Hedge

8. _____ is the difference between price and the costs of bringing to market whatever it is that is accounted as an enterprise (whether by harvest, extraction, manufacture, or purchase) in terms of the component costs of delivered goods and/or services and any operating or other expenses.

A key difficulty in measuring profit is in defining costs. Pure economic monetary profits can be zero or negative even in competitive equilibrium when accounted monetized costs exceed monetized price.

a. AAB
b. Accounting profit
c. Economic profit
d. A Random Walk Down Wall Street

9. The term _____ refers to three closely related concepts:

- The _____ model is a mathematical model of the market for an equity, in which the equity's price is a stochastic process.
- The _____ PDE is a partial differential equation which (in the model) must be satisfied by the price of a derivative on the equity.
- The _____ formula is the result obtained by solving the _____ PDE for a European call option.

Fischer Black and Myron Scholes first articulated the _____ formula in their 1973 paper, 'The Pricing of Options and Corporate Liabilities.' The foundation for their research relied on work developed by scholars such as Jack L. Treynor, Paul Samuelson, A. James Boness, Sheen T. Kassouf, and Edward O. Thorp. The fundamental insight of _____ is that the option is implicitly priced if the stock is traded.

Robert C. Merton was the first to publish a paper expanding the mathematical understanding of the options pricing model and coined the term '_____' options pricing model.

a. Black-Scholes
b. Perpetuity
c. Stochastic volatility
d. Modified Internal Rate of Return

10. A _____ is a financial contract between two parties, the seller (writer) and the buyer of the option. The put allows its buyer the right but not the obligation to sell a commodity or financial instrument (the underlying instrument) to the writer (seller) of the option at a certain time for a certain price (the strike price.) The writer (seller) has the obligation to purchase the underlying asset at that strike price, if the buyer exercises the option.

a. Bear call spread
b. Bear spread
c. Debit spread
d. Put option

11. _____ is a fee paid on borrowed assets. It is the price paid for the use of borrowed money, or, money earned by deposited funds. Assets that are sometimes lent with _____ include money, shares, consumer goods through hire purchase, major assets such as aircraft, and even entire factories in finance lease arrangements.

a. A Random Walk Down Wall Street
b. Interest
c. Insolvency
d. AAB

12. An _____ is the price a borrower pays for the use of money they do not own, and the return a lender receives for deferring the use of funds, by lending it to the borrower. _____s are normally expressed as a percentage rate over the period of one year.

_____s targets are also a vital tool of monetary policy and are used to control variables like investment, inflation, and unemployment.

a. ABN Amro
b. A Random Walk Down Wall Street
c. AAB
d. Interest rate

13. _____ is a derivative financial instrument.

The global market for exchange-traded _____s is notionally valued by the Bank for International Settlements at $3,075,400 million in 2005.

a. Eurobond
b. Economic entity
c. Education production function
d. Interest rate option

14. In finance, _____ is the process of estimating the potential market value of a financial asset or liability. they can be done on assets (for example, investments in marketable securities such as stocks, options, business enterprises, or intangible assets such as patents and trademarks) or on liabilities (e.g., Bonds issued by a company.) _____s are required in many contexts including investment analysis, capital budgeting, merger and acquisition transactions, financial reporting, taxable events to determine the proper tax liability, and in litigation.

a. Procter ' Gamble
b. Margin
c. Share
d. Valuation

15. A _____ is a payment made by a corporation to its shareholder members. When a corporation earns a profit or surplus, that money can be put to two uses: it can either be re-invested in the business (called retained earnings), or it can be paid to the shareholders as a _____. Many corporations retain a portion of their earnings and pay the remainder as a _____.

a. Dividend yield
b. Dividend puzzle
c. Special dividend
d. Dividend

16. In economic models, the _____ time frame assumes no fixed factors of production. Firms can enter or leave the marketplace, and the cost (and availability) of land, labor, raw materials, and capital goods can be assumed to vary. In contrast, in the short-run time frame, certain factors are assumed to be fixed, because there is not sufficient time for them to change.

Chapter 20. Options Markets: Introduction

a. 529 plan
b. 4-4-5 Calendar
c. Short-run
d. Long-run

17. _____ are those dividends paid out in form of additional stock shares of the issuing corporation or other corporation They are usually issued in proportion to shares owned (for example for every 100 shares of stock owned, 5% stock dividend will yield 5 extra shares). If this payment involves the issue of new shares, this is very similar to a stock split in that it increases the total number of shares while lowering the price of each share and does not change the market capitalization or the total value of the shares held

a. Time-based currency
b. The Hong Kong Securities Institute
c. Database auditing
d. Stock or scrip dividends

18. A _____ or stock divide increases or decreases the number of shares in a public company. The price is adjusted such that the before and after market capitalization of the company remains the same and dilution does not occur. Options and warrants are included.

a. Contract for difference
b. Stop order
c. Stock split
d. Stop price

19. _____ means regulating, adapting or settling in a variety of contexts:

In commercial law, _____ means the settlement of a loss incurred on insured goods. The calculation of the amounts of compensation to be paid by or to the several interests is a complicated matter. It involves much detail and arithmetic, and requires a full and accurate knowledge of the principles of the subject.

a. Asset recovery
b. Intelligent investor
c. Equity method
d. Adjustment

20. A _____ is an exchange of promises between two or more parties to do an act which is enforceable in a court of law. It is where an unqualified offer meets a qualified acceptance and the parties reach Consensus ad Idem. The parties must have the necessary capacity to _____ and the _____ must not be either trifling, indeterminate, impossible or illegal.

a. 529 plan
b. 4-4-5 Calendar
c. 7-Eleven
d. Contract

21. In banking and finance, _____ denotes all activities from the time a commitment is made for a transaction until it is settled. _____ is necessary because the speed of trades is much faster than the cycle time for completing the underlying transaction.

In its widest sense _____ involves the management of post-trading, pre-settlement credit exposures, to ensure that trades are settled in accordance with market rules, even if a buyer or seller should become insolvent prior to settlement.

a. Share
b. Clearing house
c. Procter ' Gamble
d. Clearing

22. A _____ is a financial services company that provides clearing and settlement services for financial transactions, usually on a futures exchange, and often acts as central counterparty (the payor actually pays the _____, which then pays the payee). A _____ may also offer novation, the substitution of a new contract or debt for an old, or other credit enhancement services to its members.

The term is also used for banks like Suffolk Bank that acted as a restraint on the over-issuance of private bank notes.

    a. Valuation   b. Warrant
    c. Clearing house   d. Bucket shop

23. The institution most often referenced by the word '_____' is a public or publicly traded _____, the shares of which are traded on a public stock exchange (e.g., the New York Stock Exchange or Nasdaq in the United States) where shares of stock of _____s are bought and sold by and to the general public. Most of the largest businesses in the world are publicly traded _____s. However, the majority of _____s are said to be closely held, privately held or close _____s, meaning that no ready market exists for the trading of shares.

    a. Protect   b. Corporation
    c. Depository Trust Company   d. Federal Home Loan Mortgage Corporation

24. In finance, a _____ is collateral that the holder of a position in securities, options, or futures contracts has to deposit to cover the credit risk of his counterparty (most often his broker.) This risk can arise if the holder has done any of the following:

- borrowed cash from the counterparty to buy securities or options,
- sold securities or options short, or
- entered into a futures contract.

The collateral can be in the form of cash or securities, and it is deposited in a _____ account. On U.S. futures exchanges, '_____' was formally called performance bond.

_____ buying is buying securities with cash borrowed from a broker, using other securities as collateral.

    a. Share   b. Credit
    c. Procter ' Gamble   d. Margin

25. In finance, a _____ is a standardized contract, to buy or sell a specified commodity of standardized quality at a certain date in the future, at a market determined price (the futures price.)

The price is determined by the instantaneous equilibrium between the forces of supply and demand among competing buy and sell orders on the exchange at the time of the purchase or sale of the contract.

In many cases, the items may be such non-traditional 'commodities' as foreign currencies, commercial or government paper [e.g., bonds], or 'baskets' of corporate equity ['stock indices'] or other financial instruments.

a. Heston model
b. Repurchase agreement
c. Financial future
d. Futures contract

26. The _____ (or Euribor) is a daily reference rate based on the averaged interest rates at which banks offer to lend unsecured funds to other banks in the euro wholesale money market (or interbank market.)

Euribor rates are used as a reference rate for euro-denominated forward rate agreements, short term interest rate futures contracts and interest rate swaps, in very much the same way as LIBOR rates are commonly used for Sterling and US dollar-denominated instruments. They thus provide the basis for some of the world's most liquid and active interest rate markets.

a. A Random Walk Down Wall Street
b. Exchange Rate Mechanism
c. European Monetary System
d. Euro Interbank Offered Rate

27. A put option is a right to sell a particular stock to the writer of the option at a certain price (the strike price) on or by the expiration date. If the contract writer does not have an offsetting short position in the stock that the contract is written on, the put writer is considered uncovered for the loss incurred if the current price of the stock is below the contract price. If the writer has enough cash in his brokerage account to pay for the stock at the strike price then, although he is still considered to be in a _____ position, he may also refer more specifically to his position as a cash-covered put.

a. Debit spread
b. Moneyness
c. Bear put spread
d. Naked put

28. A _____ is a transaction in which the seller of call options already owns the corresponding amount of the underlying instrument, such as shares of a stock or other securities. These owned shares provide the 'cover' as they can be handed over to the buyer of the options when he decides to exercise them, instead of having to buy the optioned shares at unfavorable market prices in the case of 'uncovered' or short call. Thus, the _____ limits the (potentially unlimited) loss that results from a short call when the price of the underlying stock moves above the strike price of the option.

a. 4-4-5 Calendar
b. Covered call
c. 7-Eleven
d. 529 plan

29. _____ is a method of hedging a portfolio of stocks against the market risk by short selling stock index futures.

This hedging technique is frequently used by institutional investors when the market direction is uncertain or volatile. Short selling index futures can offset any downturns, but it also hinders any gains.

a. Portfolio insurance
b. PAUG
c. Delivery month
d. Freight derivative

30. _____ is the discipline of identifying, monitoring and limiting risks. In some cases the acceptable risk may be near zero. Risks can come from accidents, natural causes and disasters as well as deliberate attacks from an adversary.

a. 4-4-5 Calendar
b. FIFO
c. Penny stock
d. Risk management

31. _____ is a term used to describe any option trading strategy that involves selling options. An option writer sells options to potentially profit from the decline of extrinsic value on options, sometimes referred to as time value.

_____ strategies include covered calls, naked calls and naked puts, bear call spreads, bull put spreads, ratio credit spreads, short strangles and short straddles.

a. A Random Walk Down Wall Street
b. AAB
c. ABN Amro
d. Options writing

32. In finance, a _____ is an investment strategy involving the purchase or sale of particular option derivatives that allows the holder to profit based on how much the price of the underlying security moves, regardless of the direction of price movement. The purchase of particular option derivatives is known as a long _____, while the sale of the option derivatives is known as a short _____.

An option payoff diagram for a long _____ position

A long _____ involves going long, i.e., purchasing, both a call option and a put option on some stock, interest rate, index or other underlying.

a. Bear call spread
b. Moneyness
c. Put option
d. Straddle

33. In financial mathematics, _____ defines a relationship between the price of a call option and a put option--both with the identical strike price and expiry. To derive the _____ relationship, the assumption is that the options are not exercised before expiration day, which necessarily applies to European options. _____ can be derived in a manner that is largely model independent.

a. Hull-White model
b. Cox-Ingersoll-Ross model
c. Rendleman-Bartter model
d. Put-call parity

34. _____ is a type of bond that allows the issuer of the bond to retain the privilege of redeeming the bond at some point before the bond reaches the date of maturity. In other words, on the call dates, the issuer has the right, but not the obligation, to buy back the bonds from the bond holders at the call price. Technically speaking, the bonds are not really bought and held by the issuer but cancelled immediately.

a. Coupon rate
b. Gilts
c. Bond fund
d. Callable bond

35. In finance, a _____ is a type of bond that can be converted into shares of stock in the issuing company, usually at some pre-announced ratio. It is a hybrid security with debt- and equity-like features. Although it typically has a low coupon rate, the holder is compensated with the ability to convert the bond to common stock, usually at a substantial discount to the stock's market value.

a. Corporate bond
b. Convertible bond
c. Bond fund
d. Gilts

36. _____ refers to any type of investment that yields a regular (or fixed) return.

For example, if you lend money to a borrower and the borrower has to pay interest once a month, you have been issued a fixed-income security. When a company does this, it is often called a bond or corporate bank debt (although preferred stock is also sometimes considered to be _____).

a. 4-4-5 Calendar
c. 529 plan

b. Bond market
d. Fixed income

37. In finance, the yield curve is the relation between the interest rate (or cost of borrowing) and the time to maturity of the debt for a given borrower in a given currency. For example, the current U.S. dollar interest rates paid on U.S. Treasury securities for various maturities are closely watched by many traders, and are commonly plotted on a graph such as the one on the right which is informally called 'the yield curve.' More formal mathematical descriptions of this relation are often called the _____.

The yield of a debt instrument is the annualized percentage increase in the value of the investment.

a. 7-Eleven
c. 529 plan

b. 4-4-5 Calendar
d. Term structure of interest rates

38. In finance, the term _____ describes the amount in cash that returns to the owners of a security. Normally it does not include the price variations, at the difference of the total return. _____ applies to various stated rates of return on stocks (common and preferred, and convertible), fixed income instruments (bonds, notes, bills, strips, zero coupon), and some other investment type insurance products (e.g. annuities.)

a. Macaulay duration
c. 4-4-5 Calendar

b. Yield to maturity
d. Yield

39. In finance, the _____ is the relation between the interest rate (or cost of borrowing) and the time to maturity of the debt for a given borrower in a given currency. For example, the current U.S. dollar interest rates paid on U.S. Treasury securities for various maturities are closely watched by many traders, and are commonly plotted on a graph such as the one on the right which is informally called 'the _____.' More formal mathematical descriptions of this relation are often called the term structure of interest rates.

The yield of a debt instrument is the annualized percentage increase in the value of the investment.

a. 7-Eleven
c. 4-4-5 Calendar

b. 529 plan
d. Yield curve

40. In finance, _____ is the interest that has accumulated since the principal investment, or since the previous interest payment if there has been one already. For a financial instrument such as a bond, interest is calculated and paid in set intervals.

The primary formula for calculating the interest accrued in a given period is:

$$I_A = T \times P \times R$$

where I_A is the _____, T is the fraction of the year, P is the principal, and R is the annualized interest rate.

a. AAB
c. ABN Amro

b. A Random Walk Down Wall Street
d. Accrued interest

Chapter 20. Options Markets: Introduction

41. In finance, a _____ is a debt security, in which the authorized issuer owes the holders a debt and, depending on the terms of the _____, is obliged to pay interest (the coupon) and/or to repay the principal at a later date, termed maturity.

Thus a _____ is a loan: the issuer is the borrower, the _____ holder is the lender, and the coupon is the interest. _____s provide the borrower with external funds to finance long-term investments, or, in the case of government _____s, to finance current expenditure.

 a. Puttable bond
 b. Catastrophe bonds
 c. Convertible bond
 d. Bond

42. The _____ is the market for securities, where companies and governments can raise longterm funds. The _____ includes the stock market and the bond market. Financial regulators, such as the U.S. Securities and Exchange Commission, oversee the _____s in their designated countries to ensure that investors are protected against fraud.
 a. Forward market
 b. Delta neutral
 c. Spot rate
 d. Capital market

43. _____, refers to consumption opportunity gained by an entity within a specified time frame, which is generally expressed in monetary terms. However, for households and individuals, '_____ is the sum of all the wages, salaries, profits, interests payments, rents and other forms of earnings received... in a given period of time.' For firms, _____ generally refers to net-profit: what remains of revenue after expenses have been subtracted.
 a. Accrual
 b. OIBDA
 c. Annual report
 d. Income

44. In finance, a _____ is a security that entitles the holder to buy stock of the company that issued it at a specified price, which is usually higher than the stock price at time of issue.

_____s are frequently attached to bonds or preferred stock as a sweetener, allowing the issuer to pay lower interest rates or dividends. They can be used to enhance the yield of the bond, and make them more attractive to potential buyers.

 a. Credit
 b. Clearing house
 c. Clearing
 d. Warrant

45. _____ is a company's earnings per share (EPS) calculated using fully diluted shares outstanding (i.e. including the impact of stock option grants and convertible bonds.) Diluted EPS indicates a 'worst case' scenario, one in which everyone who could have received stock without purchasing it directly for the full market value did so.

To find diluted EPS, basic EPS is calculated for each of the categories on the income statement first.

 a. Net assets
 b. Financial ratio
 c. Price/cash flow ratio
 d. Diluted earnings per share

46. _____ are the earnings returned on the initial investment amount.

Chapter 20. Options Markets: Introduction 205

In the US, the Financial Accounting Standards Board (FASB) requires companies' income statements to report _____ for each of the major categories of the income statement: continuing operations, discontinued operations, extraordinary items, and net income.

The _____ formula does not include preferred dividends for categories outside of continued operations and net income.

a. Earnings per share
b. Average accounting return
c. Inventory turnover
d. Assets turnover

47. In business and finance, a _____ (also referred to as equity _____) of stock means a _____ of ownership in a corporation (company.) In the plural, stocks is often used as a synonym for _____s especially in the United States, but it is less commonly used that way outside of North America.

In the United Kingdom, South Africa, and Australia, stock can also refer to completely different financial instruments such as government bonds or, less commonly, to all kinds of marketable securities.

a. Bucket shop
b. Margin
c. Procter ' Gamble
d. Share

48. _____ is that which is owed; usually referencing assets owed, but the term can cover other obligations. In the case of assets, _____ is a means of using future purchasing power in the present before a summation has been earned. Some companies and corporations use _____ as a part of their overall corporate finance strategy.

a. Partial Payment
b. Cross-collateralization
c. Credit cycle
d. Debt

49. In finance, 'participation' is an ownership interest in a mortgage or other loan. In particular, _____ is a cooperation of multiple lenders to issue a loan (known as participation loan) to one borrower. This is usually done in order to reduce individual risks of the lenders.

a. Securitization
b. Short positions
c. Doctrine of the Proper Law
d. Loan participation

50. In economics, the people in the _____ are the suppliers of labor. The _____ is all the nonmilitary people who are employed or unemployed. In 2005, the worldwide _____ was over 3 billion people.

a. 7-Eleven
b. 4-4-5 Calendar
c. 529 plan
d. Labor force

51. An _____ (or average value option) is a special type of option contract. For _____s the payoff is determined by the average underlying price over some pre-set period of time. This is different to the case of the usual European option, where the payoff of the option contract depends on the price of the underlying instrument at maturity.

a. Options arbitrage
b. Options spreads
c. Option screener
d. Asian option

Chapter 20. Options Markets: Introduction

52. In finance, a _____ is a type of financial option where the option to exercise depends on the underlying crossing or reaching a given barrier level. _____s were created to provide the insurance value of an option without charging as much premium. For example, if you believe that IBM will go up this year, but are willing to bet that it won't go above $100, then you can buy the barrier and pay less premium than the vanilla option.
   a. Barrier option
   b. Binary option
   c. Naked put
   d. Net volatility

53. The _____ is an American financial and commodity derivative exchange based in Chicago. The _____ was founded in 1898 as the Chicago Butter and Egg Board. Originally, the exchange was a non-profit organization.
   a. Chicago Mercantile Exchange
   b. Financial Crimes Enforcement Network
   c. Public Company Accounting Oversight Board
   d. Gamelan Council

54. The _____ are the financial markets for derivatives. The market can be divided into two, that for exchange traded derivatives and that for over-the-counter derivatives. The legal nature of these products is very different as well as the way they are traded, though many market participants are active in both.
   a. Derivatives markets
   b. Commodity tick
   c. Real estate derivatives
   d. Notional amount

55. The _____ are a type of exotic options with path dependency, among many other kind of options. The payoff depends on the optimal (maximum or minimum) underlying asset's price occurring over the life of the option. The option allows the holder to 'look back' over time to determine the payoff.
   a. Database auditing
   b. Help desk and incident reporting auditing
   c. Weighted mean
   d. Lookback options

56. A _____ is a type of derivative in which the underlying is denominated in one currency, but the instrument itself is settled in another currency at some fixed rate. Such products are attractive for speculators and investors who wish to have exposure to a foreign asset, but without the corresponding exchange rate risk.

Common types of _____ include :

- _____ futures contracts, such as a futures contract on a European stock market index which is settled in US dollars.
- _____ options, in which the difference between the underlying and a fixed strike price is paid out in another currency.
- _____ swaps, in which one counterparty pays a non-local interest rate to the other, but the notional amount is in local currency. The second party may be paying a fixed or floating rate. For example, a swap in which the notional amount is denominated in Canadian dollars, but where the floating rate is set as USD LIBOR, would be considered a _____ swap.

   a. Volatility arbitrage
   b. Dollar roll
   c. Quanto
   d. Credit default swap index

Chapter 21. Option Valuation

1. An _____ is a contract written by a seller that conveys to the buyer the right -- but not the obligation -- to buy (in the case of a call _____) or to sell (in the case of a put _____) a particular asset, such as a piece of property such as, among others, a futures contract. In return for granting the _____, the seller collects a payment (the premium) from the buyer.

For example, buying a call _____ provides the right to buy a specified quantity of a security at a set strike price at some time on or before expiration, while buying a put _____ provides the right to sell.

   a. Option
   c. Amortization
   b. AT'T Mobility LLC
   d. Annuity

2. In finance, _____ refers to the value of a security which is intrinsic to or contained in the security itself. It is also frequently called fundamental value. It is ordinarily calculated by summing the future income generated by the asset, and discounting it to the present value.
   a. Intrinsic value
   c. Accretion
   b. Amortization
   d. Alpha

3. In finance, the value of an option consists of two components, its intrinsic value and its _____. Time value is simply the difference between option value and intrinsic value. _____ is also known as theta, extrinsic value, or instrumental value.
   a. Conservatism
   c. Global Squeeze
   b. Debt buyer
   d. Time value

4. In finance, _____ is the process of estimating the potential market value of a financial asset or liability. they can be done on assets (for example, investments in marketable securities such as stocks, options, business enterprises, or intangible assets such as patents and trademarks) or on liabilities (e.g., Bonds issued by a company.) _____s are required in many contexts including investment analysis, capital budgeting, merger and acquisition transactions, financial reporting, taxable events to determine the proper tax liability, and in litigation.
   a. Procter ' Gamble
   c. Share
   b. Margin
   d. Valuation

5. A _____ is a financial contract between two parties, the buyer and the seller of this type of option. Often it is simply labeled a 'call'. The buyer of the option has the right, but not the obligation to buy an agreed quantity of a particular commodity or financial instrument (the underlying instrument) from the seller of the option at a certain time (the expiration date) for a certain price (the strike price.)
   a. Call option
   c. Bear call spread
   b. Bear spread
   d. Bull spread

6. In finance, a _____ is a position established in one market in an attempt to offset exposure to the price risk of an equal but opposite obligation or position in another market -- usually, but not always, in the context of one's commercial activity. Hedging is a strategy designed to minimize exposure to such business risks as a sharp contraction in demand for one's inventory, while still allowing the business to profit from producing and maintaining that inventory. A typical hedger might be a farmer with 2000 acres of unharvested wheat in the ground, who would rather tend his crop without the distraction of uncertain prices.
   a. Hedge
   c. 7-Eleven
   b. 4-4-5 Calendar
   d. 529 plan

Chapter 21. Option Valuation

7. A _____ is a payment made by a corporation to its shareholder members. When a corporation earns a profit or surplus, that money can be put to two uses: it can either be re-invested in the business (called retained earnings), or it can be paid to the shareholders as a _____. Many corporations retain a portion of their earnings and pay the remainder as a _____.

   a. Dividend puzzle
   b. Special dividend
   c. Dividend yield
   d. Dividend

8. The _____ is an American stock exchange. It is the largest electronic screen-based equity securities trading market in the United States. With approximately 3,200 companies, it has more trading volume per day than any other stock exchange in the world.

   a. 7-Eleven
   b. 529 plan
   c. 4-4-5 Calendar
   d. Nasdaq

9. In business and finance, a _____ (also referred to as equity _____) of stock means a _____ of ownership in a corporation (company.) In the plural, stocks is often used as a synonym for _____s especially in the United States, but it is less commonly used that way outside of North America.

   In the United Kingdom, South Africa, and Australia, stock can also refer to completely different financial instruments such as government bonds or, less commonly, to all kinds of marketable securities.

   a. Bucket shop
   b. Margin
   c. Procter ' Gamble
   d. Share

10. The term _____ refers to three closely related concepts:

    - The _____ model is a mathematical model of the market for an equity, in which the equity's price is a stochastic process.
    - The _____ PDE is a partial differential equation which (in the model) must be satisfied by the price of a derivative on the equity.
    - The _____ formula is the result obtained by solving the _____ PDE for a European call option.

    Fischer Black and Myron Scholes first articulated the _____ formula in their 1973 paper, 'The Pricing of Options and Corporate Liabilities.' The foundation for their research relied on work developed by scholars such as Jack L. Treynor, Paul Samuelson, A. James Boness, Sheen T. Kassouf, and Edward O. Thorp. The fundamental insight of _____ is that the option is implicitly priced if the stock is traded.

    Robert C. Merton was the first to publish a paper expanding the mathematical understanding of the options pricing model and coined the term '_____' options pricing model.

    a. Perpetuity
    b. Modified Internal Rate of Return
    c. Stochastic volatility
    d. Black-Scholes

11. In finance, the binomial options pricing model (BOPM) provides a generalisable numerical method for the valuation of options. The _____ was first proposed by Cox, Ross and Rubinstein (1979.) Essentially, the model uses a 'discrete-time' model of the varying price over time of the underlying financial instrument.

Chapter 21. Option Valuation

a. Binomial model
c. Perpetuity
b. Discount rate
d. Modified Internal Rate of Return

12. A _____ is a financial contract between two parties, the seller (writer) and the buyer of the option. The put allows its buyer the right but not the obligation to sell a commodity or financial instrument (the underlying instrument) to the writer (seller) of the option at a certain time for a certain price (the strike price.) The writer (seller) has the obligation to purchase the underlying asset at that strike price, if the buyer exercises the option.
   a. Bear call spread
   c. Put option
   b. Debit spread
   d. Bear spread

13. A _____ is the price of a single share of a no. of saleable stocks of the company. Once the stock is purchased, the owner becomes a shareholder of the company that issued the share.
   a. Whisper numbers
   c. Share price
   b. Trading curb
   d. Stock split

14. In financial mathematics, the _____ of an option contract is the volatility implied by the market price of the option based on an option pricing model. In other words, it is the volatility that, given a particular pricing model, yields a theoretical value for the option equal to the current market price. Non-option financial instruments that have embedded optionality, such as an interest rate cap, can also have an _____.
   a. Implied volatility
   c. Equity derivative
   b. Interest rate derivative
   d. Interest rate future

15. _____ most frequently refers to the standard deviation of the continuously compounded returns of a financial instrument with a specific time horizon. It is often used to quantify the risk of the instrument over that time period. _____ is typically expressed in annualized terms, and it may either be an absolute number ($5) or a fraction of the mean (5%).
   a. Portfolio insurance
   c. Currency swap
   b. Seasoned equity offering
   d. Volatility

16. In econometrics, an _____ model considers the variance of the current error term to be a function of the variances of the previous time period's error terms. _____ relates the error variance to the square of a previous period's error. It is employed commonly in modeling financial time series that exhibit time-varying volatility clustering, i.e. periods of swings followed by periods of relative calm.
   a. AAB
   c. A Random Walk Down Wall Street
   b. Autoregressive conditional heteroscedasticity
   d. ABN Amro

17. _____ is a method of hedging a portfolio of stocks against the market risk by short selling stock index futures.

This hedging technique is frequently used by institutional investors when the market direction is uncertain or volatile. Short selling index futures can offset any downturns, but it also hinders any gains.

   a. PAUG
   c. Delivery month
   b. Freight derivative
   d. Portfolio insurance

Chapter 21. Option Valuation

18. In economic models, the _____ time frame assumes no fixed factors of production. Firms can enter or leave the marketplace, and the cost (and availability) of land, labor, raw materials, and capital goods can be assumed to vary. In contrast, in the short-run time frame, certain factors are assumed to be fixed, because there is not sufficient time for them to change.
   a. Short-run
   b. Long-run
   c. 529 plan
   d. 4-4-5 Calendar

19. A _____ is a fungible, negotiable instrument representing financial value. They are broadly categorized into debt securities (such as banknotes, bonds and debentures), and equity securities; e.g., common stocks. The company or other entity issuing the _____ is called the issuer.
   a. Tracking stock
   b. Book entry
   c. Securities lending
   d. Security

20. A _____ is a private or public market for the trading of company stock and derivatives of company stock at an agreed price; these are securities listed on a stock exchange as well as those only traded privately.

The size of the world _____ is estimated at about $36.6 trillion US at the beginning of October 2008. The world derivatives market has been estimated at about $480 trillion face or nominal value, 12 times the size of the entire world economy.

   a. Andrew Tobias
   b. Stock market
   c. Adolph Coors
   d. Anton Gelonkin

21. A _____ is a sudden dramatic decline of stock prices across a significant cross-section of a stock market. Crashes are driven by panic as much as by underlying economic factors. They often follow speculative stock market bubbles.
   a. 7-Eleven
   b. 4-4-5 Calendar
   c. 529 plan
   d. Stock market crash

22. In finance, a _____ is a standardized contract, to buy or sell a specified commodity of standardized quality at a certain date in the future, at a market determined price (the futures price.)

The price is determined by the instantaneous equilibrium between the forces of supply and demand among competing buy and sell orders on the exchange at the time of the purchase or sale of the contract.

In many cases, the items may be such non-traditional 'commodities' as foreign currencies, commercial or government paper [e.g., bonds], or 'baskets' of corporate equity ['stock indices'] or other financial instruments.

   a. Futures contract
   b. Repurchase agreement
   c. Financial future
   d. Heston model

23. In finance, a portfolio containing options is _____ when it consists of positions with offsetting positive and negative deltas (exposure to changes in the value of the underlying instrument), and these balance out to bring the net delta of the portfolio to zero.

A related term, delta hedging is the process of setting or keeping the delta of a portfolio as close to zero as possible.

Mathematically, delta is the partial derivative $\frac{\partial V}{\partial S}$ of the instrument or portfolio's fair value with respect to the price of the underlying security.

a. Performance attribution
b. Forward market
c. Spot rate
d. Delta neutral

24. _____ in financial markets is the likelihood of fluctuations in the exchange rate of currencies. Therefore, it is a probability measure of the threat that an exchange rate movement poses to an investor's portfolio in a foreign currency. The volatility of the exchange rate is measured as standard deviation over a dataset of exchange rate movements.
a. 7-Eleven
b. 529 plan
c. 4-4-5 Calendar
d. Volatility risk

Chapter 22. Futures Markets

1. A _____ is an agreement between two parties to buy or sell an asset at a specified point of time in the future. The price of the underlying instrument, in whatever form, is paid before control of the instrument changes. This is one of the many forms of buy/sell orders where the time of trade is not the time where the securities themselves are exchanged.

   a. Constant maturity credit default swap
   b. Derivatives markets
   c. Loan Credit Default Swap Index
   d. Forward contract

2. In finance, a _____ is a standardized contract, to buy or sell a specified commodity of standardized quality at a certain date in the future, at a market determined price (the futures price.)

   The price is determined by the instantaneous equilibrium between the forces of supply and demand among competing buy and sell orders on the exchange at the time of the purchase or sale of the contract.

   In many cases, the items may be such non-traditional 'commodities' as foreign currencies, commercial or government paper [e.g., bonds], or 'baskets' of corporate equity ['stock indices'] or other financial instruments.

   a. Financial future
   b. Repurchase agreement
   c. Heston model
   d. Futures contract

3. A _____ is an exchange of promises between two or more parties to do an act which is enforceable in a court of law. It is where an unqualified offer meets a qualified acceptance and the parties reach Consensus ad Idem. The parties must have the necessary capacity to _____ and the _____ must not be either trifling, indeterminate, impossible or illegal.

   a. 4-4-5 Calendar
   b. 529 plan
   c. Contract
   d. 7-Eleven

4. In finance, a _____ in a security, such as a stock or a bond means the holder of the position owns the security and will profit if the price of the security goes up.

   Similarly, a _____ in a futures contract or similar derivative, means the holder of the position will profit if the price of the underlying security goes up. Going long is the more conventional practice of investing and is contrasted with going short

   - Short (finance)

   a. Delta hedging
   b. Long position
   c. Central Securities Depository
   d. Forward market

5. Days to Cover (DTC) is a numerical term that describes the relationship between the amount of shares in a given equity that have been short sold and the number of days of typical trading that it would require to 'cover' all _____ outstanding. For example, if there are ten million shares of XYZ Inc. that are currently short sold and the average daily volume of XYZ shares traded each day is one million, it would require ten days of trading for all _____ to be covered (10 million / 1 million.)

   a. Guaranteed investment contracts
   b. Stock or scrip dividends
   c. Cash budget
   d. Short positions

Chapter 22. Futures Markets

6. The concept was first developed in game theory and consequently zero-sum situations are often called _____s though this does not imply that the concept applies only to what are commonly referred to as games.

For 2-player finite _____s, the different game theoretic Solution concepts of Nash equilibrium, minimax, and maximin all give the same solution. In the solution, players play a mixed strategy.

   a. 4-4-5 Calendar
   b. 529 plan
   c. 7-Eleven
   d. Zero-sum game

7. _____ are futures contracts with the underlying asset being one particular stock, usually in batches of 100. When purchased, no transmission of share rights or dividends occurs. Being futures contracts they are traded on margin, thus offering leverage, and they are not subject to the short selling limitations that stocks are.
   a. Heston model
   b. Volatility swap
   c. Single-stock futures
   d. Weather derivatives

8. The _____ is an American financial and commodity derivative exchange based in Chicago. The _____ was founded in 1898 as the Chicago Butter and Egg Board. Originally, the exchange was a non-profit organization.
   a. Public Company Accounting Oversight Board
   b. Financial Crimes Enforcement Network
   c. Chicago Mercantile Exchange
   d. Gamelan Council

9. A _____ is a financial services company that provides clearing and settlement services for financial transactions, usually on a futures exchange, and often acts as central counterparty (the payor actually pays the _____, which then pays the payee). A _____ may also offer novation, the substitution of a new contract or debt for an old, or other credit enhancement services to its members.

The term is also used for banks like Suffolk Bank that acted as a restraint on the over-issuance of private bank notes.

   a. Clearing house
   b. Warrant
   c. Valuation
   d. Bucket shop

10. _____ is a major futures and options exchange for European benchmark derivatives featuring open and low-cost electronic access globally. Its electronic trading and clearing platform offers a broad range of products and amongst other, operates the most liquid fixed income markets. _____ was established in 1998 with the merger of Deutsche Terminbörse and SOFFEX (Swiss Options and Financial Futures.)
   a. AAB
   b. A Random Walk Down Wall Street
   c. ABN Amro
   d. Eurex

11. A _____ is a professionally managed type of collective investment scheme that pools money from many investors and invests it in stocks, bonds, short-term money market instruments, and/or other securities. The _____ will have a fund manager that trades the pooled money on a regular basis. Currently, the worldwide value of all _____s totals more than $26 trillion.

Since 1940, there have been three basic types of investment companies in the United States: open-end funds, also known in the US as _____s; unit investment trusts (UITs); and closed-end funds.

a. Financial intermediary
b. Net asset value
c. Trust company
d. Mutual fund

12. _____ denotes the total number of derivative contracts, like futures and options, that are currently active on a specific underlying security, having specific terms.

Namely, the total contracts for a specific strike price and expiration date, that have been traded, but have not yet expired, have not yet been closed through a closing transaction, or have not yet been terminated via early exercise. A closing transaction occurs when a counterparty that longs the contract sells, or, conversely, when a counterparty that shorts the contract buys.

a. Equity derivative
b. Open interest
c. Equity swap
d. International Swaps and Derivatives Association

13. _____ is a fee paid on borrowed assets. It is the price paid for the use of borrowed money, or, money earned by deposited funds. Assets that are sometimes lent with _____ include money, shares, consumer goods through hire purchase, major assets such as aircraft, and even entire factories in finance lease arrangements.

a. A Random Walk Down Wall Street
b. AAB
c. Insolvency
d. Interest

14. An _____ is a company whose main business is holding securities of other companies purely for investment purposes. The _____ invests money on behalf of its shareholders who in turn share in the profits and losses.

a. A Random Walk Down Wall Street
b. Unit investment trust
c. Investment company
d. AAB

15. The variation margin or _____ is not collateral, but a daily offsetting of profits and losses. Futures are marked-to-market every day, so the current price is compared to the previous day's price. The profit or loss on the day of a position is then paid to or debited from the holder by the futures exchange.

a. Delivery month
b. SPI 200 futures contract
c. Total return swap
d. Maintenance margin

16. In finance, a _____ is collateral that the holder of a position in securities, options, or futures contracts has to deposit to cover the credit risk of his counterparty (most often his broker.) This risk can arise if the holder has done any of the following:

- borrowed cash from the counterparty to buy securities or options,
- sold securities or options short, or
- entered into a futures contract.

The collateral can be in the form of cash or securities, and it is deposited in a _____ account. On U.S. futures exchanges, '_____' was formally called performance bond.

_____ buying is buying securities with cash borrowed from a broker, using other securities as collateral.

a. Procter ' Gamble
c. Margin
b. Credit
d. Share

17. The collateral can be in the form of cash or securities, and it is deposited in a _____. On U.S. futures exchanges, 'margin' was formally called performance bond.

Margin buying is buying securities with cash borrowed from a broker, using other securities as collateral.

a. Forward contract
c. Dollar roll
b. Risk-neutral measure
d. Margin account

18. _____, in bookkeeping, refers to assets, liabilities, income, and expenses recorded on individual pages of the so called book of final entry or ledger. Changes in _____ value are made by chronologically posting debit (DR) and credit (CR) entries to its page. Examples of _____ s are cash, _____ s receivable, mortgages, loans, land and buildings, common stock, sales, services provided, wages, and payroll overhead.
a. Accretion
c. Account
b. Option
d. Alpha

19. In the original and simplified sense, _____ were things of value, of uniform quality, that were produced in large quantities by many different producers; the items from each different producer are considered equivalent. It is the contract and this underlying standard that define the commodity, not any quality inherent in the product.

_____ exchanges include:

- Chicago Board of Trade
- Kansas City Board of Trade
- Euronext.liffe
- Kuala Lumpur Futures Exchange
- Bhatinda Om ' Oil Exchange
- London Metal Exchange
- New York Mercantile Exchange
- Multi Commodity Exchange
- Dalian Commodity Exchange

Markets for trading _____ can be very efficient, particularly if the division into pools matches demand segments. These markets will quickly respond to changes in supply and demand to find an equilibrium price and quantity.

a. 4-4-5 Calendar
c. Commodities
b. 529 plan
d. 7-Eleven

20. A _____ is a fungible, negotiable instrument representing financial value. They are broadly categorized into debt securities (such as banknotes, bonds and debentures), and equity securities; e.g., common stocks. The company or other entity issuing the _____ is called the issuer.

Chapter 22. Futures Markets

a. Securities lending
b. Security
c. Tracking stock
d. Book entry

21. The U.S. _____ is an independent agency of the United States government which holds primary responsibility for enforcing the federal securities laws and regulating the securities industry, the nation's stock and options exchanges, and other electronic securities markets. The SEC was created by section 4 of the SEC of 1934 (now codified as 15 U.S.C. Â§ 78d and commonly referred to as the 1934 Act.)
    a. 7-Eleven
    b. 529 plan
    c. 4-4-5 Calendar
    d. Securities and Exchange Commission

22. A _____ is a point at which a stock market will stop trading for a period of time in response to substantial drops in value.

On the New York Stock Exchange, one type of _____ is referred to as a 'circuit breaker.' These limits were put in place after Black Monday in order to reduce market volatility and massive panic sell-offs, giving traders time to reconsider their transactions.

At the start of each quarter, the NYSE sets three circuit breaker levels at levels of 10%, 20%, and 30% of the average closing price of the Dow Jones Industrial Average for the month preceding the start of the quarter, rounded to the nearest 50-point interval.

    a. Stock repurchase
    b. Common stock
    c. Trading curb
    d. Stock market index

23. _____ (in a financial context) is the assumption of the risk of loss, in return for the uncertain possibility of a reward. Only if one may safely say that a particular position involves no risk may one say, strictly speaking, that such a position represents an 'investment.' Financial _____ involves the buying, holding, selling, and short-selling of stocks, bonds, commodities, currencies, collectibles, real estate, derivatives, or any valuable financial instrument to profit from fluctuations in its price as opposed to buying it for use or for income via methods such as dividends or interest. _____ represents one of four market roles in Western financial markets, distinct from hedging, long- or short-term investing, and arbitrage.
    a. Speculation
    b. Forward market
    c. Market anomaly
    d. Central Securities Depository

24. In finance, _____ (or gearing) is borrowing money to supplement existing funds for investment in such a way that the potential positive or negative outcome is magnified and/or enhanced. It generally refers to using borrowed funds, or debt, so as to attempt to increase the returns to equity. Deleveraging is the action of reducing borrowings.
    a. Financial endowment
    b. Pension fund
    c. Limited partnership
    d. Leverage

25. In finance, a _____ is a position established in one market in an attempt to offset exposure to the price risk of an equal but opposite obligation or position in another market -- usually, but not always, in the context of one's commercial activity. Hedging is a strategy designed to minimize exposure to such business risks as a sharp contraction in demand for one's inventory, while still allowing the business to profit from producing and maintaining that inventory. A typical hedger might be a farmer with 2000 acres of unharvested wheat in the ground, who would rather tend his crop without the distraction of uncertain prices.

a. 4-4-5 Calendar
b. 529 plan
c. Hedge
d. 7-Eleven

26. _____ in finance is the risk associated with imperfect hedging using futures. It could arise because of the difference between the asset whose price is to be hedged and the asset underlying the derivative, or because of a mismatch between the expiration date of the futures and the actual selling date of the asset.

Under these conditions, the spot price of the asset, and the futures price, do not converge on the expiration date of the future.

a. Currency risk
b. Basis risk
c. Liquidity risk
d. Credit risk

27. In finance, a _____ is an option spread trade involving the purchase of options of an underlying market expiring in some named month, and the simultaneous sale of other options of the same underlying market and the same striking price in a different month.

The usual _____, also called a time spread or horizontal spread, involves the purchase of options of a named striking price expiring in a more distant month and the sale of options having the same striking price that expire in a more nearby month.

The _____ is a strategy used by the trader in an attempt to take advantage of a difference in the implied volatilities between two different months' options.

a. Calendar spread
b. Debit spread
c. Binary option
d. Put option

28. In economics and finance, _____ is the practice of taking advantage of a price differential between two or more markets: striking a combination of matching deals that capitalize upon the imbalance, the profit being the difference between the market prices. When used by academics, an _____ is a transaction that involves no negative cash flow at any probabilistic or temporal state and a positive cash flow in at least one state; in simple terms, a risk-free profit.

a. Issuer
b. Arbitrage
c. Efficient-market hypothesis
d. Initial margin

29. The _____ or spot rate of a commodity, a security or a currency is the price that is quoted for immediate (spot) settlement (payment and delivery.) Spot settlement is normally one or two business days from trade date. This is in contrast with the forward price established in a forward contract or futures contract, where contract terms (price) are set now, but delivery and payment will occur at a future date.

a. Cost of carry
b. Market price
c. Central Securities Depository
d. Spot price

30. _____ is a term used in the futures market to describe an upward sloping forward curve (as in the normal yield curve.) Such a forward curve is said to be 'in _____' (or sometimes '_____ed'.)

Formally, it is the situation where, and the amount by which, the price of a commodity for future delivery is higher than the spot price, or a far future delivery price higher than a nearer future delivery.

a. Delta One
b. Single-stock futures
c. Commodity tick
d. Contango

31. _____ proposes how rational investors will use diversification to optimize their portfolios, and how a risky asset should be priced. The basic concepts of the theory are Markowitz diversification, the efficient frontier, capital asset pricing model, the alpha and beta coefficients, the Capital Market Line and the Securities Market Line.

_____ models an asset's return as a random variable, and models a portfolio as a weighted combination of assets so that the return of a portfolio is the weighted combination of the assets' returns.

a. Market value
b. Payback period
c. Consumer basket
d. Modern portfolio theory

32. _____ is a futures market term. It describes a situation where the amount of money required for future delivery of an item is lower than the amount required for immediate delivery of that item. For example, immediate delivery of gold may cost $1,000 an ounce, whereas delivery in two months only costs $900 an ounce, with that $900 to be paid at time of delivery.

a. Delivery month
b. STIRT
c. Backwardation
d. Risk-neutral measure

Chapter 23. Futures and Swaps: Markets and Applications

1. In finance, a _____ is a standardized contract, to buy or sell a specified commodity of standardized quality at a certain date in the future, at a market determined price (the futures price.)

The price is determined by the instantaneous equilibrium between the forces of supply and demand among competing buy and sell orders on the exchange at the time of the purchase or sale of the contract.

In many cases, the items may be such non-traditional 'commodities' as foreign currencies, commercial or government paper [e.g., bonds], or 'baskets' of corporate equity ['stock indices'] or other financial instruments.

   a. Futures contract   b. Financial future
   c. Heston model   d. Repurchase agreement

2. The _____ is an American financial and commodity derivative exchange based in Chicago. The _____ was founded in 1898 as the Chicago Butter and Egg Board. Originally, the exchange was a non-profit organization.
   a. Financial Crimes Enforcement Network   b. Gamelan Council
   c. Public Company Accounting Oversight Board   d. Chicago Mercantile Exchange

3. A _____ is a futures contract on a short term interest rate (STIR.) Contracts vary, but are often defined on an interest rate index such as 3-month sterling or US dollar LIBOR.

They are traded across a wide range of currencies, including the G12 country currencies and many others.

   a. Dual currency deposit   b. Financial Future
   c. Notional amount   d. Real estate derivatives

4. A _____ is a central financial exchange where people can trade standardized futures contracts; that is, a contract to buy specific quantities of a commodity or financial instrument at a specified price with delivery set at a specified time in the future.

Though the origins of futures trading can supposedly be traced to Ancient Greek or Phoenician times, the first modern organized _____ began in 1710 at the Dojima Rice Exchange in Osaka, Japan.

The United States followed in the early 1800s.

   a. Futures Exchange   b. 529 plan
   c. 4-4-5 Calendar   d. 7-Eleven

5. _____ is a fee paid on borrowed assets. It is the price paid for the use of borrowed money, or, money earned by deposited funds. Assets that are sometimes lent with _____ include money, shares, consumer goods through hire purchase, major assets such as aircraft, and even entire factories in finance lease arrangements.
   a. Interest   b. A Random Walk Down Wall Street
   c. AAB   d. Insolvency

6. An _____ is the price a borrower pays for the use of money they do not own, and the return a lender receives for deferring the use of funds, by lending it to the borrower. _____s are normally expressed as a percentage rate over the period of one year.

_____s targets are also a vital tool of monetary policy and are used to control variables like investment, inflation, and unemployment.

   a. A Random Walk Down Wall Street
   b. AAB
   c. ABN Amro
   d. Interest rate

7. _____ is an economic concept, expressed as a basic algebraic identity that relates interest rates and exchange rates. The identity is theoretical, and usually follows from assumptions imposed in economics models. There is evidence to support as well as to refute the concept.
   a. AAB
   b. Unit price
   c. A Random Walk Down Wall Street
   d. Interest rate parity

8. The _____ started life on September 30, 1982, to take advantage of the removal of currency controls in the UK in 1979. The exchange modelled itself after the Chicago Board of Trade and the Chicago Mercantile Exchange. It initially offered futures contracts and options linked to short term interest rates.
   a. 7-Eleven
   b. 529 plan
   c. 4-4-5 Calendar
   d. London International Financial Futures Exchange

9. In economics and finance, _____ is the practice of taking advantage of a price differential between two or more markets: striking a combination of matching deals that capitalize upon the imbalance, the profit being the difference between the market prices. When used by academics, an _____ is a transaction that involves no negative cash flow at any probabilistic or temporal state and a positive cash flow in at least one state; in simple terms, a risk-free profit.
   a. Issuer
   b. Initial margin
   c. Efficient-market hypothesis
   d. Arbitrage

10. The term _____ or economic cycle refers to the fluctuations of economic activity (business fluctuations) around a long-term growth trend. The cycle involves shifts over time between periods of relatively rapid growth of output (recovery and prosperity), and periods of relative stagnation or decline (contraction or recession.) These fluctuations are often measured using the real gross domestic product.
   a. Business cycle
   b. Behavioral finance
   c. Deflation
   d. Fixed exchange rate

11. A _____, also FX future or foreign exchange future, is a futures contract to exchange one currency for another at a specified date in the future at a price (exchange rate) that is fixed on the purchase date. Typically, one of the currencies is the US dollar. The price of a future is then in terms of US dollars per unit of other currency.
   a. Currency swap
   b. Foreign exchange controls
   c. Non-deliverable forward
   d. Currency future

12. In finance, the _____ between two currencies specifies how much one currency is worth in terms of the other. For example an _____ of 102 Japanese yen to the United States dollar means that JPY 102 is worth the same as USD 1. The foreign exchange market is one of the largest markets in the world.
   a. AAB
   b. ABN Amro
   c. A Random Walk Down Wall Street
   d. Exchange rate

Chapter 23. Futures and Swaps: Markets and Applications

13. _____ is the investment strategy where an investor buys a financial instrument denominated in a foreign currency, and hedges his foreign exchange risk by selling a forward contract in the amount of the proceeds of the investment back into his base currency. The proceeds of the investment are only known exactly if the financial instrument is risk-free and only pays interest once, on the date of the forward sale of foreign currency. Otherwise, some foreign exchange risk remains.

   a. Covered interest arbitrage
   b. Triangular arbitrage
   c. Floating exchange rate
   d. Currency future

14. The term _____ refers to three closely related concepts:

   - The _____ model is a mathematical model of the market for an equity, in which the equity's price is a stochastic process.
   - The _____ PDE is a partial differential equation which (in the model) must be satisfied by the price of a derivative on the equity.
   - The _____ formula is the result obtained by solving the _____ PDE for a European call option.

   Fischer Black and Myron Scholes first articulated the _____ formula in their 1973 paper, 'The Pricing of Options and Corporate Liabilities.' The foundation for their research relied on work developed by scholars such as Jack L. Treynor, Paul Samuelson, A. James Boness, Sheen T. Kassouf, and Edward O. Thorp. The fundamental insight of _____ is that the option is implicitly priced if the stock is traded.

   Robert C. Merton was the first to publish a paper expanding the mathematical understanding of the options pricing model and coined the term '_____' options pricing model.

   a. Black-Scholes
   b. Stochastic volatility
   c. Modified Internal Rate of Return
   d. Perpetuity

15. _____ is a form of risk that arises from the change in price of one currency against another. Whenever investors or companies have assets or business operations across national borders, they face _____ if their positions are not hedged.

   - Transaction risk is the risk that exchange rates will change unfavourably over time. It can be hedged against using forward currency contracts;
   - Translation risk is an accounting risk, proportional to the amount of assets held in foreign currencies. Changes in the exchange rate over time will render a report inaccurate, and so assets are usually balanced by borrowings in that currency.

   The exchange risk associated with a foreign denominated instrument is a key element in foreign investment. This risk flows from differential monetary policy and growth in real productivity, which results in differential inflation rates.

   a. Credit risk
   b. Market risk
   c. Tracking error
   d. Currency risk

16. A _____ is an exchange of promises between two or more parties to do an act which is enforceable in a court of law. It is where an unqualified offer meets a qualified acceptance and the parties reach Consensus ad Idem. The parties must have the necessary capacity to _____ and the _____ must not be either trifling, indeterminate, impossible or illegal.
   a. 4-4-5 Calendar
   b. 7-Eleven
   c. Contract
   d. 529 plan

17. In Finance the _____ is a mathematical model for portfolio allocation developed in 1990 at Goldman Sachs by Fischer Black and Robert Litterman, and published in 1992. It seeks to overcome problems that institutional investors have encountered in applying modern portfolio theory in practice. The model starts with the equilibrium assumption that the asset allocation of a representative agent should be proportional to the market values of the available assets, and then modifies that to take into account the 'views' (i.e. the specific opinions about asset returns) of the investor in question to arrive at a bespoke asset allocation.
   a. Black-Litterman model
   b. Specific risk
   c. Capital surplus
   d. Clientele effect

18. _____ is the strategy of making buy or sell decisions of financial assets (often stocks) by attempting to predict future market price movements. The prediction may be based on an outlook of market or economic conditions resulting from technical or fundamental analysis. This is an investment strategy based on the outlook for an aggregate market, rather than for a particular financial asset.
   a. Portable alpha
   b. Market timing
   c. Divestment
   d. Late trading

19. _____ is an investment strategy that attempts to exploit short-term market inefficiencies by establishing positions in an assortment of markets with a goal to profit from relative movements across those markets. This top-down strategy focuses on general movements in the market rather than on performance of individual securities.
   a. Cash management
   b. Cash concentration
   c. Debt ratio
   d. Global tactical asset allocation

20. In business and accounting, _____s are everything of value that is owned by a person or company. The balance sheet of a firm records the monetary value of the _____s owned by the firm. The two major _____ classes are tangible _____s and intangible _____s.
   a. EBITDA
   b. Income
   c. Accounts payable
   d. Asset

21. _____ is a term used to refer to how an investor distributes his or her investments among various classes of investment vehicles (e.g., stocks and bonds.)

A large part of financial planning is finding an _____ that is appropriate for a given person in terms of their appetite for and ability to shoulder risk. This can depend on various factors; see investor profile.

   a. Investing online
   b. Investment performance
   c. Alternative investment
   d. Asset allocation

22. _____ is a method of investing in which investors modify their asset allocation according to the valuation of the markets in which they are invested. Thus, someone invested heavily in stocks might reduce his position when he perceives that other securities, such as bonds, are poised to outperform stocks. Unlike stock picking, in which the investor predicts which individual stocks will perform well, _____ involves only judgments of the future return of complete markets or sectors.

    a. Security market line   b. Market timing
    c. Divestment   d. Tactical asset allocation

23. Behavioral economics and _____ are closely related fields that have evolved to be a separate branch of economic and financial analysis which applies scientific research on human and social, cognitive and emotional factors to better understand economic decisions by, say, consumers, borrowers, investors, and how they affect market prices, returns and the allocation of resources.

The field is primarily concerned with the bounds of rationality (selfishness, self-control) of economic agents. Behavioral models typically integrate insights from psychology with neo-classical economic theory.

    a. Market structure   b. Recession
    c. Medium of exchange   d. Behavioral finance

24. _____ is the risk that the value of an investment will decrease due to moves in market factors. The five standard _____ factors are:

- Equity risk, the risk that stock prices will change.
- Interest rate risk, the risk that interest rates will change.
- Currency risk, the risk that foreign exchange rates will change.
- Commodity risk, the risk that commodity prices (e.g. grains, metals) will change.

As with other forms of risk, _____ may be measured in a number of ways. Traditionally, this is done using a Value at Risk methodology. Value at risk is well established as a risk management technique, but it contains a number of limiting assumptions that constrain its accuracy.

    a. Currency risk   b. Tracking error
    c. Market risk   d. Transaction risk

25. In finance, a _____ is a position established in one market in an attempt to offset exposure to the price risk of an equal but opposite obligation or position in another market -- usually, but not always, in the context of one's commercial activity. Hedging is a strategy designed to minimize exposure to such business risks as a sharp contraction in demand for one's inventory, while still allowing the business to profit from producing and maintaining that inventory. A typical hedger might be a farmer with 2000 acres of unharvested wheat in the ground, who would rather tend his crop without the distraction of uncertain prices.

    a. 4-4-5 Calendar   b. 7-Eleven
    c. Hedge   d. 529 plan

26. An _____ is a futures contract with an interest-bearing instrument as the underlying asset.

Examples include Treasury-bill futures, Treasury-bond futures and Eurodollar futures.

The global market for exchange-traded _____s is notionally valued by the Bank for International Settlements at $5,794,200 million in 2005.

a. Open interest
b. Equity swap
c. Interest rate derivative
d. Interest rate future

27. In finance, a _____ is a debt security, in which the authorized issuer owes the holders a debt and, depending on the terms of the _____, is obliged to pay interest (the coupon) and/or to repay the principal at a later date, termed maturity.

Thus a _____ is a loan: the issuer is the borrower, the _____ holder is the lender, and the coupon is the interest. _____s provide the borrower with external funds to finance long-term investments, or, in the case of government _____s, to finance current expenditure.

a. Bond
b. Puttable bond
c. Catastrophe bonds
d. Convertible bond

28. _____ is the risk (variability in value) borne by an interest-bearing asset, such as a loan or a bond, due to variability of interest rates. In general, as rates rise, the price of a fixed rate bond will fall, and vice versa. _____ is commonly measured by the bond's duration.

a. A Random Walk Down Wall Street
b. Official bank rate
c. International Fisher effect
d. Interest rate risk

29. A _____ is a unit that is equal to 1/100th of a percentage point. It is frequently used to express percentage point changes of less than 1%. It avoids the ambiguity between relative and absolute discussions about rates.

a. 4-4-5 Calendar
b. 529 plan
c. Bond market
d. Basis point

30. A _____ is a private investment fund open to a limited range of investors that is permitted by regulators to undertake a wider range of activities than other investment funds and also pays a performance fee to its investment manager. Each fund will have its own strategy which determines the type of investments and the methods of investment it undertakes. _____s as a class invest in a broad range of investments extending over shares, debt, commodities and beyond.

a. 4-4-5 Calendar
b. Hedge fund
c. 7-Eleven
d. 529 plan

31. In finance, a _____ is a type of bond that can be converted into shares of stock in the issuing company, usually at some pre-announced ratio. It is a hybrid security with debt- and equity-like features. Although it typically has a low coupon rate, the holder is compensated with the ability to convert the bond to common stock, usually at a substantial discount to the stock's market value.

a. Convertible bond
b. Gilts
c. Bond fund
d. Corporate bond

32. An _____ is a company whose main business is holding securities of other companies purely for investment purposes. The _____ invests money on behalf of its shareholders who in turn share in the profits and losses.

Chapter 23. Futures and Swaps: Markets and Applications

a. AAB
b. Investment Company
c. Unit investment trust
d. A Random Walk Down Wall Street

33. In e-business terms, a _____ is an organization that originated and does business purely through the internet, they have no physical store (brick and mortar) where customers can shop. Examples of large _____ companies include Amazon.com and Netflix.com. There are also many smaller, niche oriented _____ mail order companies such as women's travel accessories company Christine Columbus and fashion jewelry merchant Jewels of Denial.
   a. 529 plan
   b. 4-4-5 Calendar
   c. The Dogs of the Dow
   d. Pure play

34. An _____ is a derivative in which one party exchanges a stream of interest payments for another party's stream of cash flows. _____s can be used by hedgers to manage their fixed or floating assets and liabilities. They can also be used by speculators to replicate unfunded bond exposures to profit from changes in interest rates.
   a. Implied volatility
   b. Equity swap
   c. International Swaps and Derivatives Association
   d. Interest rate swap

35. In finance, a _____ is a derivative in which two counterparties agree to exchange one stream of cash flows against another stream. These streams are called the legs of the _____.

The cash flows are calculated over a notional principal amount, which is usually not exchanged between counterparties.

   a. Volatility swap
   b. Volatility arbitrage
   c. Local volatility
   d. Swap

36. In financial accounting, a _____ or statement of financial position is a summary of a person's or organization's balances. Assets, liabilities and ownership equity are listed as of a specific date, such as the end of its financial year. A _____ is often described as a snapshot of a company's financial condition.
   a. Statement on Auditing Standards No. 70: Service Organizations
   b. Statement of retained earnings
   c. Financial statements
   d. Balance sheet

37. _____ is the corporate management term for the act of reorganizing the legal, ownership, operational, or other structures of a company for the purpose of making it more profitable or better organized for its present needs. Alternate reasons for restructing include a change of ownership or ownership structure, demerger repositioning debt _____ and financial _____.
   a. Day trading
   b. Restructuring
   c. Cross-border leasing
   d. Concentrated stock

38. _____s are deposits denominated in United States dollars at banks outside the United States, and thus are not under the jurisdiction of the Federal Reserve. Consequently, such deposits are subject to much less regulation than similar deposits within the United States, allowing for higher margins. There is nothing 'European' about _____ deposits; a US dollar-denominated deposit in Tokyo or Caracas would likewise be deemed _____ deposits.
   a. Eurodollar
   b. AAB
   c. ABN Amro
   d. A Random Walk Down Wall Street

Chapter 23. Futures and Swaps: Markets and Applications

39. A _____ is an agreement between two parties to buy or sell an asset at a specified point of time in the future. The price of the underlying instrument, in whatever form, is paid before control of the instrument changes. This is one of the many forms of buy/sell orders where the time of trade is not the time where the securities themselves are exchanged.
   a. Derivatives markets
   b. Constant maturity credit default swap
   c. Forward contract
   d. Loan Credit Default Swap Index

40. A _____ is something for which there is demand, but which is supplied without qualitative differentiation across a market. It is a product that is the same no matter who produces it, such as petroleum, notebook paper, or milk. In other words, copper is copper.
   a. 4-4-5 Calendar
   b. 7-Eleven
   c. Commodity
   d. 529 plan

41. _____ is the provision of resources (such as granting a loan) by one party to another party where that second party does not reimburse the first party immediately, thereby generating a debt, and instead arranges either to repay or return those resources (or material(s) of equal value) at a later date. The first party is called a creditor, also known as a lender, while the second party is called a debtor, also known as a borrower.

Movements of financial capital are normally dependent on either _____ or equity transfers.

   a. Warrant
   b. Clearing house
   c. Comparable
   d. Credit

42. _____ is the risk of loss due to a debtor's non-payment of a loan or other line of credit (either the principal or interest (coupon) or both)

Most lenders employ their own models (credit scorecards) to rank potential and existing customers according to risk, and then apply appropriate strategies. With products such as unsecured personal loans or mortgages, lenders charge a higher price for higher risk customers and vice versa. With revolving products such as credit cards and overdrafts, risk is controlled through careful setting of credit limits.

   a. Credit risk
   b. Market risk
   c. Transaction risk
   d. Liquidity risk

43. In economics, business, and accounting, a _____ is the value of money that has been used up to produce something, and hence is not available for use anymore. In business, the _____ may be one of acquisition, in which case the amount of money expended to acquire it is counted as _____. In this case, money is the input that is gone in order to acquire the thing.
   a. Fixed costs
   b. Sliding scale fees
   c. Marginal cost
   d. Cost

44. In finance, the _____ approach describes a method of valuing a project, company, or asset using the concepts of the time value of money. All future cash flows are estimated and discounted to give their present values. The discount rate used is generally the appropriate cost of capital and may incorporate judgments of the uncertainty (riskiness) of the future cash flows.

a. Present value of benefits
c. Net present value
b. Discounted cash flow
d. Future-oriented

45. _____ is the balance of the amounts of cash being received and paid by a business during a defined period of time, sometimes tied to a specific project. Measurement of _____ can be used

- to evaluate the state or performance of a business or project.
- to determine problems with liquidity. Being profitable does not necessarily mean being liquid. A company can fail because of a shortage of cash, even while profitable.
- to generate project rate of returns. The time of _____s into and out of projects are used as inputs to financial models such as internal rate of return, and net present value.
- to examine income or growth of a business when it is believed that accrual accounting concepts do not represent economic realities. Alternately, _____ can be used to 'validate' the net income generated by accrual accounting.

_____ as a generic term may be used differently depending on context, and certain _____ definitions may be adapted by analysts and users for their own uses. Common terms include operating _____ and free _____.

_____s can be classified into:

1. Operational _____s: Cash received or expended as a result of the company's core business activities.
2. Investment _____s: Cash received or expended through capital expenditure, investments or acquisitions.
3. Financing _____s: Cash received or expended as a result of financial activities, such as interests and dividends.

All three together - the net _____ - are necessary to reconcile the beginning cash balance to the ending cash balance. Loan draw downs or equity injections, that is just shifting of capital but no expenditure as such, are not considered in the net _____.

a. Corporate finance
c. Shareholder value
b. Real option
d. Cash flow

Chapter 24. Portfolio Performance Evaluation

1. The _____ is a measure of the excess return (or Risk Premium) per unit of risk in an investment asset or a trading strategy it is defined as:

$$S = \frac{R - R_f}{\sigma} = \frac{E[R - R_f]}{\sqrt{\text{var}[R - R_f]}},$$

where R is the asset return, R_f is the return on a benchmark asset, such as the risk free rate of return, $E[R - R_f]$ is the expected value of the excess of the asset return over the benchmark return, and σ is the standard deviation of the asset excess return.

Note, if R_f is a constant risk free return throughout the period,

$$\sqrt{\text{var}[R - R_f]} = \sqrt{\text{var}[R]}.$$

The _____ is used to characterize how well the return of an asset compensates the investor for the risk taken. When comparing two assets each with the expected return E[R] against the same benchmark with return R_f, the asset with the higher _____ gives more return for the same risk.

    a. P/E ratio   b. Receivables turnover ratio
    c. Current ratio   d. Sharpe ratio

2. In finance, _____, also known as return on investment is the ratio of money gained or lost on an investment relative to the amount of money invested. The amount of money gained or lost may be referred to as interest, profit/loss, gain/loss, or net income/loss. The money invested may be referred to as the asset, capital, principal, or the cost basis of the investment.
    a. Rate of return   b. Stock or scrip dividends
    c. Composiition of Creditors   d. Doctrine of the Proper Law

3. The _____ is a capital budgeting metric used by firms to decide whether they should make investments. It is an indicator of the efficiency or quality of an investment, as opposed to net present value (NPV), which indicates value or magnitude.

The IRR is the annualized effective compounded return rate which can be earned on the invested capital, i.e., the yield on the investment.

    a. Internal rate of return   b. A Random Walk Down Wall Street
    c. ABN Amro   d. AAB

4. _____ measures the active return of an investment manager divided by the amount of risk the manager takes relative to a benchmark. It is used in the analysis of performance of mutual funds, hedge funds, etc. Specifically, the _____ is defined as active return divided by tracking error.
    a. Operating leverage   b. Earnings yield
    c. Asset turnover   d. Information ratio

Chapter 24. Portfolio Performance Evaluation

5. In finance, _____ is a measure of how closely a portfolio follows the index to which it is benchmarked. It measures the standard deviation of the difference between the portfolio and index returns.

Many portfolios are managed to a benchmark, normally an index.

a. Transaction risk
c. Liquidity risk
b. Tracking error
d. Market risk

6. A _____ is a professionally managed type of collective investment scheme that pools money from many investors and invests it in stocks, bonds, short-term money market instruments, and/or other securities. The _____ will have a fund manager that trades the pooled money on a regular basis. Currently, the worldwide value of all _____s totals more than $26 trillion.

Since 1940, there have been three basic types of investment companies in the United States: open-end funds, also known in the US as _____s; unit investment trusts (UITs); and closed-end funds.

a. Financial intermediary
c. Trust company
b. Mutual fund
d. Net asset value

7. _____ is a risk-adjusted measure of the so-called active return on an investment. It is the return in excess of the compensation for the risk borne, and thus commonly used to assess active managers' performances. Often, the return of a benchmark is subtracted in order to consider relative performance, which yields Jensen's _____.

a. Alpha
c. Annuity
b. Amortization
d. Option

8. In statistics, a _____ is a tabulation of the values that one or more variables take in a sample.

Univariate _____s are often presented as lists ordered by quantity showing the number of times each value appears. For example, if 100 people rate a five-point Likert scale assessing their agreement with a statement on a scale on which 1 denotes strong agreement and 5 strong disagreement, the _____ of their responses might look like:

This simple tabulation has two drawbacks.

a. Covariance
c. Variance
b. Random variables
d. Frequency distribution

9. The _____ is the weighted-average most likely outcome in gambling, probability theory, economics or finance.

In gambling and probability theory, there is usually a discrete set of possible outcomes. In this case, _____ is a measure of the relative balance of win or loss weighted by their chances of occurring.

a. AAB
c. ABN Amro
b. A Random Walk Down Wall Street
d. Expected return

Chapter 24. Portfolio Performance Evaluation

10. A _____ is a fungible, negotiable instrument representing financial value. They are broadly categorized into debt securities (such as banknotes, bonds and debentures), and equity securities; e.g., common stocks. The company or other entity issuing the _____ is called the issuer.
   a. Securities lending
   b. Book entry
   c. Tracking stock
   d. Security

11. In finance, a _____ is a position established in one market in an attempt to offset exposure to the price risk of an equal but opposite obligation or position in another market -- usually, but not always, in the context of one's commercial activity. Hedging is a strategy designed to minimize exposure to such business risks as a sharp contraction in demand for one's inventory, while still allowing the business to profit from producing and maintaining that inventory. A typical hedger might be a farmer with 2000 acres of unharvested wheat in the ground, who would rather tend his crop without the distraction of uncertain prices.
   a. 529 plan
   b. 7-Eleven
   c. 4-4-5 Calendar
   d. Hedge

12. A _____ is a private investment fund open to a limited range of investors that is permitted by regulators to undertake a wider range of activities than other investment funds and also pays a performance fee to its investment manager. Each fund will have its own strategy which determines the type of investments and the methods of investment it undertakes. _____s as a class invest in a broad range of investments extending over shares, debt, commodities and beyond.
   a. 4-4-5 Calendar
   b. Hedge fund
   c. 529 plan
   d. 7-Eleven

13. _____ is an investment management term which refers to the return of an investment manager who has intentionally and completely eliminated his market risk, or beta. The return of such a portfolio will only represent the manager's skill in selecting investments within the market, and will be independent of the direction or magnitude of the market's movement. The elimination of market risk can be accomplished through use of futures, swaps, options, or short selling.
   a. Certificate in Investment Performance Measurement
   b. Rebalancing
   c. Market timing
   d. Portable alpha

14. _____ is the process whereby an organization establishes the parameters within which programs, investments, and acquisitions are reaching the desired results. Performance Reference Model of the Federal Enterprise Architecture, 2005.

This process of measuring performance ofter requires the use of statistical evidence to determine progress toward specific defined organizational objectives.

There are many types of measurements.

   a. Cash cow
   b. Corporate Transparency
   c. Performance measurement
   d. Decentralization

Chapter 24. Portfolio Performance Evaluation

15. In finance, a _____ is a type of bond that can be converted into shares of stock in the issuing company, usually at some pre-announced ratio. It is a hybrid security with debt- and equity-like features. Although it typically has a low coupon rate, the holder is compensated with the ability to convert the bond to common stock, usually at a substantial discount to the stock's market value.
    a. Gilts
    b. Convertible bond
    c. Bond fund
    d. Corporate bond

16. _____ is a market neutral investment strategy often associated with hedge funds. It involves the simultaneous purchase of convertible securities and the short sale of the same issuer's common stock.

    The premise of the strategy is that the convertible is sometimes priced inefficiently relative to the underlying stock, for reasons that range from illiquidity to market psychology.

    a. Convertible arbitrage
    b. Forward market
    c. Long position
    d. Market price

17. _____ are securities of companies or government entities that are either already in default, under bankruptcy protection, or in distress and heading toward such a condition. The most common _____ are bonds and bank debt. While there is no precise definition, fixed income instruments with a yield to maturity in excess of 1000 basis points over the risk-free rate of return (e.g. Treasuries) are commonly thought of as being distressed.
    a. 7-Eleven
    b. Distressed securities
    c. 4-4-5 Calendar
    d. 529 plan

18. The term _____ is used to describe a nation's social, or business activity in the process of rapid industrialization. _____ are generally less-wealthy than the developed world, and are wealthier (or the wealthiest of) the developing world. According to The Economist many people find the term dated, but a new term has yet to gain much traction.
    a. A Random Walk Down Wall Street
    b. ABN Amro
    c. AAB
    d. Emerging markets

19. An investment strategy or portfolio is considered _____ if it seeks to entirely avoid some form of market risk, typically by hedging. In order to evaluate market neutrality, it is first necessary to specify the risk being avoided. For example, convertible arbitrage attempts to fully hedge fluctuations in the price of the underlying common stock.
    a. Credit event
    b. Flight-to-quality
    c. Black-Litterman model
    d. Market neutral

20. _____ is the strategy of making buy or sell decisions of financial assets (often stocks) by attempting to predict future market price movements. The prediction may be based on an outlook of market or economic conditions resulting from technical or fundamental analysis. This is an investment strategy based on the outlook for an aggregate market, rather than for a particular financial asset.
    a. Portable alpha
    b. Market timing
    c. Late trading
    d. Divestment

21. In economics and finance, _____ is the practice of taking advantage of a price differential between two or more markets: striking a combination of matching deals that capitalize upon the imbalance, the profit being the difference between the market prices. When used by academics, an _____ is a transaction that involves no negative cash flow at any probabilistic or temporal state and a positive cash flow in at least one state; in simple terms, a risk-free profit.

a. Initial margin
b. Issuer
c. Efficient-market hypothesis
d. Arbitrage

22. In finance, the _____ is used to determine a theoretically appropriate required rate of return of an asset, if that asset is to be added to an already well-diversified portfolio, given that asset's non-diversifiable risk. The model takes into account the asset's sensitivity to non-diversifiable risk (also known as systemic risk or market risk), often represented by the quantity beta (β) in the financial industry, as well as the expected return of the market and the expected return of a theoretical risk-free asset.

The model was introduced by Jack Treynor (1961, 1962), William Sharpe (1964), John Lintner (1965a,b) and Jan Mossin (1966) independently, building on the earlier work of Harry Markowitz on diversification and modern portfolio theory.

a. Capital asset pricing model
b. Hull-White model
c. Random walk hypothesis
d. Cox-Ingersoll-Ross model

23. _____ is a measure of the ability of a debtor to pay their debts as and when they fall due. It is usually expressed as a ratio or a percentage of current liabilities.

For a corporation with a published balance sheet there are various ratios used to calculate a measure of liquidity.

a. Accounting liquidity
b. Operating profit margin
c. Invested capital
d. Operating leverage

24. In financial accounting, _____s are precautions for which the amount or probability of occurrence are not known. Typical examples are _____s for warranty costs and _____ for taxes the term reserve is used instead of term _____; such a use, however, is inconsistent with the terminology suggested by International Accounting Standards Board.

a. Provision
b. Petty cash
c. Money measurement concept
d. Momentum Accounting and Triple-Entry Bookkeeping

25. In probability and statistics, the _____ of a collection of numbers is a measure of the dispersion of the numbers from their expected (mean) value. It can apply to a probability distribution, a random variable, a population or a data set. The _____ is usually denoted with the letter σ (lowercase sigma.)

a. Sample size
b. Kurtosis
c. Standard deviation
d. Mean

26. A _____ is a financial contract between two parties, the buyer and the seller of this type of option. Often it is simply labeled a 'call'. The buyer of the option has the right, but not the obligation to buy an agreed quantity of a particular commodity or financial instrument (the underlying instrument) from the seller of the option at a certain time (the expiration date) for a certain price (the strike price.)

a. Bear spread
b. Bear call spread
c. Bull spread
d. Call option

Chapter 24. Portfolio Performance Evaluation   233

27. An _____ is a contract written by a seller that conveys to the buyer the right -- but not the obligation -- to buy (in the case of a call _____) or to sell (in the case of a put _____) a particular asset, such as a piece of property such as, among others, a futures contract. In return for granting the _____, the seller collects a payment (the premium) from the buyer.

For example, buying a call _____ provides the right to buy a specified quantity of a security at a set strike price at some time on or before expiration, while buying a put _____ provides the right to sell.

a. AT'T Mobility LLC
c. Annuity

b. Amortization
d. Option

28. The term _____ refers to three closely related concepts:

- The _____ model is a mathematical model of the market for an equity, in which the equity's price is a stochastic process.
- The _____ PDE is a partial differential equation which (in the model) must be satisfied by the price of a derivative on the equity.
- The _____ formula is the result obtained by solving the _____ PDE for a European call option.

Fischer Black and Myron Scholes first articulated the _____ formula in their 1973 paper, 'The Pricing of Options and Corporate Liabilities.' The foundation for their research relied on work developed by scholars such as Jack L. Treynor, Paul Samuelson, A. James Boness, Sheen T. Kassouf, and Edward O. Thorp. The fundamental insight of _____ is that the option is implicitly priced if the stock is traded.

Robert C. Merton was the first to publish a paper expanding the mathematical understanding of the options pricing model and coined the term '_____' options pricing model.

a. Perpetuity
c. Modified Internal Rate of Return

b. Stochastic volatility
d. Black-Scholes

29. _____ is the price at which an asset would trade in a competitive Walrasian auction setting. _____ is often used interchangeably with open _____, fair value or fair _____, although these terms have distinct definitions in different standards, and may differ in some circumstances.

International Valuation Standards defines _____ as 'the estimated amount for which a property should exchange on the date of valuation between a willing buyer and a willing seller in an arm'e;s-length transaction after proper marketing wherein the parties had each acted knowledgeably, prudently, and without compulsion.'

_____ is a concept distinct from market price, which is 'e;the price at which one can transact'e;, while _____ is 'e;the true underlying value'e; according to theoretical standards.

a. Wrap account
c. T-Model

b. Debt restructuring
d. Market value

Chapter 24. Portfolio Performance Evaluation

30. A _____ is a private or public market for the trading of company stock and derivatives of company stock at an agreed price; these are securities listed on a stock exchange as well as those only traded privately.

The size of the world _____ is estimated at about $36.6 trillion US at the beginning of October 2008 . The world derivatives market has been estimated at about $480 trillion face or nominal value, 12 times the size of the entire world economy.

   a. Anton Gelonkin   b. Adolph Coors
   c. Andrew Tobias   d. Stock market

31. In Modern Portfolio Theory, the _____ is the graphical representation of the Capital Asset Pricing Model. It displays the expected rate of return for an overall market as a function of systematic (non-diversifiable) risk (beta.)

The Y-Intercept (beta=0) of the _____ is equal to the risk-free interest rate.

   a. Rebalancing   b. Security market line
   c. Certificate in Investment Performance Measurement   d. Divestment

32. _____ or Investment _____ is a set of techniques that performance analysts use to explain why a portfolio's performance differed from the benchmark. This difference between the portfolio return and the benchmark return is known as the active return. The active return is the component of a portfolio's performance that arises from the fact that the portfolio is actively managed.
   a. Convertible arbitrage   b. Delta neutral
   c. Performance attribution   d. Central Securities Depository

33. The institution most often referenced by the word '_____' is a public or publicly traded _____, the shares of which are traded on a public stock exchange (e.g., the New York Stock Exchange or Nasdaq in the United States) where shares of stock of _____s are bought and sold by and to the general public. Most of the largest businesses in the world are publicly traded _____s. However, the majority of _____s are said to be closely held, privately held or close _____s, meaning that no ready market exists for the trading of shares.
   a. Corporation   b. Federal Home Loan Mortgage Corporation
   c. Depository Trust Company   d. Protect

34. In Finance the _____ is a mathematical model for portfolio allocation developed in 1990 at Goldman Sachs by Fischer Black and Robert Litterman, and published in 1992. It seeks to overcome problems that institutional investors have encountered in applying modern portfolio theory in practice. The model starts with the equilibrium assumption that the asset allocation of a representative agent should be proportional to the market values of the available assets, and then modifies that to take into account the 'views' (i.e. the specific opinions about asset returns) of the investor in question to arrive at a bespoke asset allocation.
   a. Specific risk   b. Black-Litterman model
   c. Capital surplus   d. Clientele effect

35. In business and accounting, _____s are everything of value that is owned by a person or company. The balance sheet of a firm records the monetary value of the _____s owned by the firm. The two major _____ classes are tangible _____s and intangible _____s.

a. EBITDA
b. Asset
c. Accounts payable
d. Income

36. _____ is a term used to refer to how an investor distributes his or her investments among various classes of investment vehicles (e.g., stocks and bonds.)

A large part of financial planning is finding an _____ that is appropriate for a given person in terms of their appetite for and ability to shoulder risk. This can depend on various factors; see investor profile.

a. Investing online
b. Alternative investment
c. Investment performance
d. Asset allocation

Chapter 25. International Diversification

1. _____ in finance is a risk management technique, related to hedging, that mixes a wide variety of investments within a portfolio. Because the fluctuations of a single security have less impact on a diverse portfolio, _____ minimizes the risk from any one investment.

A simple example of _____ is the following: On a particular island the entire economy consists of two companies: one that sells umbrellas and another that sells sunscreen.

    a. 4-4-5 Calendar
    c. 529 plan
    b. 7-Eleven
    d. Diversification

2. The term _____ is used to describe a nation's social, or business activity in the process of rapid industrialization. _____ are generally less-wealthy than the developed world, and are wealthier (or the wealthiest of) the developing world. According to The Economist many people find the term dated, but a new term has yet to gain much traction.

    a. AAB
    c. ABN Amro
    b. A Random Walk Down Wall Street
    d. Emerging markets

3. The _____ is a bank that provides financial and technical assistance to developing countries for development programs (e.g. bridges, roads, schools, etc.) with the stated goal of reducing poverty.

The _____ differs from the _____ Group, in that the _____ comprises only two institutions:

- International Bank for Reconstruction and Development (IBRD)
- International Development Association (IDA)

Whereas the latter incorporates these two in addition to three more:

- International Finance Corporation (IFC)
- Multilateral Investment Guarantee Agency (MIGA)
- International Centre for Settlement of Investment Disputes (ICSID)

John Maynard Keynes (right) represented the UK at the conference, and Harry Dexter White represented the US.

The _____ was created following the ratification of the United Nations Monetary and Financial Conference | Bretton Woods agreement. The concept was originally conceived in July 1944 at the United Nations Monetary and Financial Conference.

    a. 4-4-5 Calendar
    c. 7-Eleven
    b. 529 plan
    d. World Bank

4. A _____ is a private or public market for the trading of company stock and derivatives of company stock at an agreed price; these are securities listed on a stock exchange as well as those only traded privately.

The size of the world _____ is estimated at about $36.6 trillion US at the beginning of October 2008. The world derivatives market has been estimated at about $480 trillion face or nominal value, 12 times the size of the entire world economy.

Chapter 25. International Diversification

a. Anton Gelonkin
b. Adolph Coors
c. Stock market
d. Andrew Tobias

5. A _____ is a fungible, negotiable instrument representing financial value. They are broadly categorized into debt securities (such as banknotes, bonds and debentures), and equity securities; e.g., common stocks. The company or other entity issuing the _____ is called the issuer.
   a. Securities lending
   b. Security
   c. Book entry
   d. Tracking stock

6. The _____ is one of the measures of national income and input for a given country's economy. _____ is defined as the total cost of all finished goods and services produced within the country in a stipulated period of time (usually a 365-day year.) It is sometimes regarded as the sum of profits added at every level of production (the intermediate stages) of all final goods and services produced within a country in a stipulated timeframe, and it is rarely given a monetary value.
   a. Behavioral finance
   b. Recession
   c. Macroeconomics
   d. Gross domestic product

7. _____ is a measurement of corporate or economic size equal to the share price times the number of shares outstanding of a public company. As owning stock represents owning the company, including all its equity, capitalization could represent the public opinion of a company's net worth and is a determining factor in stock valuation. Likewise, the capitalization of stock markets or economic regions may be compared to other economic indicators.
   a. Proxy fight
   b. Just-in-time
   c. Market capitalization
   d. Synthetic CDO

8. A _____, securities exchange or (in Europe) bourse is a corporation or mutual organization which provides 'trading' facilities for stock brokers and traders, to trade stocks and other securities. _____s also provide facilities for the issue and redemption of securities as well as other financial instruments and capital events including the payment of income and dividends. The securities traded on a _____ include: shares issued by companies, unit trusts and other pooled investment products and bonds.
   a. 7-Eleven
   b. 529 plan
   c. 4-4-5 Calendar
   d. Stock exchange

9. In finance, the _____ between two currencies specifies how much one currency is worth in terms of the other. For example an _____ of 102 Japanese yen to the United States dollar means that JPY 102 is worth the same as USD 1. The foreign exchange market is one of the largest markets in the world.
   a. A Random Walk Down Wall Street
   b. ABN Amro
   c. Exchange rate
   d. AAB

10. _____ is a form of risk that arises from the change in price of one currency against another. Whenever investors or companies have assets or business operations across national borders, they face _____ if their positions are not hedged.

- Transaction risk is the risk that exchange rates will change unfavourably over time. It can be hedged against using forward currency contracts;
- Translation risk is an accounting risk, proportional to the amount of assets held in foreign currencies. Changes in the exchange rate over time will render a report inaccurate, and so assets are usually balanced by borrowings in that currency.

The exchange risk associated with a foreign denominated instrument is a key element in foreign investment. This risk flows from differential monetary policy and growth in real productivity, which results in differential inflation rates.

a. Tracking error
c. Currency risk
b. Credit risk
d. Market risk

11. The term _____ or economic cycle refers to the fluctuations of economic activity (business fluctuations) around a long-term growth trend. The cycle involves shifts over time between periods of relatively rapid growth of output (recovery and prosperity), and periods of relative stagnation or decline (contraction or recession.) These fluctuations are often measured using the real gross domestic product.

a. Deflation
c. Behavioral finance
b. Business cycle
d. Fixed exchange rate

12. A _____ is a variable associated with an increased risk of disease or infection. They are correlational and not necessarily causal, because correlation does not imply causation. For example, being young cannot be said to cause measles, but young people are more at risk as they are less likely to have developed immunity during a previous epidemic.

a. Risk factor
c. 7-Eleven
b. 4-4-5 Calendar
d. 529 plan

13. _____ is a fee paid on borrowed assets. It is the price paid for the use of borrowed money , or, money earned by deposited funds . Assets that are sometimes lent with _____ include money, shares, consumer goods through hire purchase, major assets such as aircraft, and even entire factories in finance lease arrangements.

a. AAB
c. A Random Walk Down Wall Street
b. Insolvency
d. Interest

14. An _____ is the price a borrower pays for the use of money they do not own, and the return a lender receives for deferring the use of funds, by lending it to the borrower. _____s are normally expressed as a percentage rate over the period of one year.

_____s targets are also a vital tool of monetary policy and are used to control variables like investment, inflation, and unemployment.

a. ABN Amro
c. A Random Walk Down Wall Street
b. Interest rate
d. AAB

Chapter 25. International Diversification

15. _____ is an economic concept, expressed as a basic algebraic identity that relates interest rates and exchange rates. The identity is theoretical, and usually follows from assumptions imposed in economics models. There is evidence to support as well as to refute the concept.
   a. Unit price
   b. Interest rate parity
   c. AAB
   d. A Random Walk Down Wall Street

16. In economics and finance, _____ is the practice of taking advantage of a price differential between two or more markets: striking a combination of matching deals that capitalize upon the imbalance, the profit being the difference between the market prices. When used by academics, an _____ is a transaction that involves no negative cash flow at any probabilistic or temporal state and a positive cash flow in at least one state; in simple terms, a risk-free profit.
   a. Arbitrage
   b. Efficient-market hypothesis
   c. Initial margin
   d. Issuer

17. _____ is a type of risk faced by investors, corporations, and governments. It is a risk that can be understood and managed with proper aforethought and investment.

   Broadly, _____ refers to the complications businesses and governments may face as a result of what are commonly referred to as political decisions--or 'any political change that alters the expected outcome and value of a given economic action by changing the probability of achieving business objectives.'.
   a. Single-index model
   b. Mid price
   c. Capital asset
   d. Political Risk

18. An _____ represents the ownership in the shares of a foreign company trading on US financial markets. The stock of many non-US companies trades on US exchanges through the use of _____ s. _____ s enable US investors to buy shares in foreign companies without undertaking cross-border transactions.
   a. American Depository Receipt
   b. A Random Walk Down Wall Street
   c. AAB
   d. ABN Amro

19. _____ refers to the likelihood that changes in the business environment adversely affect operating profits or the value of assets in a specific country. For example, financial factors such as currency controls, devaluation or regulatory changes, or stability factors such as mass riots, civil war and other potential events contribute to companies' operational risks. This term is also sometimes referred to as political risk, however _____ is a more general term, which generally only refers to risks affecting all companies operating within a particular country.
   a. Single-index model
   b. Country Risk
   c. Capital asset
   d. Solvency

20. An _____ is an investment vehicle traded on stock exchanges, much like stocks. An ETF holds assets such as stocks or bonds and trades at approximately the same price as the net asset value of its underlying assets over the course of the trading day. Most ETFs track an index, such as the Dow Jones Industrial Average or the S'P 500.
   a. A Random Walk Down Wall Street
   b. Exchange-traded fund
   c. ABN Amro
   d. AAB

21. In business and finance, a _____ (also referred to as equity _____) of stock means a _____ of ownership in a corporation (company.) In the plural, stocks is often used as a synonym for _____ s especially in the United States, but it is less commonly used that way outside of North America.

Chapter 25. International Diversification

In the United Kingdom, South Africa, and Australia, stock can also refer to completely different financial instruments such as government bonds or, less commonly, to all kinds of marketable securities.

a. Margin
b. Procter ' Gamble
c. Bucket shop
d. Share

22. _____ is the risk that the value of an investment will decrease due to moves in market factors. The five standard _____ factors are:

- Equity risk, the risk that stock prices will change.
- Interest rate risk, the risk that interest rates will change.
- Currency risk, the risk that foreign exchange rates will change.
- Commodity risk, the risk that commodity prices (e.g. grains, metals) will change.

As with other forms of risk, _____ may be measured in a number of ways. Traditionally, this is done using a Value at Risk methodology. Value at risk is well established as a risk management technique, but it contains a number of limiting assumptions that constrain its accuracy.

a. Transaction risk
b. Currency risk
c. Tracking error
d. Market risk

23. _____ occurs when prices among different location or related goods follow similar patterns in a long period. Group of prices often move proportionally to each other and when this relation is very clear among different markets it is said that the markets are integrated. Thus _____ is an indicator that explains how much different markets are related to each other.
a. Channel stuffing
b. Market integration
c. Securities offering
d. Bonus share

24. A _____ is the direction in which a financial market is moving. _____s can be classified as primary trends, secondary trends (short-term), and secular trends (long-term.) This principle incorporates the idea that market cycles occur with regularity and persistence.
a. 4-4-5 Calendar
b. Market trend
c. 529 plan
d. 7-Eleven

25. A _____ is a sudden dramatic decline of stock prices across a significant cross-section of a stock market. Crashes are driven by panic as much as by underlying economic factors. They often follow speculative stock market bubbles.
a. 7-Eleven
b. 529 plan
c. Stock market crash
d. 4-4-5 Calendar

26. _____ or Investment _____ is a set of techniques that performance analysts use to explain why a portfolio's performance differed from the benchmark. This difference between the portfolio return and the benchmark return is known as the active return. The active return is the component of a portfolio's performance that arises from the fact that the portfolio is actively managed.

Chapter 25. International Diversification

a. Delta neutral
c. Convertible arbitrage
b. Central Securities Depository
d. Performance attribution

27. The institution most often referenced by the word '_____' is a public or publicly traded _____, the shares of which are traded on a public stock exchange (e.g., the New York Stock Exchange or Nasdaq in the United States) where shares of stock of _____s are bought and sold by and to the general public. Most of the largest businesses in the world are publicly traded _____s. However, the majority of _____s are said to be closely held, privately held or close _____s, meaning that no ready market exists for the trading of shares.

a. Corporation
c. Depository Trust Company
b. Federal Home Loan Mortgage Corporation
d. Protect

28. In finance, the _____ is used to determine a theoretically appropriate required rate of return of an asset, if that asset is to be added to an already well-diversified portfolio, given that asset's non-diversifiable risk. The model takes into account the asset's sensitivity to non-diversifiable risk (also known as systemic risk or market risk), often represented by the quantity beta (β) in the financial industry, as well as the expected return of the market and the expected return of a theoretical risk-free asset.

The model was introduced by Jack Treynor (1961, 1962), William Sharpe (1964), John Lintner (1965a,b) and Jan Mossin (1966) independently, building on the earlier work of Harry Markowitz on diversification and modern portfolio theory.

a. Hull-White model
c. Random walk hypothesis
b. Cox-Ingersoll-Ross model
d. Capital asset pricing model

29. The term _____ has three unrelated technical definitions, and is also used in a variety of non-technical ways.

- In financial economics, it refers to any asset used to make money, as opposed to assets used for personal enjoyment or consumption. This is an important distinction because two people can disagree sharply about the value of personal assets, one person might think a sports car is more valuable than a pickup truck, another person might have the opposite taste. But if an asset is held for the purpose of making money, taste has nothing to do with it, only differences of opinion about how much money the asset will produce. With the further assumption that people agree on the probability distribution of future cash flows, it is possible to have an objective _____ pricing model. Even without the assumption of agreement, it is possible to set rational limits on _____ value.
- In governmental accounting, it is defined as any asset used in operations with an initial useful life extending beyond one reporting period. Generally, government managers have a 'stewardship' duty to maintain _____s under their control. See International Public Sector Accounting Standards for details.
- In US tax accounting, it is defined as any property other than a list of exceptions. The main exceptions are anything held for sale, and any real estate or depreciable property used in business. Almost everything you own and use for personal purposes, pleasure or investment is a _____. If something is a _____ for tax purposes, gains or losses on sale or disposition are capital gains or capital losses. For individuals, however, capital losses on property held for personal use are generally not deductible. See the IRS publication Tax Facts about Capital Gains and Losses for details.

A well-known financial accounting textbook advises that the term be avoided except in tax accounting because it is used in so many different senses, not all of them well-defined. For example it is often used as a synonym for fixed assets or for investments in securities.

A common non-technical usage occurs when people ask that employees or the environment or something else be treated as a _____.

    a. Settlement date   b. Political risk
    c. Solvency   d. Capital asset

30. In business and accounting, _____s are everything of value that is owned by a person or company. The balance sheet of a firm records the monetary value of the _____s owned by the firm. The two major _____ classes are tangible _____s and intangible _____s.
    a. Accounts payable   b. EBITDA
    c. Income   d. Asset

31. In finance, _____ is the process of estimating the potential market value of a financial asset or liability. they can be done on assets (for example, investments in marketable securities such as stocks, options, business enterprises, or intangible assets such as patents and trademarks) or on liabilities (e.g., Bonds issued by a company.) _____s are required in many contexts including investment analysis, capital budgeting, merger and acquisition transactions, financial reporting, taxable events to determine the proper tax liability, and in litigation.
    a. Procter ' Gamble   b. Share
    c. Margin   d. Valuation

Chapter 26. Investment Policy and the Framework of the CFA Institute

1. _____ is an international professional designation offered by the _____ Institute (formerly known as AIMR) to financial analysts who complete a series of three examinations. In order to become a '_____ Charterholder' candidates must pass all three six-hour exams, possess a bachelor's degree (or equivalent, as assessed by the _____ institute) and have 48 months of work experience in an investment decision-making position. _____ charterholders are also obligated to adhere to a strict Code of Ethics and Standards governing their professional conduct.

   a. 529 plan
   b. 7-Eleven
   c. 4-4-5 Calendar
   d. Chartered Financial Analyst

2. A _____, securities analyst, research analyst, equity analyst, or investment analyst is a person who performs financial analysis for external or internal clients as a core part of the job.

   An analyst studies companies and other entities to arrive at the estimate of their financial value. It is normally done by analyzing financial reports, aided by follow-up interviews with company representatives and industry experts.

   a. Purchasing manager
   b. Financial Analyst
   c. Stockbroker
   d. Portfolio manager

3. _____ refers to a portfolio management strategy where the manager makes specific investments with the goal of outperforming an investment benchmark index. Investors or mutual funds that do not aspire to create a return in excess of a benchmark index will often invest in an index fund that replicates as closely as possible the investment weighting and returns of that index; this is called passive management. _____ is the opposite of passive management, because in passive management the manager does not seek to outperform the benchmark index.

   a. ABN Amro
   b. AAB
   c. A Random Walk Down Wall Street
   d. Active management

4. _____ are made by investors and investment managers.

   Investors commonly perform investment analysis by making use of fundamental analysis, technical analysis and gut feel.

   _____ are often supported by decision tools.

   a. Investment performance
   b. Investing online
   c. Asset allocation
   d. Investment decisions

5. A _____ is a pool of assets forming an independent legal entity that are bought with the contributions to a pension plan for the exclusive purpose of financing pension plan benefits.

   _____s are important shareholders of listed and private companies. They are especially important to the stock market where large institutional investors like the Ontario Teachers' Pension Plan dominate.

   a. Leverage
   b. Pension fund
   c. Leveraged buyout
   d. Limited liability company

6. The _____ is the relationship between the amount of return gained on an investment and the amount of risk undertaken in that investment. The more return sought, the more risk that must be undertaken.

There are various classes of possible investments, each with their own positions on the overall _____.

a. Fiscal sponsorship
b. Post earnings announcement drift
c. Risk-return spectrum
d. Blank endorsement

7. A _____ is a situation that involves losing one quality or aspect of something in return for gaining another quality or aspect. It implies a decision to be made with full comprehension of both the upside and downside of a particular choice.

In economics the term is expressed as opportunity cost, referring the most preferred alternative given up.

a. Break-even point
b. Capital outflow
c. Total revenue
d. Trade-off

8. Behavioral economics and _____ are closely related fields that have evolved to be a separate branch of economic and financial analysis which applies scientific research on human and social, cognitive and emotional factors to better understand economic decisions by, say, consumers, borrowers, investors, and how they affect market prices, returns and the allocation of resources.

The field is primarily concerned with the bounds of rationality (selfishness, self-control) of economic agents. Behavioral models typically integrate insights from psychology with neo-classical economic theory.

a. Recession
b. Medium of exchange
c. Market structure
d. Behavioral finance

9. _____, refers to consumption opportunity gained by an entity within a specified time frame, which is generally expressed in monetary terms. However, for households and individuals, '_____ is the sum of all the wages, salaries, profits, interests payments, rents and other forms of earnings received... in a given period of time.' For firms, _____ generally refers to net-profit: what remains of revenue after expenses have been subtracted.

a. Annual report
b. OIBDA
c. Accrual
d. Income

10. A _____ is a fungible, negotiable instrument representing financial value. They are broadly categorized into debt securities (such as banknotes, bonds and debentures), and equity securities; e.g., common stocks. The company or other entity issuing the _____ is called the issuer.

a. Security
b. Securities lending
c. Book entry
d. Tracking stock

11. The U.S. _____ is an independent agency of the United States government which holds primary responsibility for enforcing the federal securities laws and regulating the securities industry, the nation's stock and options exchanges, and other electronic securities markets. The SEC was created by section 4 of the SEC of 1934 (now codified as 15 U.S.C. § 78d and commonly referred to as the 1934 Act.)

a. 529 plan
b. 4-4-5 Calendar
c. 7-Eleven
d. Securities and Exchange Commission

Chapter 26. Investment Policy and the Framework of the CFA Institute 245

12. A _____ is a point at which a stock market will stop trading for a period of time in response to substantial drops in value.

On the New York Stock Exchange, one type of _____ is referred to as a 'circuit breaker.' These limits were put in place after Black Monday in order to reduce market volatility and massive panic sell-offs, giving traders time to reconsider their transactions.

At the start of each quarter, the NYSE sets three circuit breaker levels at levels of 10%, 20%, and 30% of the average closing price of the Dow Jones Industrial Average for the month preceding the start of the quarter, rounded to the nearest 50-point interval.

   a. Stock repurchase
   c. Stock market index
   b. Common stock
   d. Trading curb

13. _____, in accrual accounting, is any account where the asset or liability is not realized until a future date, e.g. annuities, charges, taxes, income, etc. The _____ item may be carried, dependent on type of deferral, as either an asset or liability. See also: accrual

_____ is also used in the university admissions process. It is the action by which a school rejects a student for early admission but still opts to review that student in the general admissions pool.

   a. Current asset
   c. Revenue
   b. Net profit
   d. Deferred

14. The _____ is based on common law stemming from the 1830 Massachusetts court decision - Harvard College v. Armory, 9 Pick. (26 Mass.)
   a. SIPC
   c. Williams Act
   b. Prudent man rule
   d. Rule 144A

15. In economics, a _____ is a type of retirement plan in which the amount of the employer's annual contribution is specified. Individual accounts are set up for participants and benefits are based on the amounts credited to these accounts (through employer contributions and, if applicable, employee contributions) plus any investment earnings on the money in the account. Only employer contributions to the account are guaranteed, not the future benefits. In _____s, future benefits fluctuate on the basis of investment earnings.
   a. Total revenue
   c. Fixed asset turnover
   b. Capital costs
   d. Defined contribution plan

16. In economic models, the _____ time frame assumes no fixed factors of production. Firms can enter or leave the marketplace, and the cost (and availability) of land, labor, raw materials, and capital goods can be assumed to vary. In contrast, in the short-run time frame, certain factors are assumed to be fixed, because there is not sufficient time for them to change.
   a. 529 plan
   c. Short-run
   b. 4-4-5 Calendar
   d. Long-run

17. A _____ is a professionally managed type of collective investment scheme that pools money from many investors and invests it in stocks, bonds, short-term money market instruments, and/or other securities. The _____ will have a fund manager that trades the pooled money on a regular basis. Currently, the worldwide value of all _____s totals more than $26 trillion.

Since 1940, there have been three basic types of investment companies in the United States: open-end funds, also known in the US as _____s; unit investment trusts (UITs); and closed-end funds.

    a. Mutual fund   b. Net asset value
    c. Trust company   d. Financial intermediary

18. _____ is a type of permanent life insurance based on a cash value. That is, the policy is established with the insurer where premium payments above the cost of insurance are credited to the cash value. The cash value is credited each month with interest, and the policy is debited each month by a cost of insurance (COI) charge, and any other policy charges and fees which are drawn from the cash value if no premium payment is made that month.

    a. A Random Walk Down Wall Street   b. Universal life
    c. ABN Amro   d. AAB

19. In finance, the _____ is used to determine a theoretically appropriate required rate of return of an asset, if that asset is to be added to an already well-diversified portfolio, given that asset's non-diversifiable risk. The model takes into account the asset's sensitivity to non-diversifiable risk (also known as systemic risk or market risk), often represented by the quantity beta (β) in the financial industry, as well as the expected return of the market and the expected return of a theoretical risk-free asset.

The model was introduced by Jack Treynor (1961, 1962), William Sharpe (1964), John Lintner (1965a,b) and Jan Mossin (1966) independently, building on the earlier work of Harry Markowitz on diversification and modern portfolio theory.

    a. Cox-Ingersoll-Ross model   b. Hull-White model
    c. Random walk hypothesis   d. Capital asset pricing model

20. _____ is a measure of the ability of a debtor to pay their debts as and when they fall due. It is usually expressed as a ratio or a percentage of current liabilities.

For a corporation with a published balance sheet there are various ratios used to calculate a measure of liquidity.

    a. Operating profit margin   b. Accounting liquidity
    c. Invested capital   d. Operating leverage

21. The term _____ or economic cycle refers to the fluctuations of economic activity (business fluctuations) around a long-term growth trend. The cycle involves shifts over time between periods of relatively rapid growth of output (recovery and prosperity), and periods of relative stagnation or decline (contraction or recession.) These fluctuations are often measured using the real gross domestic product.

    a. Business cycle   b. Behavioral finance
    c. Deflation   d. Fixed exchange rate

Chapter 26. Investment Policy and the Framework of the CFA Institute   247

22. In business and accounting, _____s are everything of value that is owned by a person or company. The balance sheet of a firm records the monetary value of the _____s owned by the firm. The two major _____ classes are tangible _____s and intangible _____s.

   a. Income
   c. EBITDA
   b. Accounts payable
   d. Asset

23. _____ is a term used to refer to how an investor distributes his or her investments among various classes of investment vehicles (e.g., stocks and bonds.)

A large part of financial planning is finding an _____ that is appropriate for a given person in terms of their appetite for and ability to shoulder risk. This can depend on various factors; see investor profile.

   a. Alternative investment
   c. Investment performance
   b. Investing online
   d. Asset allocation

24. In Finance the _____ is a mathematical model for portfolio allocation developed in 1990 at Goldman Sachs by Fischer Black and Robert Litterman, and published in 1992. It seeks to overcome problems that institutional investors have encountered in applying modern portfolio theory in practice. The model starts with the equilibrium assumption that the asset allocation of a representative agent should be proportional to the market values of the available assets, and then modifies that to take into account the 'views' (i.e. the specific opinions about asset returns) of the investor in question to arrive at a bespoke asset allocation.

   a. Black-Litterman model
   c. Clientele effect
   b. Capital surplus
   d. Specific risk

25. The term _____ has three unrelated technical definitions, and is also used in a variety of non-technical ways.

- In financial economics, it refers to any asset used to make money, as opposed to assets used for personal enjoyment or consumption. This is an important distinction because two people can disagree sharply about the value of personal assets, one person might think a sports car is more valuable than a pickup truck, another person might have the opposite taste. But if an asset is held for the purpose of making money, taste has nothing to do with it, only differences of opinion about how much money the asset will produce. With the further assumption that people agree on the probability distribution of future cash flows, it is possible to have an objective _____ pricing model. Even without the assumption of agreement, it is possible to set rational limits on _____ value.
- In governmental accounting, it is defined as any asset used in operations with an initial useful life extending beyond one reporting period. Generally, government managers have a 'stewardship' duty to maintain _____s under their control. See International Public Sector Accounting Standards for details.
- In US tax accounting, it is defined as any property other than a list of exceptions. The main exceptions are anything held for sale, and any real estate or depreciable property used in business. Almost everything you own and use for personal purposes, pleasure or investment is a _____. If something is a _____ for tax purposes, gains or losses on sale or disposition are capital gains or capital losses. For individuals, however, capital losses on property held for personal use are generally not deductible. See the IRS publication Tax Facts about Capital Gains and Losses for details.

A well-known financial accounting textbook advises that the term be avoided except in tax accounting because it is used in so many different senses, not all of them well-defined. For example it is often used as a synonym for fixed assets or for investments in securities.

248   *Chapter 26. Investment Policy and the Framework of the CFA Institute*

A common non-technical usage occurs when people ask that employees or the environment or something else be treated as a _____.

   a. Solvency   b. Political risk
   c. Capital asset   d. Settlement date

26. _____ refers to any type of investment that yields a regular (or fixed) return.

For example, if you lend money to a borrower and the borrower has to pay interest once a month, you have been issued a fixed-income security. When a company does this, it is often called a bond or corporate bank debt (although preferred stock is also sometimes considered to be _____).

   a. 4-4-5 Calendar   b. Bond market
   c. 529 plan   d. Fixed income

27. In economics, _____ is a rise in the general level of prices of goods and services in an economy over a period of time. The term '_____' once referred to increases in the money supply (monetary _____); however, economic debates about the relationship between money supply and price levels have led to its primary use today in describing price _____. _____ can also be described as a decline in the real value of money--a loss of purchasing power in the medium of exchange which is also the monetary unit of account.

   a. AAB   b. ABN Amro
   c. A Random Walk Down Wall Street   d. Inflation

28. _____ is a fee paid on borrowed assets. It is the price paid for the use of borrowed money, or, money earned by deposited funds. Assets that are sometimes lent with _____ include money, shares, consumer goods through hire purchase, major assets such as aircraft, and even entire factories in finance lease arrangements.

   a. A Random Walk Down Wall Street   b. Insolvency
   c. AAB   d. Interest

29. An _____ is the price a borrower pays for the use of money they do not own, and the return a lender receives for deferring the use of funds, by lending it to the borrower. _____s are normally expressed as a percentage rate over the period of one year.

_____s targets are also a vital tool of monetary policy and are used to control variables like investment, inflation, and unemployment.

   a. A Random Walk Down Wall Street   b. AAB
   c. ABN Amro   d. Interest rate

30. _____ is the risk (variability in value) borne by an interest-bearing asset, such as a loan or a bond, due to variability of interest rates. In general, as rates rise, the price of a fixed rate bond will fall, and vice versa. _____ is commonly measured by the bond's duration.

   a. A Random Walk Down Wall Street   b. International Fisher effect
   c. Official bank rate   d. Interest rate risk

Chapter 26. Investment Policy and the Framework of the CFA Institute   249

31. _____ arises from situations in which a party interested in trading an asset cannot do it because nobody in the market wants to trade that asset. _____ becomes particularly important to parties who are about to hold or currently hold an asset, since it affects their ability to trade.

Manifestation of _____ is very different from a drop of price to zero.

a. Liquidity risk
c. Tracking error
b. Credit risk
d. Currency risk

32. _____ is the risk that the value of an investment will decrease due to moves in market factors. The five standard _____ factors are:

- Equity risk, the risk that stock prices will change.
- Interest rate risk, the risk that interest rates will change.
- Currency risk, the risk that foreign exchange rates will change.
- Commodity risk, the risk that commodity prices (e.g. grains, metals) will change.

As with other forms of risk, _____ may be measured in a number of ways. Traditionally, this is done using a Value at Risk methodology. Value at risk is well established as a risk management technique, but it contains a number of limiting assumptions that constrain its accuracy.

a. Market risk
c. Tracking error
b. Currency risk
d. Transaction risk

33. In finance, the _____ is the global financial market for short-term borrowing and lending. It provides short-term liquidity funding for the global financial system. The _____ is where short-term obligations such as Treasury bills, commercial paper and bankers' acceptances are bought and sold.

a. Consumer debt
c. Cramdown
b. Debt-for-equity swap
d. Money market

34. _____ is a type of risk faced by investors, corporations, and governments. It is a risk that can be understood and managed with proper aforethought and investment.

Broadly, _____ refers to the complications businesses and governments may face as a result of what are commonly referred to as political decisions--or 'any political change that alters the expected outcome and value of a given economic action by changing the probability of achieving business objectives.' .

a. Single-index model
c. Mid price
b. Political risk
d. Capital asset

35. _____ refers to a business or organization attempting to acquire goods or services to accomplish the goals of the enterprise. Though there are several organizations that attempt to set standards in the _____ process, processes can vary greatly between organizations. Typically the word '_____' is not used interchangeably with the word 'procurement', since procurement typically includes Expediting, Supplier Quality, and Traffic and Logistics (T'L) in addition to _____.

Chapter 26. Investment Policy and the Framework of the CFA Institute

a. 529 plan
c. 7-Eleven
b. 4-4-5 Calendar
d. Purchasing

36. _____ is the value of goods/services compared to the amount paid with a currency. Currency can be either a commodity money, like gold or silver, or fiat currency like US dollars which are the world reserve currency. As Adam Smith noted, having money gives one the ability to 'command' others' labor, so _____ to some extent is power over other people, to the extent that they are willing to trade their labor or goods for money or currency.
   a. 529 plan
   c. 7-Eleven
   b. Purchasing power
   d. 4-4-5 Calendar

37. In business and finance, a _____ (also referred to as equity _____) of stock means a _____ of ownership in a corporation (company.) In the plural, stocks is often used as a synonym for _____s especially in the United States, but it is less commonly used that way outside of North America.

In the United Kingdom, South Africa, and Australia, stock can also refer to completely different financial instruments such as government bonds or, less commonly, to all kinds of marketable securities.

   a. Margin
   c. Bucket shop
   b. Procter ' Gamble
   d. Share

38. In finance, the yield curve is the relation between the interest rate (or cost of borrowing) and the time to maturity of the debt for a given borrower in a given currency. For example, the current U.S. dollar interest rates paid on U.S. Treasury securities for various maturities are closely watched by many traders, and are commonly plotted on a graph such as the one on the right which is informally called 'the yield curve.' More formal mathematical descriptions of this relation are often called the _____.

The yield of a debt instrument is the annualized percentage increase in the value of the investment.

   a. Term structure of interest rates
   c. 529 plan
   b. 7-Eleven
   d. 4-4-5 Calendar

39. In finance, the term _____ describes the amount in cash that returns to the owners of a security. Normally it does not include the price variations, at the difference of the total return. _____ applies to various stated rates of return on stocks (common and preferred, and convertible), fixed income instruments (bonds, notes, bills, strips, zero coupon), and some other investment type insurance products (e.g. annuities.)
   a. 4-4-5 Calendar
   c. Yield to maturity
   b. Yield
   d. Macaulay duration

40. In finance, the _____ is the relation between the interest rate (or cost of borrowing) and the time to maturity of the debt for a given borrower in a given currency. For example, the current U.S. dollar interest rates paid on U.S. Treasury securities for various maturities are closely watched by many traders, and are commonly plotted on a graph such as the one on the right which is informally called 'the _____.' More formal mathematical descriptions of this relation are often called the term structure of interest rates.

The yield of a debt instrument is the annualized percentage increase in the value of the investment.

Chapter 26. Investment Policy and the Framework of the CFA Institute

a. 4-4-5 Calendar
b. 529 plan
c. 7-Eleven
d. Yield curve

41. In finance, _____ is the interest that has accumulated since the principal investment, or since the previous interest payment if there has been one already. For a financial instrument such as a bond, interest is calculated and paid in set intervals.

The primary formula for calculating the interest accrued in a given period is:

$$I_A = T \times P \times R$$

where I_A is the _____, T is the fraction of the year, P is the principal, and R is the annualized interest rate.

a. Accrued interest
b. ABN Amro
c. AAB
d. A Random Walk Down Wall Street

42. In finance, _____ is the process of estimating the potential market value of a financial asset or liability. they can be done on assets (for example, investments in marketable securities such as stocks, options, business enterprises, or intangible assets such as patents and trademarks) or on liabilities (e.g., Bonds issued by a company.) _____s are required in many contexts including investment analysis, capital budgeting, merger and acquisition transactions, financial reporting, taxable events to determine the proper tax liability, and in litigation.

a. Margin
b. Valuation
c. Share
d. Procter ' Gamble

43. In finance, a _____ is a debt security, in which the authorized issuer owes the holders a debt and, depending on the terms of the _____, is obliged to pay interest (the coupon) and/or to repay the principal at a later date, termed maturity.

Thus a _____ is a loan: the issuer is the borrower, the _____ holder is the lender, and the coupon is the interest. _____s provide the borrower with external funds to finance long-term investments, or, in the case of government _____s, to finance current expenditure.

a. Convertible bond
b. Puttable bond
c. Catastrophe bonds
d. Bond

44. The _____ is the market for securities, where companies and governments can raise longterm funds. The _____ includes the stock market and the bond market. Financial regulators, such as the U.S. Securities and Exchange Commission, oversee the _____s in their designated countries to ensure that investors are protected against fraud.

a. Capital market
b. Forward market
c. Delta neutral
d. Spot rate

45. A _____ is a rare metallic chemical element of high economic value. Chemically, the _____s are less reactive than most elements, have high luster, are softer or more ductile, and have higher melting points than other metals. Historically, _____s were important as currency, but are now regarded mainly as investment and industrial commodities.

a. 7-Eleven
b. 529 plan
c. 4-4-5 Calendar
d. Precious metal

46. An _____ is a retirement plan account that provides some tax advantages for retirement savings in the United States.
  a. ABN Amro
  b. AAB
  c. A Random Walk Down Wall Street
  d. Individual Retirement Arrangement

47. _____, in bookkeeping, refers to assets, liabilities, income, and expenses recorded on individual pages of the so called book of final entry or ledger. Changes in _____ value are made by chronologically posting debit (DR) and credit (CR) entries to its page. Examples of _____s are cash, _____s receivable, mortgages, loans, land and buildings, common stock, sales, services provided, wages, and payroll overhead.
  a. Option
  b. Alpha
  c. Accretion
  d. Account

48. _____ refers to the stock of skills and knowledge embodied in the ability to perform labor so as to produce economic value. Many early economic theories refer to it simply as labor, one of three factors of production, and consider it to be a fungible resource -- homogeneous and easily interchangeable. Other conceptions of labor dispense with these assumptions.
  a. Market structure
  b. Mercantilism
  c. Behavioral finance
  d. Human capital

49. _____ is a defense in the law of torts, which bars a plaintiff from recovery against a negligent tortfeasor if the defendant can demonstrate that the plaintiff voluntarily and knowingly assumed the risks at issue inherent to the dangerous activity in which he was participating at the time of his injury.

What is usually meant by _____ is more precisely termed primary _____. It occurs when the plaintiff has either expressly or impliedly relieved the defendant of the duty to mitigate or relieve the risk causing the injury from which the cause of action arises.

  a. Uniform Securities Act
  b. Economies of scale
  c. Expedited Funds Availability Act
  d. Assumption of risk

50. _____, in a financial context, refers to the allocation of finances for retirement. This normally means the setting aside of money or other assets to obtain a steady income at retirement. The goal of _____ is to achieve financial independence, so that the need to be gainfully employed is optional rather than a necessity.
  a. 529 plan
  b. Retirement planning
  c. 4-4-5 Calendar
  d. 7-Eleven

51. In business, _____ is income that a company receives from its normal business activities, usually from the sale of goods and services to customers. Some companies also receive _____ from interest, dividends or royalties paid to them by other companies. _____ may refer to business income in general, or it may refer to the amount, in a monetary unit, received during a period of time, as in 'Last year, Company X had _____ of $32 million.'

In many countries, including the UK, _____ is referred to as turnover.

Chapter 26. Investment Policy and the Framework of the CFA Institute

a. Matching principle
b. Bottom line
c. Revenue
d. Furniture, Fixtures and Equipment

52. An _____ is a contract written by a seller that conveys to the buyer the right -- but not the obligation -- to buy (in the case of a call _____) or to sell (in the case of a put _____) a particular asset, such as a piece of property such as, among others, a futures contract. In return for granting the _____, the seller collects a payment (the premium) from the buyer.

For example, buying a call _____ provides the right to buy a specified quantity of a security at a set strike price at some time on or before expiration, while buying a put _____ provides the right to sell.

a. Annuity
b. Amortization
c. Option
d. AT'T Mobility LLC

53. The role of the _____ is to issue accounting standards in the United Kingdom. It is recognised for that purpose under the Companies Act 1985. It took over the task of setting accounting standards from the Accounting Standards Committee (ASC) in 1990.

a. A Random Walk Down Wall Street
b. ABN Amro
c. AAB
d. Accounting Standards Board

54. _____ is the field of accountancy concerned with the preparation of financial statements for decision makers, such as stockholders, suppliers, banks, employees, government agencies, owners, and other stakeholders. The fundamental need for _____ is to reduce principal-agent problem by measuring and monitoring agents' performance and reporting the results to interested users.

_____ is used to prepare accounting information for people outside the organization or not involved in the day to day running of the company.

a. 7-Eleven
b. 529 plan
c. 4-4-5 Calendar
d. Financial Accounting

55. The _____ is a private, not-for-profit organization whose primary purpose is to develop generally accepted accounting principles (GAAP) within the United States in the public's interest. The Securities and Exchange Commission (SEC) designated the _____ as the organization responsible for setting accounting standards for public companies in the U.S. It was created in 1973, replacing the Accounting Principles Board and the Committee on Accounting Procedure of the American Institute of Certified Public Accountants. The _____'s mission is 'to establish and improve standards of financial accounting and reporting for the guidance and education of the public, including issuers, auditors, and users of financial information.'

The _____ is not a governmental body.

a. World Congress of Accountants
b. Financial Accounting Standards Board
c. Federal Deposit Insurance Corporation
d. KPMG

Chapter 26. Investment Policy and the Framework of the CFA Institute

56. _____ generally refers to the buying and holding of shares of stock on a stock market by individuals and funds in anticipation of income from dividends and capital gain as the value of the stock rises. It also sometimes refers to the acquisition of equity (ownership) participation in a private (unlisted) company or a startup (a company being created or newly created.) When the investment is in infant companies, it is referred to as venture capital investing and is generally understood to be higher risk than investment in listed going-concern situations.
- a. Intellidex
- b. Open outcry
- c. Insider trading
- d. Equity investment

57. The institution most often referenced by the word '_____' is a public or publicly traded _____, the shares of which are traded on a public stock exchange (e.g., the New York Stock Exchange or Nasdaq in the United States) where shares of stock of _____s are bought and sold by and to the general public. Most of the largest businesses in the world are publicly traded _____s. However, the majority of _____s are said to be closely held, privately held or close _____s, meaning that no ready market exists for the trading of shares.
- a. Depository Trust Company
- b. Protect
- c. Federal Home Loan Mortgage Corporation
- d. Corporation

58. The _____ (FSLIC) was an institution that administered deposit insurance for savings and loan institutions in the United States. It was abolished in 1989 by the Financial Institutions Reform, Recovery and Enforcement Act, which passed responsibility for savings and loan deposit insurance to the Federal Deposit Insurance Corporation (FDIC.)

The FSLIC was created as part of the National Housing Act of 1934 in order to insure deposits in savings and loans, a year after the FDIC was created to insure deposits in commercial banks.

- a. Prudent man rule
- b. Federal Savings and Loan Insurance Corporation
- c. SIPC
- d. Securities Investor Protection Corporation

59. The _____ is a linear factor model with wealth and state variable that forecast changes in the distribution of future returns or income.

The main difference between _____ and standard CAPM is additing state variables that acknowledge the fact that investors hedge against shortfalls in consumption or against changes in the future investment opportunity set.

- a. ABN Amro
- b. AAB
- c. A Random Walk Down Wall Street
- d. Intertemporal Capital Asset Pricing Model

60. _____ in finance is the risk associated with imperfect hedging using futures. It could arise because of the difference between the asset whose price is to be hedged and the asset underlying the derivative, or because of a mismatch between the expiration date of the futures and the actual selling date of the asset.

Under these conditions, the spot price of the asset, and the futures price, do not converge on the expiration date of the future.

- a. Currency risk
- b. Basis risk
- c. Liquidity risk
- d. Credit risk

Chapter 26. Investment Policy and the Framework of the CFA Institute 255

61. The _____ is a measure of the excess return (or Risk Premium) per unit of risk in an investment asset or a trading strategy it is defined as:

$$S = \frac{R - R_f}{\sigma} = \frac{E[R - R_f]}{\sqrt{\operatorname{var}[R - R_f]}},$$

where R is the asset return, R_f is the return on a benchmark asset, such as the risk free rate of return, $E[R - R_f]$ is the expected value of the excess of the asset return over the benchmark return, and σ is the standard deviation of the asset excess return.

Note, if R_f is a constant risk free return throughout the period,

$$\sqrt{\operatorname{var}[R - R_f]} = \sqrt{\operatorname{var}[R]}.$$

The _____ is used to characterize how well the return of an asset compensates the investor for the risk taken. When comparing two assets each with the expected return E[R] against the same benchmark with return R_f, the asset with the higher _____ gives more return for the same risk.

a. Current ratio
c. Sharpe ratio
b. P/E ratio
d. Receivables turnover ratio

62. _____ is a derivative financial instrument.

The global market for exchange-traded _____s is notionally valued by the Bank for International Settlements at $3,075,400 million in 2005.

a. Economic entity
c. Education production function
b. Interest rate option
d. Eurobond

63. The term _____ refers to three closely related concepts:

- The _____ model is a mathematical model of the market for an equity, in which the equity's price is a stochastic process.
- The _____ PDE is a partial differential equation which (in the model) must be satisfied by the price of a derivative on the equity.
- The _____ formula is the result obtained by solving the _____ PDE for a European call option.

Fischer Black and Myron Scholes first articulated the _____ formula in their 1973 paper, 'The Pricing of Options and Corporate Liabilities.' The foundation for their research relied on work developed by scholars such as Jack L. Treynor, Paul Samuelson, A. James Boness, Sheen T. Kassouf, and Edward O. Thorp. The fundamental insight of _____ is that the option is implicitly priced if the stock is traded.

Robert C. Merton was the first to publish a paper expanding the mathematical understanding of the options pricing model and coined the term '_____' options pricing model.

- a. Perpetuity
- c. Stochastic volatility
- b. Modified Internal Rate of Return
- d. Black-Scholes

64. The _____ is an economic law stated as: 'In an efficient market all identical goods must have only one price.'

The intuition for this law is that all sellers will flock to the highest prevailing price, and all buyers to the lowest current market price. In an efficient market the convergence on one price is instant.

Commodities can be traded on financial markets, where there will be a single offer price, and bid price.

- a. Liability
- c. Personal property
- b. Letter of credit
- d. Law of one price

Chapter 27. The Theory of Active Portfolio Management

1. _____ refers to a portfolio management strategy where the manager makes specific investments with the goal of outperforming an investment benchmark index. Investors or mutual funds that do not aspire to create a return in excess of a benchmark index will often invest in an index fund that replicates as closely as possible the investment weighting and returns of that index; this is called passive management. _____ is the opposite of passive management, because in passive management the manager does not seek to outperform the benchmark index.
   a. AAB
   b. ABN Amro
   c. Active management
   d. A Random Walk Down Wall Street

2. In Finance the _____ is a mathematical model for portfolio allocation developed in 1990 at Goldman Sachs by Fischer Black and Robert Litterman, and published in 1992. It seeks to overcome problems that institutional investors have encountered in applying modern portfolio theory in practice. The model starts with the equilibrium assumption that the asset allocation of a representative agent should be proportional to the market values of the available assets, and then modifies that to take into account the 'views' (i.e. the specific opinions about asset returns) of the investor in question to arrive at a bespoke asset allocation.
   a. Clientele effect
   b. Black-Litterman model
   c. Specific risk
   d. Capital surplus

3. In Finance the _____ is a mathematical model for security selection published by Fischer Black and Jack Treynor in 1973. The model assumes an investor who considers that most securities are priced efficiently, but who believes he has information that can be used to predict the abnormal performance (Alpha) of a few of them; the model finds the optimum portfolio to hold under such conditions.

   In essence the optimal portfolio consists of two parts: an index fund containing all securities in proportion to their market value and an 'active portfolio' containing the securities for which the investor has made a prediction about alpha.

   a. Treynor-Black model
   b. LIBOR market model
   c. Modified Internal Rate of Return
   d. Binomial model

4. _____ is a risk-adjusted measure of the so-called active return on an investment. It is the return in excess of the compensation for the risk borne, and thus commonly used to assess active managers' performances. Often, the return of a benchmark is subtracted in order to consider relative performance, which yields Jensen's _____.
   a. Alpha
   b. Option
   c. Amortization
   d. Annuity

5. In statistics, a _____ is a tabulation of the values that one or more variables take in a sample.

   Univariate _____s are often presented as lists ordered by quantity showing the number of times each value appears. For example, if 100 people rate a five-point Likert scale assessing their agreement with a statement on a scale on which 1 denotes strong agreement and 5 strong disagreement, the _____ of their responses might look like:

   This simple tabulation has two drawbacks.

   a. Frequency distribution
   b. Covariance
   c. Variance
   d. Random variables

Chapter 27. The Theory of Active Portfolio Management

6. _____ measures the active return of an investment manager divided by the amount of risk the manager takes relative to a benchmark. It is used in the analysis of performance of mutual funds, hedge funds, etc. Specifically, the _____ is defined as active return divided by tracking error.

   a. Operating leverage
   b. Asset turnover
   c. Earnings yield
   d. Information ratio

7. In finance, a _____ is a debt security, in which the authorized issuer owes the holders a debt and, depending on the terms of the _____, is obliged to pay interest (the coupon) and/or to repay the principal at a later date, termed maturity.

   Thus a _____ is a loan: the issuer is the borrower, the _____ holder is the lender, and the coupon is the interest. _____s provide the borrower with external funds to finance long-term investments, or, in the case of government _____s, to finance current expenditure.

   a. Convertible bond
   b. Puttable bond
   c. Bond
   d. Catastrophe bonds

8. In finance, _____ or 'shorting' is the practice of selling a financial instrument that the seller does not own at the time of the sale. _____ is done with intent of later purchasing the financial instrument at a lower price. Short-sellers attempt to profit from an expected decline in the price of a financial instrument.

   a. 529 plan
   b. 4-4-5 Calendar
   c. Short ratio
   d. Short selling

9. In finance, _____ is a measure of how closely a portfolio follows the index to which it is benchmarked. It measures the standard deviation of the difference between the portfolio and index returns.

   Many portfolios are managed to a benchmark, normally an index.

   a. Liquidity risk
   b. Transaction risk
   c. Market risk
   d. Tracking error

10. The _____ of a random event or an uncertain proposition is the conditional probability that is assigned after the relevant evidence is taken into account.

    The _____ distribution of one random variable given the value of another can be calculated with Bayes' theorem by multiplying the prior probability distribution by the likelihood function, and then dividing by the normalizing constant, as follows:

    $$f_{X|Y=y}(x) = \frac{f_X(x) L_{X|Y=y}(x)}{\int_{-\infty}^{\infty} f_X(x) L_{X|Y=y}(x)\, dx}$$

gives the _____ density function for a random variable X given the data Y = y, where

- $f_X(x)$ is the prior density of X,

- $L_{X|Y=y}(x) = f_{Y|X=x}(y)$ is the likelihood function as a function of x,

- $\int_{-\infty}^{\infty} f_X(x) L_{X|Y=y}(x)\, dx$ is the normalizing constant, and

- $f_{X|Y=y}(x)$ is the posterior density of X given the data Y = y.

a. 529 plan
b. 7-Eleven
c. 4-4-5 Calendar
d. Posterior probability

11. Taking this idea further, in many cases the sum or integral of the prior values may not even need to be finite to get sensible answers for the posterior probabilities. When this is the case, the prior is called an _____. Some statisticians use _____s as uninformative priors.
a. A Random Walk Down Wall Street
b. Improper prior
c. ABN Amro
d. AAB

12. An _____ (often called organization chart or organigram(me) or organogram(me)) is a diagram that shows the structure of an organization and the relationships and relative ranks of its parts and positions/jobs. The term is also used for similar diagrams, for example ones showing the different elements of a field of knowledge or a group of languages. The French Encyclopédie had one of the first _____s of knowledge in general.
a. AAB
b. A Random Walk Down Wall Street
c. ABN Amro
d. Organizational chart

13. In business and accounting, _____s are everything of value that is owned by a person or company. The balance sheet of a firm records the monetary value of the _____s owned by the firm. The two major _____ classes are tangible _____s and intangible _____s.
a. Asset
b. Income
c. Accounts payable
d. EBITDA

14. _____ is a term used to refer to how an investor distributes his or her investments among various classes of investment vehicles (e.g., stocks and bonds.)

A large part of financial planning is finding an _____ that is appropriate for a given person in terms of their appetite for and ability to shoulder risk. This can depend on various factors; see investor profile.

a. Asset allocation
b. Investing online
c. Alternative investment
d. Investment performance

Chapter 27. The Theory of Active Portfolio Management

15. _____ is a graph created by investors to measure the risk of risky and risk-free assets. The graph displays to the investors on the return they can make by taking on a certain level of risk. It is also known as a 'reward-to-variability ratio'.

   a. Portfolio investment
   b. Divestment
   c. Dollar cost averaging
   d. Capital allocation line

16. In probability theory and statistics, _____ is a measure of how much two variables change together (variance is a special case of the _____ when the two variables are identical.)

   If two variables tend to vary together (that is, when one of them is above its expected value, then the other variable tends to be above its expected value too), then the _____ between the two variables will be positive. On the other hand, when one of them is above its expected value the other variable tends to be below its expected value, then the _____ between the two variables will be negative.

   a. Stratified sampling
   b. Covariance
   c. Frequency distribution
   d. Probability distribution

17. In statistics and probability theory, the _____ is a matrix of covariances between elements of a vector. It is the natural generalization to higher dimensions of the concept of the variance of a scalar-valued random variable.

   If entries in the column vector

   $$X = \begin{bmatrix} X_1 \\ \vdots \\ X_n \end{bmatrix}$$

   are random variables, each with finite variance, then the _____ Σ is the matrix whose (i, j) entry is the covariance

   $$\Sigma_{ij} = \operatorname{cov}(X_i, X_j) = \operatorname{E}\big[(X_i - \mu_i)(X_j - \mu_j)\big]$$

   where

   $$\mu_i = \operatorname{E}(X_i)$$

   is the expected value of the ith entry in the vector X.

   a. 7-Eleven
   b. Covariance matrix
   c. 529 plan
   d. 4-4-5 Calendar

Chapter 27. The Theory of Active Portfolio Management

18. _____ is an international professional designation offered by the _____ Institute (formerly known as AIMR) to financial analysts who complete a series of three examinations. In order to become a '_____ Charterholder' candidates must pass all three six-hour exams, possess a bachelor's degree (or equivalent, as assessed by the _____ institute) and have 48 months of work experience in an investment decision-making position. _____ charterholders are also obligated to adhere to a strict Code of Ethics and Standards governing their professional conduct.

   a. 4-4-5 Calendar
   c. 529 plan
   b. Chartered Financial Analyst
   d. 7-Eleven

19. A _____, securities analyst, research analyst, equity analyst, or investment analyst is a person who performs financial analysis for external or internal clients as a core part of the job.

An analyst studies companies and other entities to arrive at the estimate of their financial value. It is normally done by analyzing financial reports, aided by follow-up interviews with company representatives and industry experts.

   a. Stockbroker
   c. Purchasing manager
   b. Portfolio manager
   d. Financial Analyst

Chapter 1

1. a	2. d	3. d	4. d	5. c	6. a	7. c	8. b	9. c	10. d
11. d	12. c	13. c	14. b	15. b	16. c	17. c	18. a	19. d	20. d
21. d	22. c	23. a	24. d	25. d	26. d	27. b	28. d	29. b	30. a
31. d	32. c	33. b	34. d	35. a	36. c	37. d	38. d	39. c	40. c
41. b	42. d	43. d	44. d	45. d	46. b	47. b	48. d	49. d	50. d
51. d	52. a	53. a	54. b	55. c	56. d	57. d	58. a	59. a	60. b

Chapter 2

1. b	2. a	3. d	4. d	5. d	6. d	7. d	8. a	9. d	10. a
11. d	12. d	13. d	14. d	15. d	16. d	17. a	18. d	19. c	20. d
21. d	22. c	23. a	24. c	25. d	26. c	27. d	28. d	29. d	30. d
31. d	32. c	33. d	34. b	35. d	36. d	37. d	38. d	39. c	40. a
41. d	42. c	43. d	44. b	45. d	46. b	47. d	48. d	49. a	50. d
51. d	52. d	53. d	54. b	55. c	56. a	57. b	58. d	59. d	60. d
61. d	62. d	63. b	64. a	65. a	66. d	67. a	68. d	69. d	70. d
71. a	72. b	73. d	74. b	75. d	76. c	77. d	78. c	79. a	80. a
81. b	82. c	83. b	84. d	85. a	86. c	87. d	88. a	89. d	90. a
91. a	92. d	93. c	94. d	95. a					

Chapter 3

1. d	2. b	3. d	4. a	5. d	6. d	7. d	8. b	9. d	10. d
11. d	12. d	13. a	14. d	15. d	16. b	17. a	18. c	19. d	20. a
21. a	22. a	23. d	24. b	25. d	26. b	27. d	28. d	29. a	30. c
31. d	32. c	33. b	34. d	35. d	36. a	37. d	38. c	39. d	40. d
41. c	42. c	43. c	44. d	45. b	46. d	47. a	48. b	49. c	50. a
51. d	52. b	53. d	54. a	55. d	56. d	57. d	58. d	59. c	60. c
61. b	62. d	63. c	64. d	65. a	66. d	67. d	68. a	69. d	70. d
71. c	72. d	73. b	74. a	75. c	76. d	77. d	78. b	79. d	

Chapter 4

1. d	2. d	3. d	4. d	5. b	6. d	7. d	8. d	9. d	10. a
11. b	12. d	13. a	14. d	15. b	16. b	17. c	18. c	19. a	20. b
21. b	22. b	23. a	24. c	25. b	26. c	27. d	28. d	29. d	30. d
31. d	32. a	33. a	34. d	35. a	36. a	37. d	38. d	39. c	

Chapter 5

1. c	2. d	3. c	4. b	5. d	6. d	7. a	8. c	9. d	10. c
11. d	12. b	13. d	14. b	15. d	16. d	17. d	18. c	19. a	20. c
21. d	22. a	23. d	24. d	25. b	26. b	27. c	28. d	29. b	30. c
31. a	32. d	33. d	34. a	35. d	36. a	37. a	38. a	39. c	40. d
41. d	42. c	43. a	44. d	45. d	46. d	47. b	48. d	49. a	

ANSWER KEY

Chapter 6

1. b	2. d	3. d	4. d	5. b	6. a	7. d	8. b	9. b	10. b
11. a	12. b	13. b	14. c	15. d	16. b	17. d	18. d	19. d	20. d
21. b	22. d	23. d	24. b	25. a	26. c	27. d	28. d	29. c	30. d

Chapter 7

1. d	2. c	3. d	4. b	5. c	6. d	7. c	8. a	9. c	10. b
11. d	12. d	13. a	14. c	15. c	16. d	17. b	18. c	19. a	20. d
21. a	22. d	23. d	24. d	25. d	26. c	27. a	28. b	29. a	30. d
31. b	32. d	33. c	34. b	35. a	36. b	37. a	38. d	39. d	40. d

Chapter 8

1. d	2. c	3. d	4. c	5. c	6. d	7. d	8. d	9. b	10. d
11. d	12. d	13. c	14. d	15. b	16. d	17. d	18. b	19. c	20. d
21. b	22. d	23. a	24. a	25. d	26. c	27. b	28. c	29. d	30. a
31. c	32. c	33. d	34. d	35. b	36. d	37. a			

Chapter 9

1. d	2. d	3. d	4. d	5. a	6. a	7. c	8. d	9. d	10. d
11. d	12. d	13. d	14. b	15. d	16. d	17. a	18. d	19. d	20. d
21. d	22. b	23. a	24. c	25. b	26. a	27. a	28. c	29. b	30. d
31. c	32. b	33. b	34. a	35. c	36. d	37. d	38. c	39. b	40. d
41. b	42. d	43. a	44. b	45. d	46. d	47. c	48. c	49. d	50. c
51. c									

Chapter 10

1. d	2. d	3. d	4. c	5. a	6. d	7. d	8. d	9. d	10. d
11. c	12. d	13. a	14. d	15. b	16. a	17. d	18. c	19. d	20. d
21. a	22. b	23. b							

Chapter 11

1. d	2. d	3. c	4. d	5. d	6. d	7. b	8. d	9. a	10. b
11. d	12. d	13. d	14. b	15. a	16. d	17. d	18. a	19. a	20. a
21. c	22. d	23. d	24. a	25. a	26. d	27. d	28. c	29. d	30. b
31. c	32. c	33. c	34. d	35. d	36. a	37. c	38. b	39. d	40. d
41. c									

Chapter 12

1. b	2. d	3. d	4. d	5. d	6. c	7. a	8. a	9. d	10. b
11. c	12. d	13. b	14. d	15. d	16. a	17. b	18. d	19. c	20. d
21. c	22. d								

Chapter 13

1. d	2. a	3. a	4. c	5. a	6. d	7. d	8. c	9. d	10. c
11. b	12. d	13. c	14. c	15. d	16. b	17. d	18. b	19. d	20. d
21. a	22. b	23. d	24. d	25. d	26. d	27. d	28. d	29. a	30. a
31. d	32. b	33. d	34. b	35. c	36. d	37. b	38. b	39. d	40. d
41. d	42. c	43. d	44. d	45. c	46. a	47. b	48. d	49. d	

Chapter 14

1. a	2. a	3. d	4. a	5. d	6. d	7. a	8. d	9. b	10. d
11. d	12. d	13. d	14. d	15. d	16. a	17. c	18. d	19. c	20. c
21. d	22. a	23. a	24. c	25. a	26. d	27. d	28. d	29. d	30. d
31. d	32. a	33. c	34. d	35. a	36. d	37. d	38. d	39. d	40. a
41. a	42. b	43. b	44. d	45. d	46. d	47. d	48. d	49. b	50. c
51. d	52. d	53. a	54. d	55. d	56. d	57. a	58. d	59. c	60. d
61. b	62. c	63. d	64. a	65. d	66. b	67. d	68. d	69. d	70. d
71. c	72. a	73. d	74. c	75. d	76. d	77. b	78. d	79. d	80. d
81. b	82. d	83. b	84. d	85. c	86. d				

Chapter 15

1. b	2. a	3. b	4. d	5. d	6. d	7. d	8. a	9. b	10. d
11. d	12. d	13. d	14. c	15. b	16. d	17. d	18. c	19. a	20. c
21. a	22. d	23. d							

Chapter 16

1. d	2. a	3. a	4. c	5. c	6. d	7. b	8. d	9. b	10. c
11. b	12. d	13. a	14. b	15. d	16. a	17. a	18. b	19. a	20. d
21. c	22. d	23. d	24. a	25. a	26. c	27. d	28. d	29. c	30. d
31. a	32. d	33. a	34. d	35. c	36. d	37. a	38. d	39. d	40. b
41. d	42. d	43. c	44. b						

Chapter 17

1. d	2. c	3. a	4. b	5. d	6. d	7. d	8. d	9. c	10. d
11. b	12. d	13. a	14. b	15. b	16. d	17. d	18. c	19. d	20. c
21. d	22. c	23. d	24. c	25. a	26. a	27. c	28. d	29. b	30. d
31. d	32. d	33. c	34. d	35. a	36. c	37. c	38. d	39. d	40. d
41. c	42. d	43. d	44. d	45. a	46. d	47. d	48. d	49. d	50. b

Chapter 18

1. a	2. d	3. d	4. d	5. c	6. d	7. d	8. d	9. c	10. d
11. c	12. a	13. d	14. d	15. d	16. d	17. b	18. d	19. d	20. d
21. c	22. d	23. d	24. c	25. d	26. d	27. d	28. d	29. d	30. d
31. d	32. d	33. a	34. d	35. b	36. a	37. c	38. d	39. d	

ANSWER KEY

Chapter 19
1. a	2. d	3. a	4. c	5. c	6. a	7. d	8. d	9. a	10. d
11. d	12. a	13. a	14. d	15. a	16. c	17. d	18. b	19. d	20. c
21. d	22. b	23. d	24. a	25. d	26. d	27. d	28. c	29. b	30. c
31. b	32. d	33. d	34. d	35. a	36. d	37. d	38. d	39. d	40. d
41. a	42. d	43. c	44. d	45. d	46. b	47. d	48. b	49. d	50. d
51. a	52. d	53. b	54. d	55. d	56. c	57. a	58. c	59. d	60. d
61. d	62. d	63. c	64. d	65. d	66. c	67. d	68. d	69. d	70. c
71. c	72. a	73. b	74. d	75. d	76. d	77. b			

Chapter 20
1. c	2. c	3. a	4. c	5. c	6. d	7. d	8. b	9. a	10. d
11. b	12. d	13. d	14. d	15. d	16. d	17. d	18. c	19. d	20. d
21. d	22. c	23. b	24. d	25. d	26. d	27. d	28. b	29. a	30. d
31. d	32. d	33. d	34. d	35. b	36. d	37. d	38. d	39. d	40. d
41. d	42. d	43. d	44. d	45. d	46. a	47. d	48. d	49. d	50. d
51. d	52. a	53. a	54. a	55. d	56. c				

Chapter 21
1. a	2. a	3. d	4. d	5. a	6. a	7. d	8. d	9. d	10. d
11. a	12. c	13. c	14. a	15. d	16. b	17. d	18. b	19. d	20. b
21. d	22. a	23. d	24. d						

Chapter 22
1. d	2. d	3. c	4. b	5. d	6. d	7. c	8. c	9. a	10. d
11. d	12. b	13. d	14. c	15. d	16. c	17. d	18. c	19. c	20. b
21. d	22. c	23. a	24. d	25. c	26. b	27. a	28. b	29. d	30. d
31. d	32. c								

Chapter 23
1. a	2. d	3. b	4. a	5. a	6. d	7. d	8. d	9. d	10. a
11. d	12. d	13. a	14. a	15. d	16. c	17. a	18. b	19. d	20. d
21. d	22. d	23. d	24. c	25. c	26. d	27. a	28. d	29. d	30. b
31. a	32. b	33. d	34. d	35. d	36. d	37. b	38. a	39. c	40. c
41. d	42. a	43. d	44. b	45. d					

Chapter 24
1. d	2. a	3. a	4. d	5. b	6. b	7. a	8. d	9. d	10. d
11. d	12. b	13. d	14. c	15. b	16. a	17. b	18. d	19. d	20. b
21. d	22. a	23. a	24. a	25. c	26. d	27. d	28. d	29. d	30. d
31. b	32. c	33. a	34. b	35. b	36. d				

Chapter 25

1. d	2. d	3. d	4. c	5. b	6. d	7. c	8. d	9. c	10. c
11. b	12. a	13. d	14. b	15. b	16. a	17. d	18. a	19. b	20. b
21. d	22. d	23. b	24. b	25. c	26. d	27. a	28. d	29. d	30. d
31. d									

Chapter 26

1. d	2. b	3. d	4. d	5. b	6. c	7. d	8. d	9. d	10. a
11. d	12. d	13. d	14. b	15. d	16. d	17. a	18. b	19. d	20. b
21. a	22. d	23. d	24. a	25. c	26. d	27. d	28. d	29. d	30. d
31. a	32. a	33. d	34. b	35. d	36. b	37. d	38. a	39. b	40. d
41. a	42. b	43. d	44. a	45. d	46. d	47. d	48. d	49. d	50. b
51. c	52. c	53. d	54. d	55. b	56. d	57. d	58. b	59. d	60. b
61. c	62. b	63. d	64. d						

Chapter 27

| 1. c | 2. b | 3. a | 4. a | 5. a | 6. d | 7. c | 8. d | 9. d | 10. d |
| 11. b | 12. d | 13. a | 14. a | 15. d | 16. b | 17. b | 18. b | 19. d | |

www.ingramcontent.com/pod-product-compliance
Lightning Source LLC
Chambersburg PA
CBHW080728230426
43665CB00020B/2653